INDEX TO AMERICAN AUTHOR BIBLIOGRAPHIES

by

Patricia Pate Havlice

The Scarecrow Press, Inc.
Metuchen, N. J.   1971

ISBN 0-8108-0426-3

Library of Congress Catalog Card Number 73-163870

IN MEMORIAM

Edward A. Pate

1917 - 1963

A man of upright heart

Preface

The purpose of this volume is to gather together under one cover as many American author bibliographies as possible which have been published in periodicals. Many bibliographic articles are not listed in standard indexes either because they are printed in new periodicals or because no indexing tool existed at the time they appeared. The authors are nominally Americans, that is, citizens of the United States. Persons active in a professional capacity in this country for some time while legally citizens of another land are also included in this listing.

The book is arranged alphabetically by the subject of the bibliography. In cases of more than one bibliography on the same person the entries follow in alphabetical order by author with anonymous pieces listed by the first word of the title.

There is an author index at the end of the book.

I wish to thank the staff of the Newberry Library of Chicago for providing assistance in my searches. The facilities of Valparaiso University and Northern Illinois University were a valuable aid in the final stages of the compilation of this bibliography.

PPH

Abbreviations

AA	American Anthropologist
AAY	American Antiquity
ABC	American Book Collector
AL	American Literature
ALR	American Literary Realism
BAL	Bibliography of American Literature
BB	Bulletin of Bibliography and Magazine Notes
BC	Book Collector (London)
BSA	Bibliographical Society of America. Papers
C	Critique: Studies in Modern Fiction
CLA	CLA Journal
CLJ	Cornell Library Journal
CLQ	Colby Library Quarterly
GSAB	Geological Society of America. Bulletin
GSAP	Geological Society of America. Proceedings
HLB	Harvard Library Bulletin
HLQ	Huntington Library Quarterly
LC	University of Pennsylvania. Library Chronicle

LCQJ	Library of Congress. Quarterly Journal
MFS	Modern Fiction Studies
NASBM	National Academy of Sciences. Biographical Memoirs.
NLB	Newberry Library Bulletin
NYPLB	New York Public Library Bulletin
PULC	Princeton University. Library Chronicle
SB	Studies in Bibliography
TCL	Twentieth Century Literature
TLC	Texas University. Library Chronicle
TSLL	Texas Studies in Literature and Language

A

ABBE, Cleveland, 1838-1916
1. Humphreys, W. J. "Selected Bibliography," NASBM
   8:489-508 '19.

ABBE, Cleveland, Jr., 1872-1934
2. Sumner, James B. "Memorial of Cleveland Abbe, Jr.,"
   GSAP pp. 151-59 '34.

ABBOT, Henry Larcom, 1831-1927
3. Abbot, Charles Greeley "Bibliography," NASBM 13:71-
   77 '30.

ABBOTT, Edith, 1876-1957
4. Marks, R. "Published Writings of Edith Abbott,"
   Social Services Review 32:51-56 Mr '58.

ABEL, John Jacob, 1857-1938
5. MacNider, William DeB. "Bibliography," NASBM
   24:249-57 '47.

ADAM, Karl, 1876-
6. App, J.A. "Contemporary Catholic Authors: Karl
   Adam, a Modern St. Augustine," Catholic Library
   World 16:106 Jan '45.

ADAMS, Comfort Avery, 1868-1958
7. Bush, Vannevar "A Partial Bibliography," NASBM
   38:14-16 '65.

ADAMS, Henry Brooks, 1838-1918
8. Blanck, Jacob "Henry Brooks Adams," BAL 1:1-11.
9. Vandersee, Charles "Henry Adams," ALR 2:89-120
   Summer '69.

ADAMS, James Truslow, 1878-1949
10. McCracken, Mary Jane "Author Bibliography of James
    Truslow Adams," BB 15:65-68 My-Ag '34.

ADAMS, Oscar Fay, 1855-1919
11. Blanck, Jacob "Oscar Fay Adams," BAL 1:12-19.

9

ADAMS, Walter Sydney, 1876-1956
12. Joy, Alfred H. "Bibliography," NASBM 31:15-31 '58.

ADKINS, Homer Burton, 1892-1949
13. Daniels, Farrington "Bibliography," NASBM 27:308-17 '52.

ADKINS, Walter Scott, 1890-1956
14. Lonsdale, John T. "Memorial to Walter Scott Adkins," GSAP pp. 97-102 '56.
15. Lozo, F. E. "Walter Scott Adkins (1890-1956)," American Association of Petroleum Geologists. Bulletin 41:788-9 Apr '57.

ADLUM, John, 1759-1836
16. Manks, Dorothy S. "Some Early American Horticultural Writers and Their Works," Huntia 2:59-66 '65.

AGASSIZ, Alexander, 1835-1910
17. Goodale, George Lincoln "Bibliography," NASBM 7: 298-305 '13.

AGEE, James, 1909-1955
18. Fabre, Genevieve "A Bibliography of the Works of James Agee," BB 24:145-48 My-Ag '65.

AIKEN, Conrad, 1889-
19. Stallman, Robert W. "An Annotated Checklist of Conrad Aiken; a Critical Study," Wake 9:114-21.

AITKEN, Robert Grant, 1864-1951
20. Van den Bos, William H. "Bibliography," NASBM 32:8-30 '58.

ALBEE, Edward, 1928-
21. Kolin, P. C. "Classified Edward Albee Checklist," Serif 6:16-32 S '69.
22. Rule, Margaret W. "An Edward Albee Bibliography," TCL 14:35-44 Apr '68.

ALCOTT, Amos Bronson, 1799-1888
23. Blanck, Jacob "Amos Bronson Alcott," BAL 1:20-26.
24. Dinwiddie, Shirley W. and Herrnstadt, Richard L. "Amos Bronson Alcott: a Bibliography," BB 21:64-67 Jan-Apr '54; 21:92-96 My-Ag '54.

ALCOTT, Louisa May, 1832-1888
25. Blanck, Jacob "Louisa May Alcott," BAL 1:27-45.

ALDRICH, Thomas Bailey, 1836-1907
26. Blanck, Jacob "Thomas Bailey Aldrich," BAL 1:46-77.

ALEXANDER, John H., 1812-1867
27. Hilgard, J. E. "Bibliography," NASBM 1:225-26
    1877.

ALLAN, John A., 1884-1955
28. Warren, P. S. "Memorial to John A. Allan," GSAP
    pp. 89-92 '55.

ALLEE, Warder Clyde, 1885-1955
29. Schmidt, Karl Patterson "Bibliography," NASBM 30:
    28-40 '57.

ALLEN, Charles Elmer, 1872-1954
30. Smith, Gilbert M. "Bibliography," NASBM 29:12-15
    '56.

ALLEN, Don Cameron, 1903-
31. Allen, D. C. "Bibliography of Books and Articles,"
    ELH 36:291-95 Mr '69.

ALLEN, Elizabeth Ann Chase Taylor Akers, 1832-1911
32. Blanck, Jacob "Elizabeth Ann Chase Taylor Akers
    Allen," BAL 1:78-87.

ALLEN, Eugene Thomas, 1864-1964
33. Fleischer, Michael and Zies, E. G. "Bibliography,"
    NASBM 40:13-17 '69.

ALLEN, Hervey, 1889-1949
34. Cohen, Louis Henry "American First Editions;
    Hervey Allen 1889- ," Publishers' Weekly 124:914-15
    '33.

ALLEN, James Lane, 1849-1925
35. Blanck, Jacob "James Lane Allen," BAL 1:88-95.
36. Bottorff, William K. "James Lane Allen (1849-1925),"
    ALR 2:121-24 Summer '69.

ALLEN, Joel Asaph, 1838-1921
37. Chapman, Frank M. "Bibliography," NASBM 11:15-20
    '22.

ALLEN, Robert Porter, 1905-1963
38. Sprunt, A. "In Memoriam: Robert Porter Allen,"
    Auk 86:34 Jan '69.

ALLEN, Rolland Craten, 1881-1947
39. Hotchkiss, William Otis "Memorial to Rolland Craten Allen," GSAP pp. 111-16 '48.

ALLSTON, Washington, 1779-1843
40. Blanck, Jacob "Washington, Allston," BAL 1:96-102.

AMES, Joseph Sweetman, 1864-1943
41. Crew, Henry "Bibliography of Joseph S. Ames," NASBM 23:198-201 '45.

AMINOFF, Gregori, 1883-1947
42. Barth, T. F. W. "Memorial to Gregori Aminoff," American Mineralogist 33:168-71.

ANDERSON, A. H., 1901-1967
43. Pendergast, David M. "A. H. Anderson, 1901-1967," AAY 33:90-92 Jan '68.

ANDERSON, Frank Marion, 1863-1945
44. Weaver, Charles E. "Memorial to Frank Marion Anderson," GSAP pp. 141-44 '46.

ANDERSON, George Harold, 1893-1956
45. Gillson, J. L. "Memorial to George Harold Anderson," GSAP p. 103 '56.

ANDERSON, Gustavus Edwin, 1879-1940
46. Weidman, Samuel "Memorial to Gustavus Edwin Anderson," GSAP pp. 149-52 '42.

ANDERSON, John August, 1876-1959
47. Bowen, Ira S. "Bibliography," NASBM 36:14-18 '62.

ANDERSON, Kenneth Eugene, 1910-
48. Pruit, C. M. "Kenneth Eugene Anderson," Science Education 44:158-61 Apr '60.

ANDERSON, Maxwell, 1888-1959
49. Avery, Laurence G. "Addenda to the Maxwell Anderson Bibliography: The Measure," BSA 63:31-36 '69.
50. Gilbert, Vedder M. "The Career of Maxwell Anderson; a Checklist of Books and Articles," Modern Drama 2:386-94.
51. Tanselle, G. Thomas "Additions to the Bibliography of Maxwell Anderson," BSA 57:90-91 '63.

ANDERSON, Oskar, 1887-1960
52. Wold, H. "Oskar Anderson, 1887-1960," Annals of
Mathematical Statistics 32:656-60 S '61.

ANDERSON, Robert Van Vleck, 1884-1949
53. Arnold, Ralph "Memorial to Robert Van Vleck Anderson," GSAP pp. 81-84 '50.

ANDERSON, Rudolph John, 1879-1961
54. Vickery, Hubert Bradford "Bibliography," NASBM 36:
38-50 '62.

ANDERSON, Sherwood, 1876-1941
55. Gozzi, Raymond D. "A Bibliography of Sherwood Anderson's Contributions to Periodicals 1941-1946," NLB
2nd series #2 pp. 71-82 D '48.
56. Jessup, Mary E. "A Checklist of the Writings of Sherwood Anderson," Americana Collector 5:157-58 '28.
57. Tanselle, G. Thomas "Additional reviews of Sherwood
Anderson's Work," BSA 56:358-65 '62.

ANDREWS, Ernest Clayton, 1870-1948
58. Walkom, A. B. "Memorial to Ernest Clayton Andrews,"
GSAP pp. 122-26 '49.

ANDREWS, Thomas Gayleon, 1903-1954
59. Lloyd, Stewart J. "Memorial to Thomas Gayleon Andrews," GSAP pp. 105-06 '56.

ANGELL, James Rowland, 1869-1949
60. Hunter, W. S. "Partial List of Publications by James
Rowland Angell," NASBM 26:206-08 '51.

ANTHONY, Alfred Webster, 1865-1939
61. Bailey, V. "Alfred Webster Anthony: with a List of
His Publications," Auk, n. s. 58:441-43 Jl '41.

ARMSBY, Henry Prentiss, 1853-1921
62. Benedict, Francis G. "Bibliography of Henry Prentiss
Armsby," NASBM 19:280-84 '38.

ARNOLDSSON, Sverker, 1908-1959
63. Morner, M. "Sverker Arnoldsson," Hispanic American
Review 40:73-74 F '60.

ASHBURNER, Charles Albert, 1854-1889
64. Hill, Frank A. "Geological Writings of Charles Albert
Ashburner," GSAB 5:564-67 1894.
13

ASHLEY, George Hall, 1866-1951
65. Stone, Ralph W. "Memorial to George Hall Ashley,"
GSAP pp. 85-92 '51.

ATHY, Lawrence Ferdinand, 1898-1955
66. Brainerd, A. E. "Memorial to Lawrence Ferdinand
Athy," GSAP pp. 107-09 '56.

ATKINSON, George Francis, 1854-1918
67. Fitzpatrick, Harry M. "Bibliography," NASBM 29:35-
44 '56.

ATWOOD, Wallace Walter, 1872-1949
68. Cressey, G. B. "Wallace W. Atwood, 1872-1949,"
Association of American Geographers. Annals 39:298-
306.
69. Mather, Kirtley, F. "Memorial to Wallace Walter Atwood," GSAP pp. 107-12 '49.

AUDUBON, John James, 1785-1851
70. Blanck, Jacob "American First Editions: John James
Audubon, 1780-1851," Publishers' Weekly 129:832.
71. Rice, Howard C., Jr. "The World of John James
Audubon: Catalogue of an Exhibition in the Princeton
University Library 15 May-30 September, 1959," PULC
21:9-88 '59.

AUSTIN, James Bliss, 1904-
72. "James Bliss Austin, Head U.S. Steel Research Laboratory," American Ceramic Society. Bulletin 26:4-5 Jan
'47.

AUSTIN, Jane Goodwin, 1831-1894
73. Blanck, Jacob "Jane Goodwin Austin," BAL 1:103-09.

AUSTIN, Mary Hunter, 1868-1934
74. Berry, J. Wilkes "Mary Hunter Austin (1868-1934),"
ALR 2:125-31 Summer '69.
75. Powell, Lawrence Clark "Dedication to the Memory of
Mary Hunter Austin, 1868-1934," Arizona and the West
10:4 Spring '68.

AVERY, Oswald Theodore, 1877-1955
76. Dochez, A. R. "Bibliography," NASBM 32:42-49 '58.

BABCOCK, Ernest Brown, 1877-1954
77. Stebbins, G. Ledyard "Bibliography," NASBM 32:58-66 '58.

BACHE, Alexander Dallas, 1806-1867
78. Henry Joseph "Bibliography," NASBM 1:205-12 1877.

BACHMANN, Werner Emmanuel, 1901-1951
79. Elderfield, Robert C. "Bibliography," NASBM 34:19-30 '60.

BACON, Delia Salter, 1811-1859
80. Blanck, Jacob "Delia Salter Bacon," BAL 1:110-12.

BAEKELAND, Leo Hendrik, 1863-1944
81. Kettering, Charles F. "Bibliography of Leo Hendrik Baekeland," NASBM 24:297-302 '47.

BAGBY, George William, 1828-1883
82. Blanck, Jacob "George William Bagby," BAL 1:113-15.

BAGG, Rufus Mather, 1869-1946
83. Bean, E. F. "Memorial to Rufus Mather Bagg," GSAP pp. 105-07 '47.

BAILEY, John Haynes, 1909-1948
84. Ritchie, William A. "Bibliography," AAY 14:215 Jan '49.

BAILEY, Solon Irving, 1854-1931
85. Cannon, Annie J. "Bibliography of Solon I. Bailey," NASBM 15:200-03 '34.

BAIN, Harry Foster, 1871-1947
86. De Wolf, Frank W. "Memorial to H. Foster Bain," GSAP pp. 127-33 '48.

BAKER, Frank Collins, 1867-1942
87. Leighton, Morris M. "Memorial to Frank Collins Baker," GSAP pp. 167-72 '42.

BALDWIN, James, 1924-
88. Fischer, Russell G. "James Baldwin; a Bibliography, 1947-1962," BB 24:127-30 Jan-Apr '65.

BALDWIN, James (continued)
89. Kindt, Kathleen A. "James Baldwin; a Checklist; 1947-1962," BB 24:122-26 Jan-Apr '65.
90. Standley, Fred L. "James Baldwin; a Checklist, 1936-1967," BB 25:135-37 My-Ag '68.

BALDWIN, Joseph Glover, 1815-1864
91. Blanck, Jacob "Joseph Glover Baldwin," BAL 1:116-17

BALK, Robert, 1899-1955
92. Cloos, Ernst "Memorial to Robert Balk," GSAP pp. 93-100 '55.

BALL, John Rice, 1881-1953
93. Dapples, E. C. and A. L. Howland "Memorial to John Rice Ball," GSAP pp. 87-89 '53.

BALLS, Arnold Kent, 1891-1966
94. Hassid, W. Z. "Bibliography," NASBM 41:11-21 '70

BANCROFT, George, 1800-1891
95. Blanck, Jacob "George Bancroft," BAL 1:118-38.

BANCROFT, Joseph Austen, 1882-1951
96. Pelletier, R. A. "Memorial to Joseph Austen Bancroft," GSAP pp. 99-102 '58.

BANGS, John Kendrick, 1862-1922
97. Blanck, Jacob "John Kendrick Bangs," BAL 1:139-61.

BARBOUR, Erwin Hinckley, 1856-1947
98. Schultz, C. Bertrand "Memorial to Erwin Hinckley Barbour," GSAP pp. 109-17 '47.

BARBOUR, Thomas, 1884-1946
99. Bigelow, Henry B. "Bibliography," NASBM 27:28-45 '52.

BARD, James, 1851-1897
100. Brown, A. C. "Check List of the Works of James and John Bard," Art in America 37:67-78 Apr '49.

BARD, John, 1815-1856
101. Brown, A. C. "Check List of Works of James and John Bard," Art in America 37:67-78 Apr '49.

BARKER, Eugene Campbell, 1874-
102. Carroll, H. B. "Writings of Eugene Campbell Barker,"

BARKER, Eugene Campbell (continued)
Southwestern Historical Quarterly 46:360-68 Apr '43.

BARKER, George C., 1912-1958
103. Hoijer, Harry "George C. Barker," AA 60:932-33 O
'58.

BARKER, James Nelson, 1784-1858
104. Blanck, Jacob "James Nelson Barker," BAL 1:162-68.

BARLOW, Joel, 1754-1812
105. Blanck, Jacob "Joel Barlow," BAL 1:169-84.

BARNARD, Edward Emerson, 1857-1923
106. Calvert, Mary R. "Bibliography, By Topics, of the
Principal Scientific Papers of Edward Emerson Barnard,"
NASBM 11:18-23 '23.

BARNARD, Frederick Augustus Porter, 1809-1889
107. Davenport, Charles B. "Scientific Bibliography of F.
A. P. Barnard," NASBM 20:268-72 '39.

BARNARD, John Gross, 1815-1882
108. Abbot, Henry L. "List of the More Important Papers
Published by General J. C. Barnard," NASBM 5:229
'05.

BARNES, Djuna, 1892-
109. Hipkiss, Robert A. "Djuna Barnes (1892-   ) - a
Bibliography," TCL 14:161-63 O '68.

BARNHART, John Hendley, 1871-1949
110. Rickett, H. W. "John Hendley Barnhart," Torrey Botanical Club Bulletin 77:167-75 My '50.

BARRELL, Joseph, 1869-1919
111. Gregory, Herbert E. "Memorial of Joseph Barrell,"
GSAB 34:18-44 '23.
112. Schuchert, Charles "Bibliography," NASBM 12:35-40
'29.

BARROWS, Harlan H., 1877-1960
113. Cobby, C. C. and G. F. White "Harlan H. Barrows,"
Association of American Geographers. Annals 51:399-
400 D '61.

BARTH, John, 1930-
114. Bryer, Jackson R. "Two Bibliographies," C 6:86-89
17

BARTH, John (continued)
Fall '63.

BARTLETT, Harley Harris, 1886-1960
115. Voss, E. G. "Harley Harris Bartlett," Torrey Botanical Club Bulletin 88:51-56 Jan '61.

BARTLETT, William H. C., 1804-1893
116. Holden, Edward S. "Bibliography," NASBM 7:192-93 '13.

BARTON, Donald Clinton, 1889-1939
117. Pratt, Wallace E. "Memorial to Donald Clinton Barton," GSAP pp. 153-66 '39.

BARTON, George H., 1852-1933
118. Lane, Alfred C. "Memorial of George H. Barton," GSAP pp. 161-71 '34.

BARTON, Roy Franklin, 1883-1947
119. Kroeber, A. L. "Bibliography," AA 51:95 '49.

BARTRAM, John Greer, 1893-1955
120. Dott, Robert H. "Memorial to John Greer Bartram," GSAP pp. 101-06 '55.

BARTRAM, William, 1793-1823
121. "Bartonia," Philadelphia Botanical Club D 31 '31.

BARUS, Carl, 1856-1935
122. Lindsay, R. B. "Bibliography," NASBM 22:193-213 '43.

BASTIN, Edson Sunderland, 1878-1953
123. Anderson, Alfred L. "Memorial to Edson Sunderland Bastin," GSAP pp. 87-92 '54.

BATEMAN, Harry, 1882-1946
124. Murnaghan, F. D. "Bibliography," NASBM 25:248-56 '49.

BATHER, Francis Arthur, 1863-1934
125. Raymond, Percy E. "Memorial of F. A. Bather," GSAP pp. 173-86 '34

BAUM, L(yman) Frank, 1856-1919
126. Martin, Dick "A Chronological Checklist of the Published Writings," ABC Special Number pp. 28-31 D '62.

BAYLEY, William Shirley, 1861-1943
127. Leighton, Morris M. "Memorial to William Shirley Bayley," GSAP pp. 105-15 '43.

BEAL, Carl Hugh, 1889-1946
128. Levorsen, A. I. "Memorial to Carl Hugh Beal," GSAP pp. 145-47 '46.

BEARD, Charles Austin, 1874-1948
129. Rule, John C. and Ralph D. Handen "Bibliography of Works on Carl Lotus Becker and Charles Austin Beard, 1945-1963," History and Theory 5:302-14 '66.
130. Tanselle, G. Thomas "Charles A. Beard in the 'Freeman'," BSA 57:226-29 '63.

BEAUBIEN, Paul L. 1903-1962
131. Steen, Charlie R. "Publications of Paul L. Beaubien," AAY 29:486 Apr '64.

BECKER, Carl Lotus, 1873-1945
132. Rule, John C. and Ralph D. Handen "Bibliography of Works on Carl Lotus Becker and Charles Austin Beard, 1945-1963," History and Theory 5:302-14 '66.

BECKER, George Ferdinand, 1847-1919
133. Day, Arthur L. "Memorial of George Ferdinand Becker," GSAB 31:14-25 '20.
134. Evans, Isabel P. "Bibliography of George Ferdinand Becker," NASBM 11:15-19 '22.

BEECHER, Charles Emerson, 1856-1904
135. Dall, William Healey "Bibliography," NASBM 6:66-70 '09.
136. Schuchert, Charles "Memoir of Charles Emerson Beecher," GSAB 16:541-48 '05.

BEER, William, 1849-1927
137. Hellman, Florence S. "Writings of William Beer, 1849-1927," BSA 20:85-90 '26.

BELKNAP, Jeremy, 1744-1798
138. Blanck, Jacob "Jeremy Belknap," BAL 1:185-91.

BELL, Alexander Graham, 1847-1922
139. Osborne, Harold S. "Bibliography of the writings and addresses of Alexander Graham Bell," NASBM 23:20-29 '45.

BELL, Earl Hoyt, 1903-1963
140. Haring, Douglas G. "Earl Hoyt Bell," AA 66:614-15 Je '64.

BELLAMY, Edward, 1850-1898
141. Blanck, Jacob "Edward Bellamy," BAL 1:192-196.
142. Bowman, Sylvia E. "Edward Bellamy (1850-1898)," ALR #1 pp. 7-12 Fall '67.

BELLOW, Saul, 1915-
143. Schneider, Harold W. "Two Bibliographies: Saul Bellow and William Styron," C 3:71-86 Summer '60.

BENEDICT, Francis Gano, 1870-1957
144. DuBois, Eugene F. and Oscar Riddle "Bibliography," NASBM 32:79-99 '58.

BENEDICT, Ruth Fulton, 1887-1948
145. Chandler, Mary E. "Bibliography 1922-1948," AA 51: 463-68 '49.

BENEDICT, Stanley Rossiter, 1884-1936
146. McCollum, Elmer Verner "Bibliography," NASBM 27: 172-77 '52.

BENÉT, Stephen Vincent, 1898-1943
147. Johnson, Merle "American First Editions: Stephen Vincent Benét," Publishers' Weekly 121:290-91 '32.
148. Maddocks, Gladys Louise "Stephen Vincent Benét: a Bibliography," BB 20:142-46 S-D '51; 20:158-60 Jan-Apr '52.

BENGSTON, Nels August, 1879-1963
149. Van Royen, W. "Nels August Bengtson," Association of American Geographers. Annals 58:603-05 S '68.

BENHAM, Rhoda Williams, 1894-1957
150. Silva, M. and E. L. Hazen "Rhoda Williams Benham, 1894-1957," Mycologia 49:601-03 Jl '57.

BENJAMIN, Park, 1809-1864
151. Blanck, Jacob "Park Benjamin," BAL 1:197-207.

BENNETT, Emerson, 1822-1905
152. Blanck, Jacob "Emerson Bennett," BAL 1:208-15.

BENNETT, Wendell C., 1905-1953
153. Rouse, Irving "Bibliography," AAY 19:268-70 Jan '54.

BERGQUIST, Stanard Gustav, 1892-1956
154. Smith, Richard A. "Memorial to Stanard Gustav Bergquist," GSAP pp. 111-15 '56.

BERKEY, Charles Peter, 1867-1955
155. Kerr, Paul F. "Bibliography," NASBM 30:50-56 '57.

BERMAN, Harry, 1902-1944
156. Larsen, Esper S. "Memorial to Harry Berman,"
GSAP pp. 151-54 '44.

BERNAYS, Edward L., 1891-
157. "Public Relations, Edward L. Bernays and the American Scene," BB 20:1-86 Supplement S-D '50; 21:237-40
My-Ag '56; 22:21-24 S-D '56.

BERRY, Edward Wilber, 1875-1945
158. Stephenson, Lloyd W. "Memorial to Edward Wilber
Berry," GSAP pp. 193-214 '45.

BEYER, Samuel Walker, 1865-1931
159. Bain, H. Foster "Memorial of Samuel Walker Beyer,"
GSAB 43:44-46 '33.

BIANCO, Margery Williams, 1881-1944
160. Moore, A. C. "Margery Williams Bianco, 1881-1944,"
Horn Book 21:164-65 My '45.

BIERCE, Ambrose, 1842-1914?
161. Blanck, Jacob "Ambrose Gwinnett Bierce," BAL 1:
216-27.
162. Blanck, Jacob "BAL Addenda," BSA 55:47 '61.
163. Fatout, Paul "Ambrose Bierce (1842-1914)," ALR #1
pp. 13-19 Fall '67.
164. Tanselle, G. Thomas "BAL Addendum: Ambrose
Bierce - Entry No. 1112," BSA 62:451 '68.

BIGELOW, Henry Bryant, 1879-
165. "Bibliography of Henry Bryant Bigelow," Deep Sea Research #3 Supplement xviii-xx D '55.

BILLINGS, John Shaw, 1838-1913
166. Marson, J. "John Shaw Billings as a Bibliographer,"
Medical Library Association Bulletin 57:390 O '69.

BINGHAM, Hiram, 1875-1956
167. Patterson, J. E. "Hiram Bingham, 1875-1956," Hispanic American Historical Review 37:134-37 F '57.

BIRD, Robert Montgomery, 1806-1854
168. Blanck, Jacob "Robert Montgomery Bird," BAL 1: 228-34.

BISHOP, Elizabeth, 1911-
169. McNally, Nancy L. "Checklist of Elizabeth Bishop's Published Writings," TCL 11:201 Jan '66.

BISHOP, John Peale, 1892-1944
170. Patrick, J. Max and Robert W. Stallman "John Peale Bishop: a Checklist," PULC 7:62-79 N '45.

BLACK, Glenn A., 1900-1964
171. Kellar, James H. "Glenn A. Black 1900-1964," AAY 31:402-05 Jan '66.

BLACKMUR, Richard Palmer, 1904-1965
172. Baker, Carlos "R. P. Blackmur: a Checklist," PULC 3:99-106 Apr '42.

BLAKE, Francis Gilman, 1887-1952
173. Paul, John Rodman "Bibliography," NASBM 28:21-29 '54.

BLAKE, Robert Pierpont, 1886-1950
174. "Robert Pierpont Blake: Bibliography," Harvard Journal of Asiatic Studies 14:xv-xvii Je '51.

BLAKE, William Phipps, 1826-1910
175. Raymond, Rossiter W. "Memoir of William Phipps Blake," GSAB 22:36-47 '11.

BLAKESLEE, Albert Francis, 1874-1954
176. Sinnott, Edmund W. "Bibliography," NASBM 33:24-28 '59.

BLICHFELDT, Hans Frederik, 1873-1945
177. Bell, E. T. "Bibliography," NASBM 26:188-89 '51.

BLISS, Gilbert Ames, 1876-1951
178. McShane, E. J. "Bibliography," NASBM 31:46-53 '58.

BOAS, Franz, 1858-1942
179. Lowie, Robert H. "Selected Bibliography," NASBM 24:321 '47.

BOGORAS, Waldemar, d. 1936
180. Boas, Franz "Partial Bibliography," AA 39:314-15 '37.

BOKER, George Henry, 1823-1890
181. Blanck, Jacob "George Henry Boker," BAL 1:235-50.
182. Taylor, George H. "Check-list to the Writings By and About George H. Boker," ABC 5:372-74.

BOLTWOOD, Bertram Borden, 1870-1927
183. Kovarik, Alois F. "Bibliography," NASBM 14:95-96 '32.

BONNER, Tom Wilkerson, 1910-1961
184. Houston, W. V. "Bibliography," NASBM 38:25-32 '65.

BORN, Kendall Eugene, 1908-1947
185. Glenn, L. C. "Memorial to Kendall Eugene Born," GSAP pp. 119-23 '47.

BOSS, Lewis, 1846-1912
186. Boss, Benjamin "Bibliography," NASBM 9:255-60 '19.

BOURNE, Randolph Silliman, 1886-1918
187. True, Michael D. "The Achievement of an American Literary Radical: A Bibliography of the Writings of Randolph Silliman Bourne," NYPLB 69:523-36 O '65.
188. Tanselle, G. Thomas "Randolph Bourne: a Supplementary Note," NYPLB 70:327-30 My '66.
189. True, Michael D. "Writings about Randolph Bourne," NYPLB 70:331-37 My '66.

BOWDITCH, Henry Pickering, 1840-1911
190. Cannon, W. B. "Bibliography," NASBM 10:195-96 '19.

BOWEN, Norman Levi, 1887-1956
191. Schairer, J. F. "Memorial to Norman Levi Bowen," GSAP pp. 117-21 '56.

BOWIE, William, 1872-1940
192. Fleming, J. A. and H. D. Harradon "Bibliography of William Bowie," NASBM 26:79-98 '51.
193. Heck, Nicholas H. "Memorial to William Bowie," GSAP pp. 163-66 '40.

BOWMAN, Amos, 1839-1894
194. Ami, H. M. "Memorial of Amos Bowman," GSAB 6:441-42 1895.

BOWMAN, Isaiah, 1878-1950
195. Carter, George F. "Bibliography," NASBM 33:55-64 '59.

BOWMAN, Isaiah (continued)
196. Mather, Kirtley F. "Memorial to Isaiah Bowman,"
GSAP pp. 93-94 '51.

BOWNE, Borden Parker, 1847-1910
197. Steinkraus, Warren E. "A Check List of Writings By
and About Borden P. Bowne (1847-1910)," NYPLB 73:
398-414 Je '69.

BOWNOCKER, John Adams, 1865-1928
198. Stauffer, Clinton R. "Memorial of John Adams Bownocker," GSAP 40:17-22 '30.

BOYD, James, 1888-1944
199. "James Boyd: a Checklist," PULC 6:77-81 F '45.

BOYESEN, Hjammar Hjorth, 1848-1895
200. Blanck, Jacob "Hjammar Hjorth Boyesen," BAL 1:
251-60.

BRACKENRIDGE, Hugh Henry, 1748-1816
201. Blanck, Jacob "Hugh Henry Brackenridge," BAL 1:
261-68.

BRADSTREET, Anne, c. 1612-1672
202. Svendsen, J. Lester "Anne Bradstreet in England: A
Bibliographical Note," AL 13:63-65 '41-42.

BRAINARD, John Gardiner Calkins, 1796-1828
203. Blanck, Jacob "John Gardiner Calkins Brainard,"
BAL 1:269-74.

BRAINERD, George Walton, 1909-1956
204. "George Walton Brainerd, 1909-1956," Masterkey 30:
73-75 My '56.
205. Hoijer, Harry and Ralph L. Beals "George Walton
Brainerd 1909-1956," AA 58:908-12 O '56.
206. Smith, Watson "Bibliography," AAY 22:167-68 O '56.

BRAMKAMP, Richard Allan, 1910-1958
207. Woodford, A. O. and G. F. Brown "Memorial to
Richard Allan Bramkamp," GSAP pp. 111-13 '58.

BRANNER, John Casper, 1850-1924
208. Penrose, R. A. F., Jr. "Memorial to John Casper
Branner," GSAB 36:15-44 '25.
209. Penrose, R. A. F., Jr. "Publications of John Casper
Branner," NASBM 11:9-20 '22.

BRANSON, Edwin Bayer, 1877-1951
210. Longwell, Chester R. "Memorial to Edwin Bayer Branson," GSAP pp. 85-89 '50.

BRAY, William Crowell, 1879-1946
211. Hildebrand, Joel Henry "Bibliography," NASBM 26: 20-24 '51.

BREASTED, James Henry, 1865-1935
212. Wilson, John A. "James Henry Breasted Bibliography," NASBM 18:115-21 '38.

BREWER, William Henry, 1825-1910
213. Chittenden, Russell H. "Bibliography," NASBM 12: 316-23 '29.

BRIDGE, Josiah, 1890-1953
214. Currier, L. S. "Memorial to Josiah Bridge," GSAP pp. 93-96 '53.

BRIDGES, Calvin Blackman, 1889-1938
215. Morgan, T. H. "Bibliography," NASBM 22:41-48 '43.

BRIDGMAN, Percy Williams, 1882-1961
216. Kemble, Edwin C. and Francis Birch "Bibliography," NASBM 41:50-67 '70.

BRIGGS, Charles Frederick, 1804-1877
217. Blanck, Jacob "Charles Frederick Briggs," BAL 1: 275-78.

BRITTON, Nathaniel Lord, 1859-1934
218. Barnhart, John Hendley "Bibliography," NASBM 19: 160-202 '38.

BROADHEAD, Garland Carr, 1827-1918
219. Keyes, Charles R. "Memorial of Garland Carr Broadhead," GSAB 30:13-27 '19.

BROCK, Reginald Walter, 1874-1935
220. Williams, M. Y. "Memorial of Reginald Walter Brock," GSAP pp. 157-70 '35.

BROMFIELD, Louis, 1896-1956
221. Derrenbacher, Merle "Louis Bromfield: a Bibliography," BB 17:112 S-D '41; 17:141-45 Jan-Apr '42.

BROOKS, Alfred Hulse, 1871-1924
222. Smith, Philip A. "Memorial of Alfred Hulse Brooks,"
GSAB 37:15-48 '26.

BROOKS, Charles Ernest Pelham, 1888-1959
223. Rigby, M. K. and M. Rigby "Annotated Bibliography
on Selected Works of Charles Ernest Pelham Brooks,"
Meteorological Abstracts and Bibliography 10:99-130
Jan '59.

BROOKS, Charles Franklin, 1891-1958
224. Van Valkenburg, S. "Charles F. Brooks, 1891-1958,"
Association of American Geographers. Annals 49:463-
65 D '59.

BROOKS, Charles Timothy, 1813-1883
225. Blanck, Jacob "Charles Timothy Brooks," BAL 1:
279-97.

BROOKS, Cleanth, 1906-
226. Stallman, R. W. "Cleanth Brooks; a Checklist of His
Critical Writings," Kansas City University Review 14:
317-24 Summer '48.

BROOKS, Maria Gowen, 1794?-1845
227. Blanck, Jacob "Maria Gowen Brooks," BAL 1:298-
301.

BROOKS, William Keith, 1848-1908
228. Conklin, Edwin Grant "Bibliography," NASBM 7:79-
88 '13.

BROUWER, Dirk, 1902-1966
229. Clemence, G. M. "Bibliography," NASBM 41:76-87
'70.

BROWN, Amos Peaslee, 1864-1917
230. Penrose, R. A. F., Jr. "Memorial of Amos P.
Brown," GSAB 29:13-17 '18.

BROWN, Charles Brockden, 1771-1810
231. Blanck, Jacob "Charles Brockden Brown," BAL 1:
302-09.
232. Green, David B. "Charles Brockden Brown, America's
First Important Novelist: a Checklist of Biography and
Criticism," BSA 60:349-63 '66.
234. Johnson, Merle "American First Editions: Charles
Brockden Brown (1771-1810)," Publishers' Weekly 121:
26

BROWN, Charles Brockden (continued)
2422 '32.
235. Krause, Sidney J. "A Census of the Works of Charles Brockden Brown," Serif 3:27-55 D '66.

BROWN, Charles Harvey, 1875-1960
236. Crawford, H. "Bibliography of Charles Harvey Brown," College and Research Libraries 8:380-84 Jl '47.

BROWN, Ernest William, 1866-1938
237. Schlesinger, Frank and Dirk Brouwer "Bibliography of Ernest William Brown," NASBM 21:262-73 '41.

BROWN, John, 1800-1859
238. "John Brown, American Abolitionist, 1800-1859; a List of Clippings from the Scrap Books of Eugene V. Debs," Tamiment Institute Library Bulletin #38 pp. 2-4 Ag '63.

BROWN, Leonard, 1837-1914
239. Wright, L. "Leonard Brown: Poet and Populist," Iowa Journal of History and Politics 46:227-65 Jl '48.

BROWN, Thomas Clachar, 1882-1934
240. Mather, Kirtley F. "Memorial of Thomas Clachar Brown," GSAP pp. 203-07 '34.

BROWN, William Henry, 1884-1939
241. Perez, C. B. "William Henry Brown," Philippine Journal of Science 72:245-47 Jl '40.

BROWN, William Hill, 1766-1793
242. Blanck, Jacob "William Hill Brown," BAL 1:310-11.

BROWNE, Charles Farrar, 1834-1867
243. Blanck, Jacob "Charles Farrar Browne," BAL 1:312-24.

BROWNELL, Henry Howard, 1820-1872
244. Blanck, Jacob "Henry Howard Brownell," BAL 1:325-30.

BROWNELL, William Crary, 1851-1928
245. Fletcher, Frank "A Bibliography of William Crary Brownell," BB 20:242-44 Jan-Apr '53.

BRUCE, Everend Lester, 1884-1949
246. Hawley, J. E. "Memorial to Everend Lester Bruce,"
American Mineralogist 35:264-67 Mr '50.

BRUSH, George Jarvis, 1831-1912
247. Dana, Edward S. "Bibliography," NASBM 10:112 '19.

BRYAN, Kirk, 1888-1950
248. Larsen, Esper S., Jr. "Memorial to Kirk Bryan,"
GSAP pp. 91-96 '50.

BRYANT, William Cullen, 1794-1878
249. Blanck, Jacob "William Cullen Bryant," BAL 1:331-
84.

BUCHER, Walter Hermann, 1888-1956
250. Bradley, W. H. "Bibliography," NASBM 40:26-34 '69.

BUCK, Pearl, 1892-
251. Brenni, Vito J. "Pearl Buck: a Selected Bibliography," BB 22:65-69 My-Ag '57; 22:94-96 S-D '57.

BUCKLEY, Ernest Robertson, 1872-1912
252. Buehler, H. A. "Memoir of Ernest Robertson Buckley," GSAB 24:44-48 '13.

BUCKLEY, Oliver Ellsworth, 1887-1959
253. Kelly, Mervin J. "Bibliography," NASBM 37:28-32
'64.

BUEHLER, Henry Andrew, 1876-1944
254. McQueen, H. S. "Memorial to Henry Andrew Buehler,"
GSAP pp. 155-62 '44.

BUMP, James Dye, 1903-1959
255. Green, Morton "Memorial to James Dye Bump,"
GSAP pp. 83-85 '60.

BUMSTEAD, Henry Andrews, 1870-1920
256. Page, Leigh "Bibliography," NASBM 13:124 '30.

BUNNER, Henry Cuyler, 1855-1896
257. Blanck, Jacob "Henry Cuyler Bunner," BAL 1:385-99.

BURDETTE, Robert Jones, 1844-1914
258. Blanck, Jacob "Robert Jones Burdette," BAL 1:400-
12.

28

BURGESS, George Kimball, 1874-1932
259. Briggs, Lyman J. and Wallace R. Brode "Bibliography," NASBM 30:65-72 '57.

BURGH, Robert Frederick, 1907-1962
260. Smith, Watson "Bibliography," AAY 28:85-86 Jl '62.

BURKITT, Robert James, 1869-1945
261. Osborne, Lilly de Jongh and J. Alden Mason "Bibliography," AA 47:610 '45.

BURNETT, Frances Eliza Hodgson (Townsend), 1840-1924
262. Blanck, Jacob "Frances Eliza Hodgson Burnett," BAL 1:413-32.

BURROUGHS, John, 1837-1921
263. Blanck, Jacob "John Burroughs," BAL 1:433-48.
264. Garrison, Joseph M., Jr. "John Burroughs; a Checklist of Published Literary Criticism Including Essays on Natural History Containing Literary Criticism or Comment," BB 24:95-96 My-Ag '64.

BURROWS, Edwin Grant, 1891-1958
265. Barnett, James H. "Edwin Grant Burrows," AA 61: 97-98 F '59.

BURT, Struthers, 1882-1954
266. Wainwright, Alexander D. "A Check List of the Writings of Struthers Burt '04," PULC 19:123-48 Spring '58.

BUTLER, Benjamin Franklin, 1818-1893
267. Cary, Richard "A Dozen Ben Butler Letters," CLQ 6:486-97 S '64.

BUTLER, Ormond Rourke, 1877-1940
268. Milhus, I. E. "Ormond Rourke Butler, 1877-1940; with a List of His Published Papers," Phytopathologist 32:449-50 Je '42.

BUTLER, William Howard Allen, 1825-1902
269. Blanck, Jacob "William Howard Allen Butler," BAL 1:449-59.

BUTTS, Charles, 1863-1946
270. Bevan, Arthur "Memorial to Charles Butts," GSAP pp. 125-29 '47.

BUWALDA, John Peter, 1886-1954
271. Campbell, Ian and Robert P. Sharp "Memorial to John Peter Buwalda," GSAP pp. 107-12 '55.

BYBEE, Halbert Pleasant, 1888-1957
272. Bullard, Fred M. "Memorial to Halbert Pleasant Bybee," GSAP pp. 89-94 '57.

BYNNER, Edwin Lassetter, 1842-1893
273. Blanck, Jacob "Edwin Lassetter Bynner," BAL 1:460-62.

BYRNE, Brian Oswald Donn, 1887-1928
274. Blanck, Jacob "Brian Oswald Donn Byrne," BAL 1: 463-70.
275. Wetherbee, Winthrop, Jr. "(Brian Oswald) Donn Byrne - a Bibliography," BB16:66-67 S-D '37; 16:96 Jan-Apr '38; 16:117-18 My-Ag '38; 16:160-61 Jan-Apr '39; 16:179-80 My-Ag '39.

C

CABLE, George Washington, 1844-1925
276. Blanck, Jacob "George Washington Cable," BAL 2:1-14.
277. Butcher, Philip "George Washington Cable (1844-1925)," ALR #1 pp. 20-25 Fall '67.

CAHAN, Abraham, 1860-1951
278. Marovitz, Sanford E. and Lewis Fried "Abraham Cahan (1860-1951); an Annotated Bibliography," ALR 3: 197-243 Summer '70.

CAHN, Edmond Nathaniel, 1906-1964
279. "Bibliography of the Writings of Edmond Cahn," New York University Law Review 40:278-84 Apr '65.

CAIN, James M. 1892-
280. Hagemann, E. R. and Philip C. Curham "James M. Cain, 1922-1958: a Selected Checklist," BB 23:57-61 S-D '60.

CALHOUN, Fred Harvey Hall, 1874-1959
281. Gunter, Herman "Memorial to Fred Harvey Hall Calhoun," GSAP pp. 115-16 '59.

CALHOUN, John Caldwell, 1782-1850
282. Schultz, H. S. "Century of Calhoun Biographies,"
South Atlantic Quarterly 50:248-54 Apr '51.

CALVERT, George Henry, 1803-1889
283. Blanck, Jacob "George Henry Calvert," BAL 2:15-24.

CALVERT, Philip Powell, 1871-
284. Schmieder, R. G. and M. E. Phillips "Bibliography
of Philip P. Calvert," Entomological News 62:3-40
Jan '51.

CALVIN, Samuel, 1840-1911
285. Shimek, B. "Memoir of Samuel Calvin," GSAB 23:4-
12 '12.

CAMPBELL, Douglas Houghton, 1859-1953
286. Steere, William Campbell "Bibliography," NASBM 29:
55-63 '56.

CAMPBELL, Henry Donald, 1862-1934
287. Roberts, Joseph K. "Memorial of Henry Donald
Campbell," GSAP pp. 209-12 '34.

CAMPBELL, Marius Robinson, 1858-1940
288. Ashley, George H. "Memorial to Marius Robinson
Campbell," GSAP pp. 171-83 '40.

CAMPBELL, Robert Burns, 1892-1955
289. Gunter, Herman "Memorial to Robert Burns Campbell," GSAP pp. 113-14 '55.

CAMPBELL, William Wallace, 1862-1938
290. Wright, W. H. "Bibliography of William Wallace
Campbell," NASBM 25:58-74 '49.

CAPOTE, Truman, 1924-
291. Wall, Richard J. and Carl L. Craycraft "A Checklist of Works About Truman Capote," NYPLB 71:165-
72 Mr '67.

CAPPS, Stephen Reid, 1881-1948
292. Smith, Philip S. "Memorial to Stephen Reid Capps,"
GSAP pp. 127-37 '49.

CARLSON, Anton Julius, 1875-1956
293. Dragstedt, Lester R. "Bibliography," NASBM 35:
16-32 '61.

CARLETON, William McKendree, 1845-1912
294. Blanck, Jacob "William McKendree Carleton," BAL 2:25-41.

CARLTON, Robert see HALL, Baynard Rush

CARMAN, William Bliss, 1861-1929
295. Blanck, Jacob "William Bliss Carman," BAL 2:42-76.

CARNEY, Frank, 1868-1934
296. Thomas, Norman L. "Memorial of Frank Carney," GSAP pp. 213-19 '34.

CAROTHERS, Wallace Hume, 1896-1937
297. Adams, Roger "Bibliography of Wallace Hume Carothers," NASBM 20:304-09 '39.

CARPENTER, Franklin R., 1848-1910
298. Hofman, H. O. "Memoir of Franklin R. Carpenter," GSAB 22:48-52 '11.

CARRYL, Guy Wetmore, 1873-1904
299. Blanck, Jacob "Guy Wetmore Carryl," BAL 2:77-82.

CARTY, John Joseph, 1861-1932
300. Jewett, Frank B. "List of John J. Carty's Published Writings and Addresses," NASBM 18:86-91 '38.

CARVER, George Washington, 1864-1943
301. Guzman, Jessie Parkhurst "George Washington Carver: a Classified Bibliography," BB 21:13-16 My-Ag '53; 21:34-38 S-D '53.

CARY, Alice, 1820-1871
302. Blanck, Jacob "Alice Cary," BAL 2:83-96.

CARY, Phoebe, 1824-1871
303. Blanck, Jacob "Phoebe Cary," BAL 2:97-106.

CASE, Clarence Marsh, 1874-1946
304. Penchef, E. "Writings of Clarence Marsh Case," Sociology and Social Resarch 31:188-93 Jan '47.

CASE, Ermine Cowles, 1871-1953
305. Kellum, Lewis B. "Memorial to Ermine Cowles Case," GSAP pp. 93-101 '54.

CASE, Shirley Jackson, 1872-1947
306. Jennings, L. B. "Bibliography of the Writings of Shirley Jackson Case," Journal of Religion 29:47-58 Jan '49.

CASTLE, William Ernest, 1867-1962
307. Dunn, L. C. "Bibliography," NASBM 38:64-80 '65.

CATHCART, Stanley Holman, 1889-1953
308. Willard, Bradford "Memorial to Stanley Holman Cathcart," GSAP pp. 97-99 '53.

CATHER, Willa, 1876-1947
309. Cary, Richard "A Willa Cather Collection," CLQ 8: 82-95 Je '68
310. Du Bose, La Rocque "American First Editions at TxU IX Willa Cather (1876-1947)," TLC 5:44-47 Spring '55.
311. Hinz, John P. "Willa Cather in Pittsburgh," New Colophon 2:198-207.
312. Hutchinson, Phyllis Martin "Reminiscences of Willa Cather as a Teacher; With a Contribution Toward a Bibliography of Her Writings," NYPLB 60:263-88 Je '56; 60:338-56 Jl '56; 60:378-400 Ag '56.
313. Jessup, Mary E. "A Bibliography of the Writings of Willa Cather," Americana Collector 6:67 '28.

CATHERWOOD, Mary Hartwell, 1847-1902
314. Blanck, Jacob "BAL Addenda," BSA 55:47 '61.
315. Blanck, Jacob "Mary Hartwell Catherwood," BAL 2: 107-16.
316. Price, R. "Mary Hartwell Catherwood; a Bibliography," Illinois State Historical Society Journal 33:68-77 Mr '40.

CATTELL, James McKeen, 1860-1944
317. Pillsbury, W. B. "Partial List of Publications by James McKeen Cattell," NASBM 25:10-16 '49.

CAWEIN, Madison Julius, 1865-1914
318. Blanck, Jacob "Madison Julius Cawein," BAL 2:117-28.

CHADWICK, George Halcott, 1876-1953
319. Goldring, Winifred "Memorial to George Halcott Chadwick," GSAP pp. 101-06 '53.

CHAMBERLAIN, Alexander Francis, 1865-1914
320. Gilbertson, Albert N. "Bibliography," AA 16:343-48

CHAMBERLAIN, Alexander Francis (continued)
'14.

CHAMBERLIN, Rollin Thomas, 1881-1948
321. Bowen, Norman L. "Memorial to Rollin Thomas Chamberlin," GSAP pp. 135-43 '48.
322. Pettijohn, F. J. "Bibliography," NASBM 41:104-10 '70.

CHAMBERLIN, Thomas Chrowder, 1843-1928
323. Chamberlin, Rollin Thomas "A Bibliography of the Published Works of Thomas Chrowder Chamberlin (1843-1928)," NASBM 15:394-407 '34.
324. Willis, Bailey "Memorial of Thomas Chrowder Chamberlin," GSAB 40:23-45 '30.

CHANDLER, Charles Frederick, 1836-1925
325. Bogert, Marston Taylor "Bibliography," NASBM 14: 179-81 '32.

CHANDLER, Raymond, 1888-1959
326. "Some Uncollected Authors I: Raymond Chandler," BC 2:209-11 Autumn '53.

CHANNING, William Ellery, 1818-1901
327. Blanck, Jacob "William Ellery Channing," BAL 2: 129-33.

CHAPIN, James Henry, 1832-1892
328. Davis, W. M. "Memorial of James Henry Chapin," GSAB 4:406-08 1893.

CHAPMAN, Frank Michler, 1864-1945
329. Gregore, William King "Bibliography," NASBM 25: 133-45 '49.

CHAPMAN, John Jay, 1862-1933
330. Stocking, David M. "A Checklist of the Writings of John Jay Chapman," BB 20:146-48 S-D '51; 20:162-65 Jan-Apr '52.

CHARLES, Vera Katherine, 1877-1954
331. Cash, E. K. "Vera Katherine Charles," Mycologia 47:264-65 Mr '55.

CHASE, Mary Ellen, 1887-
332. Cary, Richard "A Bibliography of the Published Writings of Mary Ellen Chase," CLQ 6:34-45 Mr '62.

CHAUVENET, William, 1820-1870
333. Coffin, J. H. C. "Bibliography," NASBM 1:243-44
1877.

CHENEY, George Monroe, 1893-1952
334. Seinmes, Douglas R. "Memorial to George Monroe
Cheney," GSAP pp. 103-06 '54.

CHESNUTT, Charles Waddell, 1858-1932
335. Burris, A. M. "American First Editions: Charles
Waddell Chesnutt," Publishers' Weekly 131:2033 '37.
336. Keller, Dean H. "Charles Waddell Chesnutt (1858-
1932)," ALR #3 pp. 1-4 Summer '68.

CHILD, Charles Manning, 1869-1954
337. "Annotated Bibliography of the Scientific Publications
of Professor Charles Manning Child, L. H. Hyman
and C. D. Van Cleve," Physiological Zoology 11:105-
25 Apr '38.
338. Hyman, Libbie H. "Bibliography," NASBM 30:87-103
'57.

CHILD, Lydia Maria Francis, 1802-1880
339. Blanck, Jacob "Lydia Maria Francis Child," BAL
2:134-56.

CHINARD, Gilbert, 1881-
340. Rice, Howard C., Jr. "Men and Nature in the New
World: A Check List of the Writings of Gilbert Chinard," PULC 26:147-96 Spring '65.

CHITTENDEN, Russell Henry, 1856-1943
341. Vickery, Hubert Bradford "Bibliography," NASBM 24:
94-104 '47.

CHIVERS, Thomas Holley, 1809-1858
342. Blanck, Jacob "Thomas Holley Chivers," BAL 2:157-
59.

CHOPIN, Kate (Katherine) O'Flaherty, 1851-1904
343. Blanck, Jacob "Kate O'Flaherty Chopin," BA1 2:160-
61.
344. Seyersted, Per "Kate Chopin (1851-1904)," ALR 3:
153-59 Spring '70.

CHURCHILL, Winston, 1871-1947
345. Titus, Warren I. "Winston Churchill (1871-1947),"
ALR #3 pp. 26-31 Fall '67.

CLAPP, Charles Horace, 1883-1934
346. Deiss, Charles "Memorial of Charles Horace Clapp," GSAP pp. 171-82 '35.

CLAPP, Frederick Gardner, 1879-1944
347. Washburne, Chester W. "Memorial to Frederick Gardner Clapp," GSAP pp. 163-69 '44.

CLARK, Bruce Lawrence, 1880-1945
348. Camp, Charles L. "Memorial to Bruce Lawrence Clark," GSAP pp. 149-53 '46.

CLARK, Henry James, 1826-1873
349. Packard, A. S., Jr. "List of Scientific Papers and Works," NASBM 1:327-28 1877.

CLARK, Robert Watson, d. 1947
350. Heald, K. C. "Memorial to Robert Watson Clark," GSAP pp. 139-40 '49.

CLARK, Walter Van Tilburg, 1909-
351. Kuehl, John R. "Walter Van Tilburg Clark: a Bibliography," BB 22:18-20 S-D '56.

CLARK, William Bullock, 1860-1917
352. Clarke, John M. "Bibliography," NASBM 9:13-18 '19.
353. Clarke, John M. "Memorial of William Bullock Clark," GSAB 29:21-29 '18.

CLARK, William Mansfield, 1884-1964
354. Vickery, Hubert Bradford "Bibliography," NASBM 39:27-36 '67.

CLARK, William Otterbein, 1874-1952
355. Cox, Doak C. "Memorial to William Otterbein Clark," GSAP pp. 107-10 '54.

CLARK, Willis Gaylord, 1808-1841
356. Blanck, Jacob "Willis Gaylord Clark," BAL 2:162-68.

CLARKE, Frank Wigglesworth, 1847-1931
357. Williams, Lucia K. "Publications by Frank Wigglesworth Clarke," NASBM 15:146-65 '34.

CLARKE, John Mason, 1857-1925
358. Clarke, Noah T. and Clara Mae LeVene "Bibliography," NASBM 12:223-44 '29.
359. Schuchert, Charles "Memorial of John Mason Clarke,"

CLARKE, John Mason (continued)
GSAB 37:49-93 '26.

CLARKE, McDonald, 1798-1842
360. Blanck, Jacob "McDonald Clarke," BAL 2:169-72.

CLAUSEN, Roy Elwood, 1891-1956
361. Jenkins, James A. "Bibliography," NASBM 39:50-54 '67.

CLAYPOLE, Edward Waller, 1835-1901
362. Comstock, Theodore B. "Memoir of Edward Waller Claypole," GSAB 13:487-97 '02.

CLELAND, Herdman Fitzgerald, 1869-1935
363. Raymond, Percy E. "Memorial of Herdman Fitzgerald Cleland," GSAP pp. 183-88 '35.

CLEMENS, Samuel Langhorne, 1835-1910
364. Beebe, Maurice and John Feaster "Criticism of Mark Twain; a Selected Checklist," MFS 14:93-139 Spring '68.
365. Blanck, Jacob "BAL Addendum 3479: Twain's 'A Dog's Tale,' " BSA 62:617 '68.
366. Blanck, Jacob "Samuel Langhorne Clemens," BAL 2: 173-254.
367. Branch, Edgar M. "A Chronological Bibliography of the Writings of Samuel Clemens to June 8, 1867," AL 18:109-59 '46-'47.
368. Mobley, Laurence E. "Mark Twain and the Golden Era," BSA 58:8-23 '64.
369. Roper, Gordon "Check List of Canadian Editions of Mark Twain's Work," ABC 10:28-29 Je '60.

CLINTON, George Perkins, 1867-1937
370. McCormick, Florence A. "Bibliography," NASBM 20: 189-96 '39.

CLOUGH, Wilson Ober, 1894-
371. Hillier, R. L. "Bibliography of Wilson O. Clough," University of Wyoming. Publications. 25:5-12 Jl '61.

COBB, Collier, 1862-1934
372. Prouty, William F. "Memorial of Collier Cobb," GSAP pp. 189-94 '35.

COBBETT, William, 1762-1835
373. Manks, Dorothy S. "Some Early American Horticul-

COBBETT, William (continued)
tural Writers and Their Works," Huntia 2:66-110 '65.

COBLENTZ, William Weber, 1873-1962
374. "Bibliography," Journal of the Optical Society of
America 36:62-71 '46.
375. Meggers, William F. "Bibliography," NASBM 39:80-
102 '67.

COFFIN, Robert P. Tristram, 1892-1955
376. Cary, Richard "A Bibliography of Robert P. Tristram
Coffin," CLQ 7:170-89 D '65; 7:270-99 Je '66; 7:355-
82 D '66.
377. Cary, Richard "A Bibliography of Robert P. Tristram
Coffin: Addenda," CLQ 8:22-28 Mr '68.

COFFMAN, George Raleigh, 1880-1958
378. "List of the Writings of George Raleigh Coffman,"
Studies in Philology 48:457-60 Jl '51.

COGHILL, George Ellett, 1872-1941
379. Herrick, C. Judson "Bibliography," NASBM 22:268-
73 '43.

COHEN, Morris Raphael, 1880-1947
380. Kuhn, Martin Arno "Morris Raphael Cohen: a Bibliography: Journal of the History of Ideas Special Supplement '57.

COHN, Edwin Joseph, 1892-1953
381. Esdall, John T. "Bibliography," NASBM 35:73-84 '61.

COKER, William Chambers, 1872-1953
382. Couch, J. N. and V. D. Matthews "William Chambers
Coker," Mycologia 46:378-83 My '54.

COLE, Fay-Cooper, 1881-1961
383. Eggan, Fred and E. Arsenio Manuel "Bibliography of
Fay-Cooper Cole," AA 65:645-48 Je '63.

COLE, George Watson, 1850-1939
384. "List of the Printed Productions of George Watson
Cole 1870-1935," BB 15:183-86 My-Ag '36; 16:11-12
S-D '36; 16:32-35 Jan-Apr '37.

COLLIER, Arthur James, 1866-1939
385. Richardson, G. B. "Memorial to Arthur James Collier," GSAP pp. 181-85 '39.
38

COMPTON, Arthur Holly, 1892-1962
386. Allison, Samuel K. "Bibliography," NASBM 38:99-110 '65.

COMPTON, Karl Taylor, 1887-1954
387. Bartlett, E. L. "Writings of Karl Taylor Compton," Technology Review 57:89-92 D '54.

COMSTOCK, Cyrus Ballou, 1831-1910
388. Abbot, Henry L. "Bibliography," NASBM 7:201 '13.

COMSTOCK, George Cary, 1855-1934
389. Stebbins, Joel "Bibliography," NASBM 20:175-82 '39.

COMSTOCK, Theodore Bryant, 1849-1915
390. Ries, Heinrich "Memorial of Theodore Bryant Comstock," GSAB 27:12-15 '16.

CONANT, James Bryant, 1893-
391. Protor, V. "Bibliography of James B. Conant," Journal of General Education 5:48-56 O '50.

CONDIT, Donald Dale, 1886-1955
392. Weeks, Lewis G. "Memorial to Donald Dale Condit," GSAP pp. 115-19 '55.

CONKLIN, Edwin Grant, 1863-1952
393. Harvey, E. Newton "Bibliography," NASBM 31:75-91 '58.

CONNOLLY, Joseph Peter, 1890-1947
394. Graton, L. C. "Memorial to Joseph Peter Connolly," American Mineralogist 33:176-77.
395. McLaughlin, Donald H. "Memorial to Joseph Peter Connolly," GSAP pp. 135-39 '47.

COOK, Charles Wilford, 1882-1933
396. Hobbs, William K. "Memorial to Charles Wilford Cook," GSAP pp. 181-84 '33.

COOK, George Hamell, 1818-1889
397. Gilbert, G. K. "Bibliography," NASBM 4:143-44 '02.
398. Smock, John C. "Geological Writings of George H. Cook," GSAB 5:569-71 1894.

COOKE, John Esten, 1830-1886
399. Blanck, Jacob "John Esten Cooke," BAL 2:255-65.
400. Wegelin, Oscar "A Bibliography of the Separate Writ-

COOKE, John Esten (continued)
ings of John Esten Cooke," Americana Collector 1:96-
99 '25.

COOKE, Josiah Parson, 1827-1894
401. Jackson, Charles L. "A List of the More Important
Publications of Josiah Parson Cooke," NASBM 4:180-
83 '02.

COOKE, Rose Terry, 1827-1892
402. Blanck, Jacob "Rose Terry Cooke," BAL 2:266-75.
403. Downey, Jean "Rose Terry Cooke: a Bibliography,"
BB 21:159-63 My-Ag '55.

COOPER, James Fenimore, 1789-1851
404. Blanck, Jacob "James Fenimore Cooper," BAL 2:276-
310.

COOPER, John Montgomery, 1881-1949
405. Stine, Jane "Anthropological Bibliography 1914-1949,"
AA 52:69-74 '50.

COOPER, Paul Lemen, 1909-1961
406. Kivett, Marvin F. "Bibliography," AAY 27:572 Apr
'62.

COOPER, Peter, 1791-1883
407. Spalding, C. Sumner "Peter Cooper: a Critical Bibliography of His Life and Works," NYPLB 45:723-45
S '41.

COOPER, Susan Augusta Fenimore, 1813-1894
408. Blanck, Jacob "Susan Augusta Fenimore Cooper,"
BAL 2:311-15.

COPE, Edward Drinker, 1840-1897
409. Osborn, Henry Fairfield et al. "Bibliography of Edward Drinker Cope 1859-1915," NASBM 13:172-317
'30.

COREY, Lewis (formerly Louis C. Fraina), 1892-1953
410. Corey, E. "Lewis Corey (Louis C. Fraina) 1892-
1953; A Bibliography with Autobiographical Notes,"
Labor History 4:103-31 Spring '63.

COTTON, John, 1584-1652
411. Etulain, Richard W. "John Cotton: a Checklist of
Relevant Materials," Early American Literature 4:

COTTON, John (continued)
64-69.

COTTRELL, Frederick Gardner, 1877-1948
412. Bush, Vannevar "Bibliography of Frederick Gardner Cottrell," NASBM 27:8-11 '52.

COUCH, John Nathaniel, 1896-
413. Shanor, L. "John Nathaniel Couch," Elisha Mitchell Scientific Society. Journal 84:5-7 Spring '68.

COUES, Elliott, 1842-1899
414. Allen, J. A. "List of Principal Works and Papers," NASBM 6:426-46 '09.

COULTER, John Merle, 1851-1928
415. Arthur, J. C. "Bibliography," NASBM 14:109-23 '32.

COUNCILMAN, William Thomas, 1854-1933
416. Cushing, Harvey "Bibliography," NASBM 18:168-74 '38.

COX, Guy Henry, 1881-1921
417. Dake, C. L. "Memorial of Guy H. Cox," GSAB 34: 15-18 '23.

COXE, Louis, 1918-
418. Johnson, E. D. H. "A Checklist of the Writings of Louis Coxe," PULC 25:16-20 Autumn '63.

COZZENS, Frederic Swartwout, 1818-1869
419. Blanck, Jacob "Frederic Swartwout Cozzens," BAL 2:316-19.

COZZENS, James Gould, 1903-
420. Meriwether, James B. "A James Gould Cozzens Check List," C 1:57-63 Winter '58.

CRAFTS, James Mason, 1839-1917
421. Cross, Charles R. "Bibliography," NASBM 9:169-77 '19.

CRAIG, Hardin, 1875-
422. Johnson F. R. "Bibliography of the Writings of Hardin Craig from 1901 to 1940," Philological Quarterly 20:527-31 Jl '41.

CRANCH, Christopher Pearse, 1813-1892
423. Blanck, Jacob "Christopher Pearse Cranch," BAL 2: 320-28.

CRANDALL, Vaughan, J. , 1922-1963
424. Hunt, D. E. et al. "Vaughan J. Crandall," Child Development 35:593-94 S '64.

CRANE, Hart, 1899-1932
425. Bloomingdale, Judith "Three Decades in Periodical Criticism of Hart Crane's 'The Bridge,' " BSA 57:360-71 '63.
426. Radhuber, Stanley G. "Hart Crane: an Annotated Bibliography," Dissertation, University of Michigan '69.
427. Robinson, Jethro "The Hart Crane Collection," Columbia Library Columns 4:3-7 F '55.
428. Rowe, H. D. "Hart Crane: a Bibliography," TCL 1: 94-113 Jl '55.
429. White, William "Hart Crane: Bibliographical Addenda," BB 24:35 S-D '63.

CRANE, Stephen, 1871-1900
430. Beebe, Maurice and Thomas A. Gullason "Criticism of Stephen Crane: a Selected Checklist with an Index to Studies of Separate Works," MFS 5:282-91 Autumn '59.
431. Blanck, Jacob "Stephen Crane," BAL 2:329-38.
432. Braunstein, Simeon "A Checklist of Writings by and About Stephen Crane in The Fra," Stephen Crane Newsletter 3:8.
433. Fraser, Robert S. "The Thoth Annual Bibliography of Stephen Crane Scholarship," Thoth 9:58-61.
434. Hudspeth, Robert N. "A Bibliography of Stephen Crane Scholarship: 1893-1962," Thoth 4:30-58 Winter '63.
435. Hudspeth, Robert N. "The Thoth Annual Bibliography of Stephen Crane Scholarship," Thoth 5:85-87; 6 pp. 31-33 '65; 7 pp. 76-77; 8:98-99.
436. Jones, Claude E. "Stephen Crane: A Bibliography of His Short Stories and Essays," BB 15:149-50 S-D '35; 15:170 Jan-Apr '36.
437. Katz, Joseph "CALM Addendum No. 1: Stephen Crane," BSA 63:130 '69.
438. Katz, Joseph "Quarterly Checklist of Stephen Crane Scholarship," Stephen Crane Newsletter #1 pp. 4-6.
439. Katz, Joseph "Toward a Descriptive Bibliography of Stephen Crane The Black Riders," BSA 59:150-57 '65.
440. Katz, Joseph and Matthew J. Bruccoli "Toward a Descriptive Bibliography of Stephen Crane: 'Spanish-
42

CRANE, Stephen (continued)
American War Songs,' " BSA 61:267-69 '67.
441. Monteiro, George " 'Grand Opera for the People:' An Unrecorded Stephen Crane Printing," BSA 63:29-30 '69.

CRAPSEY, Adelaide, 1878-1914
442. Blanck, Jacob "Adelaide Crapsey," BAL 2:339-40.

CRAWFORD, Francis Marion, 1854-1909
443. Blanck, Jacob "Francis Marion Crawford," BAL 2: 341-63.

CRAWFORD, Ralph Dixon, 1873-1950
444. Worcester, P. G. "Memorial to Ralph Dixon Crawford," GSAP pp. 97-99 '50.

CREW, Henry, 1859-1953
445. Meggers, William F. "Bibliography," NASBM 37:46-54 '64.

CROOK, Alja Robinson, 1864-1930
446. Farrington, Oliver C. "Memorial of Alja Robinson Crook," GSAB 42:19-25 '32.

CROSBY, Irving Ballard, 1891-1959
447. Shrock, Robert R. "Memorial to Irving Ballard Crosby," GSAP pp. 117-20 '59.

CROSBY, William Otis, 1850-1926
448. Shimer, H. W. and Waldemar Lindgren "Memorial of William Otis Crosby," GSAB 38:34-45 '27.

CROSS, Charles Whitman, 1854-1949
449. Larsen, Esper S., Jr. "Bibliography," NASBM 32: 105-12 '58.

CULVER, Garry Eugene, 1849-1938
450. Culver, Harold E. "Memorial to Garry E. Culver," GSAP pp. 143-46 '38.

CUMMINS, Maria Susanna, 1827-1866
451. Blanck, Jacob "Maria Susanna Cummins," BAL 2:364-66.

CUNNINGHAM, Harry Allen, 1891-
452. Pruitt, C. M. "Harry Allen Cunningham," Science Education 44:4-5 F '60.

CURTIS, George William, 1824-1892
453. Blanck, Jacob "George William Curtis," BAL 2:367-93.

CURTIS, Heber Doust, 1872-1942
454. Aitken, Robert G. "Complete Professional Bibliography," NASBM 22:285-94 '43.

CUSHING, Harvey, 1869-1939
455. MacCallum, W. G. "Bibliography of Harvey Cushing," NASBM 22:55-70 '43.

CUSHING, Henry Platt, 1860-1921
456. Kemp, James F. "Memorial of Henry Platt Cushing," GSAB 33:44-55 '22.

CUSHMAN, Joseph Augustine, 1881-1949
457. Henbest, Lloyd G. "Joseph Augustine Cushman and the Contemporary Epoch in Micropaleontology," GSAP pp. 95-101 '51.

CUYLER, Robert Hamilton, 1908-1944
458. Bullard, Fred M. "Memorial to Robert Hamilton Cuyler," GSAP pp. 171-74 '44.

D

DAKE, Charles Laurence, 1883-1934
459. Brown, John S. "Memorial of Charles Laurence Dake," GSAP pp. 195-200 '35.

DALGLIESH, Alice, 1893-
460. "Books by Alice Dalgliesh," Horn Book 23:66, 136 Mr '47.

DALL, William Healey, 1845-1927
461. Bartsch, Paul et al. "Bibliography and Short Biographical Sketch of William Healey Dall," Smithsonian Miscellaneous Collections 104:17-96.
462. Woodring, W. P. "Selected Bibliography," NASBM 31: 107-13 '58.

DALLENBACH, Karl M., 1887-
463. McGrade, M. C. "Bibliography of the Writings of Karl M. Dallenbach," American Journal of Psychology 71:41-49 Mr '58.

DALY, Reginald Aldworth, 1871-1957
464. Billings, Marland P. "Memorial to Reginald Aldworth Daly," GSAP pp. 115-21 '58.
465. Birch, Francis "Bibliography," NASBM 34:54-64 '60.

DANA, Edward Salisbury, 1849-1935
466. Knopf, Adolph "Bibliography of Edward S. Dana," NASBM 18:359-64 '38.
467. Schuchert, Charles "Memorial of Edward Salisbury Dana," GSAP pp. 201-14 '35.

DANA, James Dwight, 1813-1895
468. Le Conte, Joseph "Memoir of James Dwight Dana," GSAB 7:461-79 1896.
469. Pirsson, Louis V. "Bibliography," NASBM 9:83-92 '19.

DANA, John Cotton, 1856-1929
470. Johnson, H. and B. Winser "Bibliography: John Cotton Dana, Author," Library Quarterly 7:68-98 Jan '37.

DANA, Richard Henry, Sr., 1787-1879
471. Blanck, Jacob "Richard Henry Dana, Sr.," BAL 2: 394-99.

DANA, Richard Henry, Jr., 1815-1882
472. Blanck, Jacob "Richard Henry Dana, Jr.," BAL 2: 400-10.
473. Hart, James. D. "The Other Writings of Richard Henry Dana," Colophon pt. 19.
474. Johnson, Merle "American First Editions: Richard Henry Dana, Jr., 1815-1882," Publishers' Weekly 119: 2891-92 '31.

DANE, George Ezra, 1904-1941
475. Mood, F. "Chronological Bibliography of the Publications of George Ezra Dane," California Folklore Quarterly 1:93 Jan '42.

DARTON, Nelson Horatio, 1865-1948
476. King, Philip B. "Memorial to Nelson Horatio Darton," GSAP pp. 145-69 '48.

DAVENPORT, Charles Benedict, 1866-1944
477. Riddle, Oscar "Bibliography," NASBM 25:92-110 '49.
478. Steggerda, M. "Abridged Bibliography of Dr. Davenport's Writings on Human Heredity and Eugenics," Eugenical News 29:8-10 Mr '44.
479. Steggerda, M. "Charles Benedict Davenport (1866-

DAVENPORT, Charles Benedict (continued)
1944) the Man and His Contributions to Physical Anthropology," American Journal of Physical Anthropology n. s. 2:179-85 Je '44.

DAVIDSON, Daniel Sutherland, 1900-1952
480. Hallowell, A. Irving and Erna Gunther "Daniel Sutherland Davidson; 1900-1952," AA 56:873-76 '54.

DAVIDSON, George, 1825-1911
481. Davenport, Charles B. "Bibliography of George Davidson," NASBM 18:205-17 '38.

DAVIS, Bergen, 1869-1958
482. Webb, Harold W. "Bibliography," NASBM 34:79-82 '60.

DAVIS, Charles Albert, 1861-1916
483. Lane, Alfred C. "Memorial of Charles A. Davis," GSAB 28:14-40 '17.

DAVIS, Charles Augustus, 1795-1867
484. Blanck, Jacob "Charles Augustus Davis," BAL 2:411-14.

DAVIS, H. L. , 1896-1960
485. Kellogg, George "H. L. Davis, 1896-1960: a Bibliography," TSLL 5:294-303 Summer '63.

DAVIS, Rebecca Harding, 1831-1910
486. Stemple, Ruth M. "Rebecca Harding Davis, 1831-1910: a Check List," BB 22:83-85 S-D '57.

DAVIS, Richard Harding, 1864-1916
487. Blanck, Jacob "Richard Harding Davis," BAL 2:415-27.
488. Solensten, John M. "Richard Harding Davis (1864-1916)," ALR 3:160-66 Spring '70.

DAVIS, William Morris, 1850-1934
489. Daly, Reginald A. "Bibliography," NASBM 23:281-303 '45.

DAVISSON, Clinton Joseph, 1881-1958
490. Kelly, Mervin J. "Bibliography," NASBM 36:81-84 '62.
491. "Published Writings of C. J. Davisson," Bell System Technical Journal 30:1035-37 O '51.

DAWES, Rufus, 1803-1859
492. Blanck, Jacob "Rufus Dawes," BAL 2:428-31.

DAWSON, George M., 1849-1901
493. Ami, H. M. "Bibliography," GSAB 13:502-09 '02.

DAY, David Talbot, 1859-1925
494. Darton, N. H. "Memorial to David Talbot Day,"
GSAP pp. 185-91 '33.

DEAN, Bashford, 1867-1928
495. Gregory, William K. "Memorial of Bashford Dean,"
GSAB 41:16-25 '31.

DEBO, Angie, 1890-
496. Poulton, Helen J. "Angie Debo: a Check-list," BB
22:15-17 S-D '56.

de BORHEGYI, Stephan F., 1921-1969
497. Wendorf, Fred "A Bibliography of Stephan F. de Borhegyi," AAY 35:196-200 Apr '70.

DECKER, Charles Elijah, 1868-1958
498. Branson, Carl C. "Memorial to Charles Elijah Decker," GSAP pp. 123-26 '58.

DE FOREST, John William, 1826-1906
499. Blanck, Jacob "John William De Forest," BAL 2:432-
37.
500. Editors of American Literary Realism Realism "John
William De Forest (1826-1906): a Critical Bibliography
of Secondary Comment," ALR #4 pp. 1-56 Fall '68.
501. Hagemann, E. R. "A Checklist of Critical Comments
in The Nation of John William De Forest, 1866-1879,"
ALR #4 pp. 76-79 Fall '68.
502. Hagemann, E. R. "A Checklist of the Writings of John
William De Forest (1826-1906)," SB 8:185-94 '56.
503. Hagemann, E. R. "A John William De Forest Supplement, 1970," ALR 3:148-52 Spring '70.
504. Light, James F. "John William De Forest (1826-
1906)," ALR #1 pp. 32-35 Fall '67.

De GOLYER, Everette Lee, 1886-1956
505. Denison, A. Rodger "A Bibliography," NASBM 33:72-
86 '59.
506. Pratt, Wallace E. "Memorial to Everette Lee De
Golyer," GSAP pp. 95-103 '57.

DEISS, Charles Frederick, 1903-1959
507. Patton, John B. "Memorial to Charles Frederick Deiss," GSAP pp. 121-24 '59.

DELAND, Margaretta, 1857-1945
508. Humphrey, James III "The Works of Margaretta Deland," CLQ 2:134-40 N '48.

De LEON, Daniel, 1852-1914
509. Lazarus, Louis "Daniel De Leon Bibliography," Tamiment Institute Library Bulletin pp. 2-9 S/O '59.

DELL, Floyd, 1887-
510. Tanselle, G. Thomas "Floyd Dell in the 'Friday Literary Review,'" BSA 57:371-76 '63.

DEMOREST, Max Harrison, 1910-1942
511. Fenneman, Nevin M. "Memorial to Max Harrison Demorest," GSAP pp. 173-77 '42.

DEMPSTER, Arthur Jeffrey, 1886-1950
512. Allison, Samuel King "Bibliography," NASBM 27:330-33 '52.

DENNIE, Joseph, 1868-1812
513. Blanck, Jacob "Joseph Dennie," BAL 2:438-42.

DENSLOW, William Wallace, 1856-1915
514. Martin, Dick "W. W. Denslow: a Chronological Checklist of His Published Work," ABC 51:17-21 D '64.

DERBY, George Horatio, 1823-1861
515. Blanck, Jacob "George Horatio Derby," BAL 2:443-45.

DERBY, Orville Adelbert, 1851-1915
516. Branner, John C. "Memorial of Orville A. Derby," GSAB 27:15-21 '16.

DETWILER, Samuel Randall, 1890-1957
517. Nicholas J. S. "Bibliography," NASBM 35:100-11 '61.

DeVOTO, Bernard, 1897-1955
518. Lee, Robert Edson "The Easy Chair Essays of Bernard DeVoto," BB 23:64-69 S-D '60.

DE VRIES, Peter, 1910-
519. Bowden, Edwin T. "Peter De Vries - The First Thirty Years: a Bibliography, 1934-1964," TSLL 6:545-70 Supplement '65.

DEWEY, John, 1859-1952
520. Boydston, Jo Ann "The John Dewey Bibliography,"
BSA 62:67-75 '68.
521. Cressman, P. "Psychology of John Dewey," Psycho-
logical Review 49:461-62 S '42.
522. "Opere di Dewey (1939-1950)," Rivista Critica di Storia
della Filosofia 6:442-53 O '51.
523. Pillsbury, W. B. "Selected Bibliography," NASBM 30:
121-24 '57.

De WOLF, Frank Walbridge, 1881-1957
524. Scott, Harold W. "Memorial to Frank Walbridge De
Wolf," GSAP pp. 105-08 '57.

DICKERSON, Roy Ernest, 1877-1944
525. Stephenson, Lloyd W. "Memorial to Roy Ernest Dickerson," GSAP pp. 175-79 '44.

DICKEY, James, 1923-
526. Glancy, Eileen K. "James Dickey: a Bibliography,"
TCL 15:45-61 Apr '69.

DICKINSON, Emily, 1830-1886
527. Birss, John Howard "Emily Dickinson: A Biographical Note," Notes and Queries 164:421 '32.
528. Blanck, Jacob "Emily Elizabeth Dickinson," BAL 2:
446-54.
529. Treis, Susan "Emily Dickinson: A Check List of
Criticism, 1930-1966," BSA 61:359-85 '67.
530. White, William "Emily Dickinsoniana: an Annotated
Checklist of Books About the Poet," BB 26:100-05 O-
D '69.
531. White, William "Homage to Emily Dickinson: Tributes
by Creative Artists," BB 20:112-15 My-Ag '51.

DILLARD, Hardy Cross, 1902-
532. Tillman, Jeanne "A Selected Bibliography of Writings
by Hardy Cross Dillard," Virginia Journal of International Law v. 8 Apr '68.

DILLER, Joseph Silas, 1850-1928
533. Collier, A. J. "Memorial of Joseph Silas Diller,"
GSAB 40:61-80 '30.

DINSMOOR, William Bell, 1886-
534. "Bibliography of William Bell Dinsmoor," Hesperia
35:87-92 Apr '66.

49

D'INVILLIERS, Edward Vincent, 1857-1928
535. Ashley, George H. "Memorial of Edward Vincent D'Invilliers," GSAP pp. 221-24 '34.

DIXON, Roland Burrage, 1875-1934
536. Tozzer, A. M. and A. L. Kroeber "Bibliography," AA 38:297-300 '36.

DODGE, Bernard Ogilvie, 1872-1960
537. Robbins, William J. "Bibliography," NASBM 36:113-24 '62.

DODGE, Mary Abigail, 1833-1896
538. Blanck, Jacob "Mary Abigail Dodge," BAL 2:455-63.

DODGE, Mary Elizabeth Mapes, 1831-1905
539. Blanck, Jacob "Mary Elizabeth Mapes Dodge," BAL 2:464-73.

DODGE, Raymond, 1871-1942
540. Miles, Walter R. "Bibliography," NASBM 29:116-22 '56.

DODGE, Richard Elwood, 1868-1952
541. Visher, Stephen S. "Memorial to Richard Elwood Dodge," GSAP pp. 95-96 '52.

DONALDSON, Henry Herbert, 1857-1938
542. Conklin, Edwin G. "Bibliography of Henry H. Donaldson," NASBM 20:238-43 '39.

DONNELLY, Ignatius Loyola, 1831-1901
543. Blanck, Jacob "Ignatius Loyola Donnelly," BAL 2:474-79.

DOOLITTLE, Hilda, 1886-1961
544. Bryer, Jackson R. and P. Roblyer "H. D.: a Preliminary Checklist," Contemporary Literature 10:632-75 Autumn '69.

DORSEY, George A., 1868-1931
545. Cole, Fay-Cooper "Bibliography," AA 33:414 '31.

DOS PASSOS, John, 1896-1970
546. Kallich, Martin "A Bibliography of John Dos Passos," BB 19:231-35 My-Ag '49.
547. Reinhart, Virginia S. "John Dos Passos, 1950-1966, Bibliography," TCL 13:167-78 O '67.

DOS PASSOS, John (continued)
548. White, William "John Dos Passos and His Reviewers,"
     BB 20:45-47 My-Ag '50.
549. White, William "More Dos Passos: Bibliographical
     Addenda," BSA 45:156-58 '51.

DOWNING, Major Jack see DAVIS, Charles Augustus.

DRAKE, Joseph Rodman, 1795-1820
550. Blanck, Jacob "Joseph Rodman Drake," BAL 2:480-84.
551. Johnson, Merle and John H. Birss "American First
     Editions: Joseph Rodman Drake, 1795-1820," Pub-
     lishers' Weekly 127:1926 '35.

DRAKE, Noah Fields, 1864-1945
552. Miser, Hugh D. "Memorial to Noah Fields Drake,"
     GSAP pp. 141-48 '47.

DRAPER, Henry, 1837-1882
553. Barker, George F. "List of Henry Draper's Pub-
     lished Papers," NASBM 3:138-39 1895.

DRAPER, John William, 1811-1882
554. Barker, George F. "Publications of John William
     Draper," NASBM 2:383-88 1886.

DRAPER, John William, 1893-
555. Singer, A. E. "John W. Draper, Vita and Bibliogra-
     phy," West Virginia University Philological Papers 13:
     2-10 '61.

DREISER, Theodore, 1871-1945
556. Elias, Robert H. "The Library's Dreiser Collection,"
     LC 17:78-80 '50.
557. Salzman, Jack "Theodore Dreiser (1871-1945)," ALR
     2:132-38 Summer '69.

DRESSER, John Alexander, 1866-1954
558. Douglas, George Vibert "Memorial to John Alexander
     Dresser," GSAP pp. 109-11 '57.

DRYDEN, Hugh Latimer, 1898-1965
559. Hunsaker, Jerome C. and Robert C. Seaman, Jr.
     "Bibliography," NASBM 40:53-68 '69.

DUANE, William, 1872-1935
560. Bridgman, P. W. "Bibliography," NASBM 18:35-41
     '38.

DUBINSKY, David, 1892-1960
561. Oko, D. K. "David Dubinsky and the International
Ladies' Garment Workers' Union; a Selected Bibliography," Labor History 9:116-26 Supplement Spring '68.

DuBOIS, Eugene Floyd, 1882-1959
562. Aub, Joseph C. "Bibliography," NASBM 36:137-45 '62.

DUCASSE, Curt John, 1881-
563. Taylor, R. "Writings of Curt John Ducasse to December 31, 1951," Philosophy and Phenomenological Research 13:196-202 S '52.

DUGANNE, Augustine Joseph Hickey, 1823-1884
564. Blanck, Jacob "Augustine Joseph Hickey Duganne,"
BAL 2:485-97.

DUGGAR, Benjamin Minge, 1872-1956
565. Walker, J. C. "Bibliography," NASBM 32:122-31 '58.

DUMBLE, Edwin Theodore, 1852-1927
566. Simonds, Frederic William "Memorial of Edwin Theodore Dumble," GSAB 39:18-29 '28.

DUMBLETON, Joseph, fl. 1740-50
567. Cohen, Henning "The poems of Joseph Dumbleton,
1740-1750," BB 20:220 S-D '52.

DUNBAR, Paul Laurence, 1872-1906
568. Blanck, Jacob "Paul Laurence Dunbar," BAL 2:498-
505.
569. Burris, Andrew M. "Bibliography of the Works of
Paul Laurence Dunbar," Americana Collector 5:69-73
'27.

DUNLAP, William, 1766-1839
570. Blanck, Jacob "William Dunlap," BAL 2:506-18.

DUNN, Gano Sillick, 1870-1953
571. Bush, Vannevar "Bibliography," NASBM 28:40-44 '54.

DUNNE, Peter Masten, 1889-1957
572. Bannon, J. F. "Peter Masten Dunne, S. J., 1889-
1957," Hispanic American Historical Review 37:229-33
My '57.

DUSENBERRY, Verne, 1906-1966
573. Malouf, Carling "Verne Dusenberry," AA 70:326-27

DUSENBERRY, Verne (continued)
Apr '68.

DUTTON, Clarence Edward, 1841-1912
574. Diller, J. S. "Memoir of Clarence Edward Dutton," GSAB 24:10-18 '13.
575. Longwell, Chester R. "Bibliography," NASBM 32:142-45 '58.

DWIGHT, Timothy, 1752-1817
576. Blanck, Jacob "Timothy Dwight," BAL 2:519-30.

E

EAKLE, Arthur Starr, 1862-1931
577. Palache, Charles "Memorial of Arthur Starr Eakle," GSAB 43:46-52 '33.

EAMES, Wilberforce, 1855-1937
578. Stark, Lewis M. "The Writings of Wilberforce Eames," NYPLB 59:515-19 O '55.

EAST, Edward Murray, 1879-1938
579. Jones, Donald F. "Bibliography of Edward Murray East," NASBM 23:233-42 '45.

EASTLAKE, William
580. Angell, Richard C. "Eastlake; at Home and Abroad," New Mexico Quarterly 34:204-09 '64.

EASTMAN, Charles Rochester, 1868-1918
581. Dean, Bashford "Memorial of Charles Rochester Eastman," GSAB 30:27-36 '19

EATON, Harry Nelson, 1880-1944
582. Smith, Burnett "Memorial to Harry Nelson Easton," GSAP pp. 181-84 '44.

EATON, Joseph Edmund, 1895-1958
583. Corey, W. H. "Memorial of Joseph Edmund Eaton," GSAP pp. 127-28 '58.

ECKEL, Edwin Clarence, 1875-1941
584. Spencer, Arthur C. "Memorial to Edwin Clarence Eckel," GSAP pp. 179-87 '42.

EDEL, May Mandelbaum, 1909-1964
585. Bunzel, Ruth L. "May Mandelbaum Edel," AA 68:986-89 Ag '66.

EDISON, Thomas Alva, 1847-1931
586. Kennelly, Arthur E. "Bibliography," NASBM 15:304 '34.

EGGLESTON, Edward, 1837-1902
587. Blanck, Jacob "Edward Eggleston," BAL 3:1-15.
588. Randel, William "Edward Eggleston (1837-1902)," ALR #1 pp. 36-44 Fall '67.

EIGENMANN, Carl H., 1863-1927
589. Styneger, Leonhard "Bibliography," NASBM 18:324-36 '38.

EISENHART, Luther Pfahler, 1876-1965
590. Lefschetz, Solomon "Bibliography," NASBM 40:81-90 '69.

ELDRIDGE, George Homans, 1854-1905
591. Cross, Whitman "Memoir of George H. Eldridge," GSAB 17:681-87 '06.

ELIOT, Alice C. see JEWETT, Sarah Orne

ELIOT, T. S., 1888-1965
592. Fry, Varian "A Bibliography of the Writings of Thomas Stearns Eliot," Hound and Horn 1:214-18 '28.
593. Malawsky, Beryl York "T. S. Eliot: a Check List; 1952-1964," BB 25:59-61 My-Ag '67.

ELKIN, William Lewis, 1855-1933
594. Schlesinger, Frank "Bibliography of William Lewis Elkin," NASBM 18:187-88 '38.

ELLISON, Ralph Waldo, 1914-
595. Lillard, R. S. "A Ralph Waldo Ellison Bibliography (1914-1967)," ABC 19:18-22 N '68.
596. Polsgrove, Carol "Addenda to 'A Ralph Waldo Ellison Bibliography (1914-1968),'" ABC 20:11-12 N-D '69.

EMBREE, John Fee, 1908-1950
597. Pikelis, Anna "Bibliography," AA 53:379-82 '51.

EMERSON, Ralph Waldo, 1803-1882
598. Blanck, Jacob "BAL Addenda Ralph Waldo Emerson

EMERSON, Ralph Waldo (continued)
Entry No. 5272," BSA 61:124-26 '67.
599. Blanck, Jacob "Ralph Waldo Emerson," BAL 3:16-70.
600. Booth, Robert A. and Roland Stromberg "A Bibliography of Ralph Waldo Emerson, 1908-1920," BB 19:180-83 S-D '48.
601. Bryer, Jackson R. and Robert A. Rees "A Checklist of Emerson Criticism, 1951-1961," Emerson Society Quarterly #37. Reprinted by Transcendental Books.
602. Cameron, Kenneth Walter "Recent Emerson Bibliography," Emerson Society Quarterly #10 pp. 51-53; #14 pp. 96-99 '59.
603. Cameron, Kenneth W. "Current Bibliography on Ralph Waldo Emerson," Emerson Society Quarterly #19 pp. 97-98; #27 pp. 50-53; #37 pp. 88-92; #43 pp. 145-50; #48 pp. 100-05; #50 pp. 38-42.
604. Cooke, George W. "Bibliography of Ralph Waldo Emerson," Unity 51:168 My 14 '03.
605. Fairchild, Salome Cutler "Best Editions of Ralph Waldo Emerson," BB 3:58-59 '093.
606. Gordon, John D. "Ralph Waldo Emerson, 1803-1882; Catalogue of an Exhibition from the Berg Collection," NYPLB 57:392-408 Ag '53; 57:433-60 S '53.
607. Ireland, Alexander "Emerson Bibliography," Athenaeum p. 53 Jan 13 1883.
608. Jones, Gardner Maynard "Ralph Waldo Emerson," Public Library Bulletin, Salem, Mass. 6:44-47 D '01.
609. Jugaku, Bunsho "A Bibliography of Ralph Waldo Emerson in Japan from 1878 to 1935," Emerson Society Quarterly 46:53-89. Reprinted Kyoto, 1947.
610. Kennedy, William Sloane "A Bibliography of Emerson," The Literary World 11:183-85 My 22 1880.
611. Marble, Annie Russell "First Edition of Emerson," The Critic 42:430-36 My '03.
612. Steeves, H. R. "Bibliographical Notes on Emerson," Modern Language Notes 32:431-34 N '17.

EMERSON, Robert, 1903-1959
613. Rabinowitch, Eugene "Bibliography," NASBM 35:128-31 '61.

EMERSON, Rollins Adams, 1873-1947
614. Emerson, Sterling Howard "Bibliography of Rollins Adams Emerson," NASBM 25:320-23 '49.

EMMET, William Le Roy, 1859-1941
615. Whitney, Willis R. "A Comprehensive - But Not Complete - Bibliography of the Writings of W. L. R. Em-

EMMET, William Le Roy (continued)
met," NASBM 22:249-50 '43.

EMMONS, Samuel Franklin, 1841-1911
616. Hague, Arnold "Bibliography," NASBM 7:330-34 '13.
617. Hague, Arnold "Memoir of Samuel Franklin Emmons,"
GSAB 23:12-28 '12.

EMMONS, William Harvey, 1876-1949
618. Levorsen, A. I. "Memorial to William Harvey Emmons," GSAP pp. 151-57 '49.

ENGERRAND, George Charles Marius, 1877-1961
619. Campbell, T. N. "George Charles Marius Engerrand,"
AA 64:1052-56 O '62.

ENGLE, Paul, 1908-
620. Weber, Richard B. "Paul Engle; a Checklist," Books
at Iowa #5 pp. 11-37.

ENGLISH, Thomas Dunn, 1819-1902
621. Blanck, Jacob "Thomas Dunn English," BAL 3:71-81.

ERLANGER, Joseph, 1874-1965
622. Davis, Hallowell "Bibliography," NASBM 41:130-39 '70.

EVERETT, Alexander Hill, 1790-1847
623. Somkin, Fred "The Writings of Alexander Hill Everett
(1790-1847)," BB 23:238-39 Jan-Apr '63.

EWING, James, 1866-1943
624. Murphy, James B. "Bibliography of James Ewing,"
NASBM 26:52-60 '51.

EYMAN, Alice Frances, 1921-1969
625. Witthoft, John "Bibliography of Frances Eyman,"
AA 72:89 F '70.

F

FAIRCHILD, David Grandison, 1869-1934
626. Lawrence, G. H M. "Bibliography of the Writings of
David Fairchild," Huntia 1:79-102 '64.

FAIRCHILD, Herman LeRoy, 1850-1938
627. Chadwick, George Halcott "Memorial to Herman LeRoy
Fairchild," GSAP pp. 185-222 '44.

FAIRFIELD, Sumner Lincoln, 1803-1844
628. Blanck, Jacob "Sumner Lincoln Fairfield," BAL 3:82-85.

FARLOW, William Gilson, 1844-1919
629. Piquet, A. P. D. "Publications," NASBM 11:18-22 '22.

FARRELL, James T., 1904-
630. Branch, Edgar M. "Bibliography of James T. Farrell: a Supplement," ABC 17:9-19 My '67.

FARRINGTON, Oliver Cummings, 1864-1933
631. Roy, Sharat K. "Memorial: Oliver Cummings Farrington," GSAP pp. 193-209 '33.

FAULKNER, John, 1901-1963
632. White, Helen and Redding S. Sugg, Jr. "John Faulkner: an Annotated Check List of His Published Works and of His Papers," SB 23:217-29 '70.

FAULKNER, William, 1897-1962
633. Beebe, Maurice "Criticism of William Faulkner: a Selected Checklist," MFS 13:115-61 Spring '67.
634. Beebe, Maurice "Criticism of William Faulkner: a Selected Checklist with an Index to Studies of Separate Works," MFS 2:150-64 Autumn '56.
635. Longley, John L. and Robert Daniel "Faulkner's Critics; a Selective Bibliography," Perspective 3:202-08 '50.
636. Meriwether, James B. "The Literary Career of William Faulkner: Catalogue of an Exhibition in the Princeton University Library," PULC 21:111-64 Spring '60.
637. Perry, Bradley T. "Faulkner Critics; a Bibliographical Breakdown," Faulkner Studies 2:60-64.
638. Perry, Bradley "A Selected Bibliography of Critical Works on William Faulkner," University of Kansas City Review 18:159-64.
639. Runyan, Harry "Faulkner's Non-fiction Prose; an Annotated Checklist," Faulkner Studies 3:67-69 '54.
640. Sidney, George "An Addition to the Faulkner Canon: The Hollywood Writings," TCL 6:172-74 Jan '61.
641. Sleeth, Irene L. "William Faulkner: a Bibliography of Criticism," TCL 8:18-43 Apr '62.
642. Starke, Aubrey "An American Comedy; an Introduction to a Bibliography of William Faulkner," Colophon pt 19 '34.
643. Woodworth, S. D. "Sélection Bibliographique d'ouvrages ou d'articles sur William Faulkner en France," La

FAULKNER, William (continued)
Revue des Lettres Modernes #27-29 pp. 191-96.

FAWCETT, Edgar, 1847-1904
644. Blanck, Jacob "Edgar Fawcett," BAL 3:86-102.

FAY, Theodore Sedgwick, 1807-1898
645. Blanck, Jacob "Theodore Sedgwick Fay," BAL 3:103-10.

FEJOS, Paul, 1897-1963
646. Bidney, David "Paul Fejos," AA 66:110-15 F '64.

FELLOWS, Robert Ellsworth, 1915-1949
647. Cloos, Ernst, and John C. Reed "Memorial to Robert Ellsworth Fellows," GSAP pp. 159-62 '49.

FENNEMAN, Nevin M., 1865-1945
648. Bucher, Walter "Memorial to Nevin M. Fenneman," GSAP pp. 215-28 '45.

FENNER, Clarence Norman, 1870-1949
649. Wright, Fred E. "Memorial to Clarence Norman Fenner," GSAP pp. 103-07 '51.

FERBER, Edna, 1887-1968
650. Brenni, Vito J. and Betty Lee Spencer "Edna Ferber: a Selected Bibliography," BB 22:152-56 S-D '58.

FERMI, Enrico, 1901-1954
651. Allison, Samuel K. "Bibliography," NASBM 30:137-55 '57.

FERNALD, Merritt Lyndon, 1873-1950
652. Lohnes, Katharine Fernald and Lazella Schwarten "Bibliography of M. L. Fernald," NASBM 28:65-98 '54.

FERRELL, William, 1817-1891
653. Abbe, Cleveland "Publications of William Ferrel," NASBM 3:300-09 1895.

FETTKE, Charles Reinhard, 1888-1959
654. Finn, Fenton H. "Memorial to Charles Reinhard Fettke," GSAP pp. 125-32 '59.

FEWKES, Jesse Walter, 1850-1930
655. Hough, Walter "Bibliography," NASBM 15:268-83 '34.
656. Hough, Walter "Selected Bibliography," AA 33:95-

FEWKES, Jesse Walter (continued)
97 '31.

FEWKES, Vladimir J. , 1901-1941
657. Mason, J. Alden "Bibliography," AAY 8:116-17 Jl '42.

FICKE, Arthur Davison, 1883-1945
658. Blanck, Jacob "American First Editions: Arthur Davison Ficke 1883- ," Publishers' Weekly 124:513.

FIELD, Eugene, 1850-1895
659. Blanck, Jacob "Eugene Field," BAL 3:111-41.

FIELD, Rachel Lyman, 1894-1942
660. Titzell, J. "Rachel Field, 1894-1942; with List of Her Books Since 1927," Horn Book 18:225 Jl '42.

FIELDS, James Thomas, 1816?-1881
661. Blanck, Jacob "James Thomas Fields," BAL 3:142-58.

FINCH, John Wellington, 1873-1951
662. Harrison, Thomas S. "Memorial to John Wellington Finch," GSAP pp. 97-100 '52.

FINCH, Ruy Herbert, 1890-1957
663. MacDonald, Gordon A. "Memorial to Ruy Herbert Finch," GSAP pp. 117-21 '57.

FISCHER, Herman Otto Laurenz, 1888-1960
664. Stanley W. M. and W. Z. Hassid "Bibliography," NASBM 40:103-12 '69.

FISHER, Cassius Asa, 1872-1930
665. Bain, H. Foster "Memorial of Cassius Asa Fisher," GSAB 43:53-57 '33.

FISHER, Lloyd Wellington, 1897-1951
666. Willard, Bradford "Memorial to Lloyd Wellington Fisher," GSAP pp. 109-11 '51.

FISHER, Vardis, 1895-
667. Kellog, George "Vardis Fisher; a Bibliography,"· ABC 14:37-39 S '63.
668. Kellogg, George "Vardis Fisher: a Bibliography," Bookmark (University of Idaho) v. 13 #3 Supplement.

FISKE, John, 1842-1901
669. Blanck, Jacob "John Fiske," BAL 3:159-79.

FITCH, Asa, 1809-1879
670. Russell, L. M. "Notes on the Entomological Writings of Asa Fitch, M. D. with Special Reference to His Catalogues and Reports," Entomological Society of America. Annals 53:326-37 My '60.

FITCH, John, 1743-1798
671. "List of Works in the New York Public Library Relating to Henry Hudson, the Hudson River, Robert Fulton, Early Steam Navigation, etc." NYPLB 13:585-613 '09.

FITCH, William Clyde, 1865-1909
672. Blanck, Jacob "William Clyde Fitch," BAL 3:180-86.
673. Lowe, John Adams "Reading List of William Clyde Fitch," BB 7:30-31 Jl '12.

FITZGERALD, F. Scott, 1896-1940
674. Beebe, Maurice and Jackson R. Bryer "Criticism of F. Scott Fitzgerald: a Selected Checklist," MFS 7:82-94 Spring '61.
675. Bruccoli, Matthew J. "Checklist," Fitzgerald newsletter #1 p. 3; #2 p. 3; #3 p. 3; #4 p. 3; #5 p. 3; #6 pp. 3-4; #7 p. 5; #8 pp. 2-4; #9 pp. 4-6; #10 pp. 3-4; #12 pp. 2-4; #13 pp. 4-6; #14 pp. 3-7; #15 pp. 7-8; #16 pp. 8-9; #17 pp. 11-12; #18 pp. 6-8; #19 pp. 7-8; #20 pp. 8-10; #21 pp. 7-10; #22 pp. 3-4; #23 pp. 6-8; #24 pp. 7-11; #25 pp. 9-12; #26 pp. 9-10; #28 pp. 9-13; #29 pp. 11-13; #30 pp. 3-4; #31 pp. 5-6; #32 pp. 6-7; #33 pp. 3-4; #34 pp. 3-5; #35 pp. 8-9; #36 pp. 9-10; #37 pp. 6-7; #38 pp. 6-10; #39 pp. 17-18.
676. Bruccoli, Matthew J. "F. Scott Fitzgerald's First Book Appearance," BSA 59:58 '65.
677. Bryer, Jackson R. "F. Scott Fitzgerald: a Review of Research and Scholarship," TSLL 5:147-63 Spring '63.
678. Bryer, Jackson R. "F. Scott Fitzgerald and His Critics: a Bibliographical Record," BB 23:155-58 Jan-Apr '62; 23:180-83 My-Ag '62; 23:201-08 S-D '62.
679. Bryer, Jackson R. "F. Scott Fitzgerald as Book Reviewer," BSA 60:369-70 '66.
680. Piper, Henry Dan "F. Scott Fitzgerald: a Check List," PULC 12:196-208 Summer '51.
681. Porter, Bernard H. "The First Publications of F. Scott Fitzgerald," TCL 5:176-82 Jan '60.
682. Vallette, Jacques "Bibliographie Récente de Scott Fitzgerald," Mercure de France #1150 pp. 330-32 '59.
683. White, William "Two Versions of F. Scotts Fitzgerald's 'Babylon Revisited: a Textual and Bibliographi-

FITZGERALD, F. Scott (continued)
cal Study,' " BSA 60:439-52 '66.

FITZGERALD, Zelda Sayre, 1900-1948
684. Piper, Henry Dan "Zelda Sayre Fitzgerald: a Check
List," PULC 12:209-10 Summer '51.

FLEMING, John Adam, 1877-1956
685. Tuve, Merle A. "Bibliography," NASBM 39:112-40 '67.

FLETCHER, Alice Cunningham, 1838-1923
686. Hough, Walter "Bibliography," AA 25:257-58 '23.

FLETCHER, Harris Francis, 1892-
687. Grant, I. F. "Bibliography of the Writings of Harris
Francis Fletcher," Journal of English and Germanic
Philology 60:847-54 O '61.

FLINT, Timothy, 1780-1840
688. Blanck, Jacob "Timothy Flint," BAL 3:187-93.

FOERSTE, August Frederick, 1862-1936
689. Bassler, R. S. "Memorial of August F. Foerste,"
GSAP pp. 143-57 '36.

FOLIN, Otto, 1867-1934
690. Trimble, Harry C. "Bibliography of Otto Folin,"
NASBM 27:72-82 '52.

FONTAINE, William M., 1879-1911
691. Watson, Thomas L. "Memorial of William M. Fontaine," GSAB 25:6-13 '14.

FOOTE, Albert E., 1846-1895
692. Kunz, George F. "Memoir of Albert E. Foote,"
GSAB 7:481-85 1896.

FORBES, Alexander, 1882-1965
693. Fenn, Wallace O. "Bibliography," NASBM 40:132-41
'69.

FORBES, Stephen Alfred, 1844-1930
694. Oesterling, H. C. "Bibliography," NASBM 15:26-54 '34.

FORD, James Alfred, 1911-1968
695. Willey, Gordon R. "James Alfred Ford, 1911-1968,"
AAY 34:62-71 Jan '69.

FORD, Paul Leicester, 1865-1902
696. Blanck, Jacob "Paul Leicester Ford," BAL 3:194-210.

FORD, William Ebenezer, 1878-1939
697. Knopf, Adolph "Memorial to William Ebenezer Ford,"
GSAP pp. 187-93 '39.

FORESTER, Frank see HERBERT, Henry William.

FOSHAG, William Frederick, 1894-1956
698. Ross, Clarence S. "Memorial of William Frederick
Foshag," GSAP pp. 123-26 '56.

FOSTER, Hannah Webster, 1759-1840
699. Blanck, Jacob "Hannah Webster Foster," BAL 3:211.

FOWLER, Henry Weed, 1878-1965
700. Phillips, Venia T. and Maurice E. Phillips "Writings
of Henry Weed Fowler, Published from 1897 to 1965,"
Academy of Natural Sciences of Philadelphia. Proceedings 117:173-212 '65.

FOX, John William, Jr., 1862-1919
701. Blanck, Jacob "John William Fox," BAL 3:212-16.
702. Titus, Warren I. "John Fox, Jr. (1862-1919)," ALR
#3 pp. 5-8 Summer '68.

FOYE, Wilbur Garland, 1886-1935
703. Perkins, Edward H. "Memorial of Wilbur Garland
Foye," GSAP pp. 249-54 '35.

FRAENKEL, Michael
704. McCord, Howard "Michael Fraenkel; a Biographical
and Bibliographical Sketch," Research Studies (Washington State University) 35:341-44.

FRAINA, Louis C. see COREY, Lewis.

FRANKLIN, Benjamin, 1706-1790
705. Conway, Eleanor "Dr. Abeloff's Franklin Collection,"
New York Historical Society. Quarterly Bulletin 26:
65-66 '42.
706. "Catalogue of Franklin Exhibition in the Library of
Congress," American Philosophical Society. Papers
100:385-416.
707. "Franklin in France, 1814-1830; a Bibliography,"
American Philosophical Society. Papers 100:122-28.
708. "Franklin Literature," Education for Victory 3:24-25

FRANKLIN, Benjamin (continued)
D 20 '44.
709. Pettengill, G. E. "Check List of Franklin Imprints in the Library of the Franklin Institute," Franklin Institute Journal 246:351-58 O '48.

FRAZER, Persifor, 1844-1909
710. Penrose, R. A. F., Jr. "Memoir of Persifor Frazer," GSAB 21:5-12 '10.

FREDERIC, Harold, 1856-1898
711. Blanck, Jacob "Harold Frederic," BAL 3:217-23.
712. Editors of American Literary Realism "Harold Frederic (1856-1898): a Critical Bibliography of Secondary Comment," ALR #2 pp. 1-70 Spring '68.
713. Katz, Joseph BAL Addendum: Harold Frederic's 'Gloria Mundi' - Entry 6293; The First Four Printings of Harold Frederic's 'Gloria Mundi,' " BSA 63:197-98 '69.
714. O'Donnell, Thomas F. "Harold Frederic (1856-1898)," ALR 1:39-44.
715. Woodward, Robert H. "The Frederic Bibliographies: Errata," Frederic Herald 3:3-4.
716. Woodward, Robert H. "Frederic's Collection of Reviews: Supplement to the Checklist of Contemporary Review of Frederic's Writings," ALR #2 pp. 84-89 Spring '68.
717. Woodward, Robert H. "Harold Frederic: a Bibliography," SB 13:247-57 '60.
718. Woodward, Robert H. "Harold Frederic: Supplemental Critical Bibliography of Secondary Comment," ALR 3: 95-147 Spring '70.
719. Woodward, Robert H. and Stanton Garner "Frederic's Short Fiction: a Checklist," ALR #2 pp. 73-76 Spring '68.

FREEMAN, John Ripley, 1855-1932
720. Bush, Vannevar "Bibliography," NASBM 17:182-87 '37.

FREEMAN, Mary E. Wilkins, 1852-1930
721. Blanck, Jacob "BAL Addenda," BSA 55:152-53 '61.
722. Blanck, Jacob "Mary Eleanor Wilkins Freeman," BAL 3:224-43.
723. O'Connor, Rober B. "BAL Addenda M. E. W. Freeman - Entry No. 6380," BSA 61:127 '67.
724. Westbrook, Perry D. "Mary E. Wilkins Freeman (1852-1930)," ALR 2:139-42 Summer '69.

FRENEAU, Philip Morin, 1752-1832
725. Blanck, Jacob "Philip Morin Freneau," BAL 3:244-56.
726. Johnson, Merle "American First Editions: Philip Freneau (1752-1832)," Publishers' Weekly 122:213-14 '32.
727. Leary, Lewis "Philip Freneau in Charleston," South Carolina History and Geneology Magazine 42:89-98.
728. Leary, Lewis Gaston, Jr. "An Unlisted Item in the Bibliography of Philip Freneau," AL 6:331 '34-'35.
729. Thomas, Owen P., Jr. "Philip Freneau: a Bibliography of Biographical, Critical and Historical Scholarship," Proceedings of the New Jersey Historical Society 75:197-205.

FROST, Edwin Brant, 1866-1935
730. Struve, Otto "Bibliography of Edwin Brant Frost," NASBM 19:40-51 '38.

FROST, Robert, 1874-1963
731. Boutell, H. S. "A Bibliography of Robert Frost," Colophon pt 2.
732. Melcher, Frederic G. "Robert Frost and His Books," Colophon #2 pp. 1-7 '30.
733. Parameswaran, Uma "Robert Frost: a Bibliography of Articles and Books, 1958-1964," BB 25:46-48 Jan-Apr '67; 25:58 My-Ag '67.

FULLER, Henry Blake, 1857-1929
734. Blanck, Jacob "Henry Blake Fuller," BAL 3:257-61.
735. Williams, Kenny Jackson "Henry Blake Fuller (1857-1929)," ALR #3 pp. 9-13 Summer '68.

FULLER, Homer T., 1838-1908
736. Hovey, Edmund Otis "Memoir of Homer T. Fuller," GSAB 20:617-18 '09.

FULLER, Sarah Margaret (Marches d'Ossoli), 1810-1850
737. Blanck, Jacob "Sarah Margaret Fuller," BAL 3:262-69.

FULTON, Robert, 1765-1815
738. "List of Works in the New York Public Library Relating to Henry Hudson, the Hudson River, Robert Fulton, Early Steam Navigation, etc.," NYPLB 13:585-613 '09.

FURLONG, Eustace L., 1874-1950
739. Chaney, Ralph W. "Memorial to Eustace L. Furlong," GSAP pp. 113-14 '51.

GABB, William More, 1839-1878
740. Dall, William H. "Bibliography," NASBM 6:356-61 '09.

GALE, Hoyt Stoddard, 1876-1952
741. Hewett, D. F. "Memorial to Hoyt Stoddard Gale," GSAP pp. 107-13 '53.

GALE, Zona, 1874-1938
742. Simonson, Harold P. "Zona Gale (1874-1938)," ALR #3 pp. 14-17 Summer '68.

GALLAGHER, William Davis, 1808-1894
743. Blanck, Jacob "William Davis Gallagher," BAL 3: 270-74.

GALLATIN, Albert Eugene, 1881-1952
744. Wainwright, Alexander D. "A Checklist of the Writings of Albert Eugene Gallatin," PULC 14:141-51 Spring '53.

GALLIHER, Edgar Wayne, 1907-1945
745. Hoots, Harold W. "Memorial to Edgar Wayne Galliher," GSAP pp. 229-33 '45.

GAMBLE, James Lawder, 1883-1959
746. Loeb, Robert F. "Bibliography," NASBM 36:156-60 '62.

GANN, Thomas William Francis, 1867-1938
747. Thompson, J. E. S. "Bibliografías de antropólogos; Thomas William Francis Gann, 1867-1938," Boletín Bibliográfico de Antropología Americana 4:158-60 Mr '40.

GARDNER, Julia Anna, 1882-1960
748. Ladd, Harry S. "Memorial to Julia Anna Gardner," GSAP pp. 87-92 '60.

GARLAND, Hamlin, 1860-1940
749. Bryer, Jackson R. and Eugene Harding "Hamlin Garland (1860-1940): a Bibliography of Secondary Comment," ALR 3:290-387 Fall '70.
750. Pizer, Donald "Hamlin Garland: a Bibliography of Newspaper and Periodical Publications (1885-1895),"

GARLAND, Hamlin (continued)
BB 22:41-44 Jan-Apr '57.
751. Pizer, Donald "Hamlin Garland (1860-1940)," ALR #1
pp. 45-51 Fall '67.

GARRETT, George Palmer, Jr., 1929-
752. Meriwether, James B. "A Checklist of the Writings
of George Garrett," PULC 25:33-39 Autumn '63.

GATSCHET, Albert Samuel, 1832-1907
753. M. J. "Bibliography," AA 9:567-70 '07.

GAY, Frederick Parker, 1874-1939
754. Dochez, A. R. "Bibliography," NASBM 28:108-16 '54.

GEIGER, Theodor, 1891-1952
755. Agersnap, T. "Bibliography of Theodor Geiger,"
Acta Sociologica 1:80-84 '55.

GEIST, Otto William, 1888-1963
756. Skarland, Ivar "Bibliography," AAY 29:485 Apr '64.

GENTH, Frederick Augustus, 1820-1893
757. Barker, George F. "Scientific Papers, etc., Published by F. A. Genth," NASBM 4:222-31 '02.

GEORGE, Henry, 1839-1897
758. "Manuscripts and Books of Henry George," NYPLB
29:611-16 S '25.

GESELL, Arnold Lucius, 1880-1961
759. Miles, Walter R. "Bibliography," NASBM 37:74-96 '64.

GHERARDI, Bancroft, 1873-1941
760. Buckley, Oliver E. "Bibliography," NASBM 30:174-77
'57.

GIBBS, Josiah Willard, 1839-1903
761. Hastings, Charles S. "Bibliography," NASBM 6:391-
93 '09.

GIBBS, Wolcott, 1822-1908
762. Clarke, F. W. "Bibliography," NASBM 7:19-22 '13.

GIDDINGS, James Louis, 1909-1964
763. Larsen, Helge "James Louis Giddings, 1909-1964,"
AAY 31:398-401 Jan '66.
764. Rainey, Froelich "J. Louis Giddings," AA 67:1503-07

GIDDINGS, James Louis (continued)
   D '65.

GIDLEY, James Williams, 1866-1931
765. Lull, Richard Swann "Memorial of James Williams
   Gidley," GSAB 43:57-68 '33

GIFFORD, Edward Winslow, 1887-1959
766. Heizer, Robert F. "Bibliography," AAY 25:259 O '59.

GILBERT, Grove Karl, 1843-1918
767. Wood, B. D. and G. B. Cottle "Bibliography," GSAB
   31:45-64 '20.

GILBERT, Katherine Everett, 1886-1952
768. "Katherine Everett Gilbert's Writings on Aesthetics:
   a Selected Bibliography," Journal of Aesthetics 11:76-
   78 '52.

GILDER, Richard Watson, 1844-1909
769. Blanck, Jacob "Richard Watson Gilder," BAL 3:275-
   88.

GILL, Theodore Nicholas, 1837-1914
770. Dall, William Healey "Bibliography of Theodore Nicholas Gill," NASBM 8:322-43 '19.

GILLET, Joseph Eugene, 1888-1958
771. "Publications of Joseph Eugene Gillet," Hispanic Review 27:18-29 Jan '59.

GILLETTE, John Morris, 1866-1949
772. Reinhardt, J. M. "John M. Gillette: Partial Bibliography," Sociology and Social Research 34:351-55 My
   '50.

GILLIN, John Philip, 1907-
773. "Bibliografias de Antropólogos: John Gillin," Boletín
   Bibliografía Antropólogia Americana 3:192-93 My '39.

GILLIS, James Louis, 1857-1917
774. Mumm, B. and A. R. Ottley "James L. Gillis in
   Print," News Notes of California Libraries 52:654-58
   O '57.

GILMORE, Charles Whitney, 1874-1945
775. Lewis, G. Edward "Memorial to Charles Whitney Gilmore," GSAP pp. 235-43 '45.

GINSBERG, Allen, 1926-
776. Menkin, Edward Z. "Allen Ginsberg: a Bibliography and Biographical Sketch," Thoth 8:35-44.

GIRTY, George Herbert, 1870-1939
777. Williams, James S. "Memorial to George Herbert Girty," GSAP pp. 195-205 '39.

GLASGOW, Ellen, 1873-1945
778. Egly, William H. "Bibliography of Ellen Anderson Gholson Glasgow," BB 17:47-50 S-D '40.
779. Quenenbery, W. D., Jr. "Ellen Glasgow: a Critical Bibliography," BB 22:201-06 My-Ag '59; 22:230-36 S-D '59.

GLENN, Leonidas Chalmers, 1871-1951
780. Jewell, W. B. and C. W. Wilson, Jr. "Memorial to Leonidas Chalmers Glenn," GSAP pp. 101-04 '52.
781. Jewell, W. B. and C. W. Wilson, Jr. "Memorial of Leonidas Chalmers Glenn," Tennessee Academy of Science. Journal 27:170-72 Jl '52.

GOGGIN, John Mann, 1916-1963
782. Rouse, Irving "Bibliography," AAY 29:373-75 Jan '64.
783. Sturtevant, William C. "John Mann Goggin," AA 66:385-94 Apr '64.

GOLDENWEISER, Alexander A., 1880-1940
784. Wallis, Wilson D. "Bibliography," AA 43:253-55 '41.

GOLDSCHMIDT, Richard Benedict, 1878-1958
785. Stern, Curt "Bibliography," NASBM 39:174-92 '67.

GOLDSCHMIDT, Victor Moritz, 1888-1947
786. Oftedal, Ivar "Memorial to Victor Moritz Goldschmidt," GSAP pp. 153-54 '48.

GOLDTHWAIT, James Walter, 1880-1947
787. White, George W. "Memorial to James Walter Goldthwait," GSAP pp. 171-82 '48.

GOMBERG, Moses, 1866-1947
788. Bailar, John C., Jr. "Bibliography," NASBM 41:166-73 '70.

GOOCH, Frank Austin, 1852-1929
789. Van Name, Ralph G. "Bibliography of Frank Austin Gooch," NASBM 15:126-35 '34.

GOODALE, George Lincoln, 1839-1923
790. Jackson, Robert Tracy "Bibliography," NASBM 11:9-19 '22.

GOODPASTURE, Ernest William, 1886-1960
791. Long, Esmond R. "Bibliography," NASBM 38:133-44 '65.

GORDON, Caroline, 1895-
792. Griscom, Joan "Bibliography of Caroline Gordon," C 1:74-78 Winter '56.

GORDON, Charles Henry, 1857-1934
793. Hall, George Martin "Memorial of Charles Henry Gordon," GSAP pp. 225-31 '34.

GORDON, Clarence Everitt, 1876-1951
794. Lull, Richard S. "Memorial to Clarence Everitt Gordon," GSAP pp. 105-06 '52.

GORDON, Samuel George, 1897-1952
795. Parrish, W. "Memorial to Samuel George Gordon," American Mineralogist 38:305-08 Mr '53.

GORTNER, Ross Aiken, 1885-1942
796. Lind, Samuel Colville "Bibliography of Ross Aiken Gortner," NASBM 23:161-80 '45.

GOUDKOFF, Paul Pavel, 1880-1955
797. Laiming, Boris, H. E. Thalmann and George Tunell "Memorial to Paul Pavel Goudkoff," GSAP pp. 127-31 '55.

GOULD, Augustus Addison, 1805-1866
798. Wyman, Jeffries "Bibliography," NASBM 5:106-13 '05.

GOULD, Benjamin Athrop, 1824-1896
799. Comstock, George C. "Bibliography," NASBM 10:171-80 '19.

GOULD, Charles Newton, 1868-1949
800. Clifton, Roland L. "Memorial to Charles Newton Gould," GSAP pp. 165-74 '49.

GRABAU, Amadeus William, 1870-1946
801. Shimer, Hervey W. "Memorial to Amadeus William Grabau," GSAP pp. 155-66 '46.

GRAHAM, William A. P., 1899-1934
802. Grout, F. F. "Memorial of William A. P. Graham,"
GSAP pp. 233-36 '34.

GRANGER, Walter, 1872-1941
803. Simpson, George Gaylord "Memorial to Walter Granger,"
GSAP pp. 159-72 '41.

GRASTY, John Sharshall, 1880-1930
804. Maynard, Poole "Memorial of John Sharshall Grasty,"
GSAB 42:25-30 '32.

GREEN, Otis Howard, 1898-
805. Lloyd, P. M. and U. J. DeWinter "Publications of
Otis Howard Green," Hispanic Review 37:12-22 Jan '69.

GREENE, Edmund Fisk see FISKE, John.

GREGORY, Charles Oscar, 1902-
806. "Bibliography of Works by Charles Oscar Gregory,"
Virginia Law Review 53:919-23 My '67.

GREGORY, Herbert Ernest, 1869-1952
807. Longwell, Chester R. "Memorial to Herbert Ernest
Gregory," GSAP pp. 115-23 '53.

GRIERSON, Francis, 1848-1927
808. Simonson, Harold P. "Francis Grierson - a Biographical Sketch and Bibliography," Illinois State Historical
Society. Journal 54:198-203.

GRIGAUT, Paul LeRoy, 1905-1968
809. "Paul LeRoy Grigaut: a Bibliography," Detroit. Institute of Arts. Bulletin 47: no. 3-4:60-62 '68.

GRISWOLD, Rufus Wilmot, 1815-1857
810. Blanck, Jacob "Rufus Wilmot Griswold," BAL 3:289-
304.

GROUT, Frank Fitch, 1880-1958
811. Thiel, George A. "Memorial to Frank Fitch Grout,"
GSAP pp. 129-33 '58.

GROVES, Ernest Rutherford, 1877-1946
812. Odum, H. W. "Ernest R. Groves and His Work,"
Social Forces 25:202-06 D '46.

GRUMMERE, Amelia Mott, 1859-1937
813. Hewitt, A. B. "Bibliography of the Writings of Amelia Mott Grummere," Friends Historical Association. Bulletin 27:91-96 Autumn '38.

GUDGER, Eugene Willis, 1866-
814. "Bibliography of Dr. E. W. Gudger's Contributions to the History of Ichthyology (1905-1951)," Isis 42:237-42 '51.

GUINEY, Louise Imogen, 1861-1920
815. Blanck, Jacob "Louise Imogen Guiney," BAL 3:305-18.

GURLEY, William Frank Eugene, 1854-1943
816. Chamberlin, Rollin T. "Memorial to William Frank Eugene Gurley," GSAP pp. 135-40 '43.

GUTENBERG, Beno, 1889-1960
817. Richter, Charles F. "Memorial to Beno Gutenberg," GSAP pp. 93-104 '60.

GUTHRIE, A. B., Jr. 1901-
818. Etulain, Richard W. "A. B. Guthrie: a Bibliography," Western American Literature 4:133-38.

GUTTERIDGE, Harold Cooke, 1876-1953
819. Hamson, C. J. "Publications of Professor H. C. Gutteridge," International and Comparative Law Quarterly 3:386-92 Jl '54.

GUYOT, Arnold, 1807-1884
820. Dana, James D. "List of the Writings of Professor Arnold Guyot," NASBM 2:345-47 1886.

H

HACKETT, Charles Wilson, 1888-1951
821. Cumberland, C. C. "Writings of Charles Wilson Hackett: a Bibliography," Hispanic American Historical Review 32:144-52 F '52.

HAEBERLIN, Herman Karl, 1891-1918
822. Boas, Franz "Bibliography of Herman K. Haeberlin," AA 21:74 '19.

HAGUE, Arnold, 1840-1917
823. Iddings, Joseph P. "Bibliography," NASBM 9:36-38 '19.

HAGUE, Arnold (continued)
824. Iddings, Joseph P. "Memorial of Arnold Hague,"
GSAB 29:35-48 '18.

HAINES, Helen Elizabeth, 1872-1961
825. Sive, M. R. "Helen E. Haines: a Annotated Bibliography," Journal of Library History 5:146-64 Apr '70.

HALBERSTADT, Baird, 1860-1934
826. Ashley, George H. "Memorial of Baird Halberstadt,"
GSAP pp. 159-62 '36.

HALE, Edward Everett, 1822-1909
827. Holloway, Jean "A Checklist of the Writings of Edward
Everett Hale," BB 21:89-92 My-Ag '54; 21:114-20 S-D
'54; 21:140-43 Jan-Apr '55.

HALE, George Ellery, 1868-1938
828. Adams, Walter S. "Bibliography of George Ellery
Hale," NASBM 21:218-41 '41.

HALE, Sarah Josepha Buell, 1788-1879
829. Blanck, Jacob "Sarah Josepha Buell Hale," BAL 3:
319-40.

HALL, Arthur Lewis, 1872-1955
830. Haughton, Sidney H. "Memorial of Arthur Lewis Hall,"
GSAP pp. 137-40 '56.

HALL, Asaph, 1829-1907
831. Horigan, William D. "Published Writings of Asaph
Hall," NASBM 6:276-309 '09.

HALL, Baynard Rush, 1798-1863
832. Blanck, Jacob "Baynard Rush Hall," BAL 3:341-43.

HALL, Christopher Webber, 1845-1911
833. Winchell, Newton H. "Memoir of Christopher Webber
Hall," GSAB 23:28-30 '12.

HALL, Edwin Herbert, 1855-1938
834. Bridgman, P. W. "Bibliography," NASBM 21:87-94
'41.

HALL, George Martin, 1891-1941
835. Amick, H. C. "Bibliography of George Martin Hall,"
Tennessee Academy of Sciences, Journal 16:343-44 O
'41. Reprinted American Mineralogist 27:199 Mr '42

HALL, George Martin (continued)
and GSAP pp. 175-76 '42.
836. Singewald, J. T. "George Martin Hall (1891-1941) with
List of His Publications," American Association of
Petroleum Geologists. Bulletin 25:1830 S '41.
837. Singewald, Joseph T., Jr. "Memorial to George Martin Hall," GSAP pp. 173-76 '41.

HALL, Granville Stanley, 1846-1924
838. Wilson, Louis N. "Bibliography of the Published Writings of G. Stanley Hall," NASBM 12:155-80 '29.

HALL, Hazel, 1886-1924
839. Saul, George Brandon "Hazel Hall: a Chronological
List of Acknowledged Verses in the Periodicals," TCL
1:34-36 Apr '55.

HALL, James, 1793-1868
840. Blanck, Jacob "James Hall," BAL 3:344-55.
841. Eckert, Robert P., Jr. "The Path of the Pioneer,"
Colophon n.s. 1:404-21.

HALL, James, 1811-1898
842. Stevenson, John J. "Memoir of James Hall," GSAB
10:425-51 1899.

HALLECK, Fitz-Greene, 1790-1867
843. Blanck, Jacob "Fitz-Greene Halleck," BAL 3:356-65.
844. Johnson, Merle and John J. Birss "American First
Editions: Fitz-Greene Halleck, 1790-1867," Publishers'
Weekly 127:2306.

HALLET, Richard Matthews, 1887-1967
845. Cary, Richard "A Bibliography of Richard Matthews
Hallet," CLQ 7:453-63 Je '67.

HALLOWELL, Alfred Irving, 1892-
846. "Writings of Hallowell," Psychiatry 3:481-82 Ag '40.

HALPINE, Charles Graham, 1827-1868
847. Blanck, Jacob "Charles Graham Halpine," BAL 3:366-71.

HALSTED, William Stewart, 1852-1922
848. MacCallum, W. G. "Bibliography," NASBM 17:163-70
'37.

HAMILTON, Edith, 1867-1963
849. Parker, Franklin and Joyce Parker "Edith Hamilton at
94: a Partial Bibliography," BB 23:183-84 My-Ag '62.

HAMILTON, Gail see DODGE, Mary Abigail.

HAMILTON, Peggy-Kay, 1922-1959
850. Kerr, Paul F. "Memorial to Peggy-Kay Hamilton,"
GSAP pp. 133-35 '59.

HAMMETT, Dashiell, 1894-1961
851. Stoddard, Roger E. "Some Uncollected Authors XXI:
Dashiell Hammett, 1894-1961," BC 11:71-78 Spring '62.

HANCE, James Harold, 1880-1955
852. Culver, Harold E. "Memorial to James Harold Hance,"
GSAP pp. 123-25 '57.

HAND, Learned, 1872-1961
853. Breuer, Ernest Henry   "Learned Hand, January 27,
1872-August 18, 1961:   a Bibliography," Law Library
Journal 59:284-94 '59.   Reprinted New York State Library, 1964.

HANSEN, James Edward, 1898-
854. "James Edward Hansen, Enamel Division Trustee,"
American Ceramic Society. Bulletin 19:237 Je '40.

HANSEN, William Webster, 1909-1949
855. Bloch, Felix "Bibliography," NSBM 27:135-37 '52.

HARDY, Arthur Sherburne, 1847-1930
856. Blanck, Jacob "Arthur Sherburne Hardy," BAL 3:372-
76.

HARLAND, Henry, 1861-1905
857. Blanck, Jacob "Henry Harland," BAL 3:377-83.

HARPER, Robert Almer, 1862-1946
858. Thom, Charles "Harper Bibliography," NASBM 25:
238-40 '49.

HARRADON, Harry Durward, 1883-1949
859. Fleming, J. A. "Harry Durward Harradon, 1883-1949,"
Journal of Geophysical Research 55:88-90 Mr '50.

HARRIMAN, Philip Lawrence, 1894-1968
860. "Writings of Harriman," Psychiatry 4:326-27 My '41.

HARRINGTON, John Peabody, 1884-1961
861. Glemser, Karlena "Bibliography of the Writings of
John Peabody Harrington," AA 65:376-81 Apr '63.

HARRIS, George Washington, 1814-1869
862. Blanck, Jacob "George Washington Harris," BAL 3:
384-86.

HARRIS, Gilbert Dennison, 1864-1952
863. Olsson, Axel A. "Memorial to Gilbert Dennison Harris," GSAP pp. 125-30 '53.

HARRIS, Joel Chandler, 1848-1908
864. Blanck, Jacob "BAL Addendum Joe Chandler Harris -
Entry No. 7115," BSA 61:266 '67.
865. Blanck, Jacob "Joel Chandler Harris," BAL 3:387-401.
866. Turner, Arlin "Joel Chandler Harris (1848-1908),"
ALR #3 pp. 18-23 Summer '68.

HARRISON, Constance Cary, 1843-1920
867. Blanck, Jacob "Constance Cary Harrison," BAL 3:402-
11.

HARRISON, Ross Granville, 1870-1959
868. Wilens, Sally "Bibliography," NASBM 35:155-62 '61.

HART, Edwin Bret, 1874-1953
869. Elvehjem, Conrad A. "Bibliography of E. B. Hart,"
NASBM 28:135-61 '54.

HARTE, Francis Brett, 1836-1902
870. Blanck, Jacob "Francis Brett Harte," BAL 3:412-78.
871. De Gruson, Gene "An Unlocated Bret Harte - Joaquin
Miller Book," BSA 61:60 '67.
872. Morrow, Patrick "Bret Harte (1836-1902)," ALR 3:
167-77 Spring '70.
873. Stewart, George R., Jr. "A Bibliography of the Writings of Bret Harte in the Magazines and Newspapers of
California 1857-1871," University of California. Publications in English 3:119-70.

HARVEY, Edmund Newton, 1887-1959
874. Johnson, Frank H. "Bibliography," NASBM 39:242-66
'67.

HASS, Wilbert Henry, 1906-1959
875. Sohn, I. G. "Memorial to Wilbert Henry Hass," GSAP
pp. 105-06 '60.

HASTINGS, Charles Sheldon, 1848-1932
876. Uhler, Horace S. "Bibliography of Charles S. Hastings," NASBM 20:288-91 '39.

HASTINGS, John Beazley, 1858-1942
877. Berkey, Charles P. "Memorial to John B. Hastings," GSAP pp. 189-94 '42.

HATCHER, John B., 1861-1904
878. Scott, W. B. "Memoir of John B. Hatcher," GSAB 16:548-55 '05.

HAVENS, Raymond Dexter, 1880-1958
879. "Bibliography of Raymond Dexter Havens," ELH 7:v-vii D '40.

HAWKES, John
880. Bryer, Jackson R. "Two Bibliographies," C 6:89-94 Fall '63.

HAWTHORNE, Julian, 1846-1934
881. Bassan, Maurice "The Literary Career of Julian Hawthorne: a Selected Checklist," BB 24:157-62 My-Ag '65.
882. Monteiro, George "Additions to the Bibliography of Julian Hawthorne," BB 25:64 My-Ag '67.
883. Monteiro, George "Further Additions to the Bibliography of Julian Hawthorne," BB 27:6-7 Jan/Mr '70.

HAWTHORNE, Nathaniel, 1804-1864
884. Adkins, Nelson F. "Notes on the Hawthorne Canon," BSA 60:364-67 '66.
885. Blanck, Jacob "Nathaniel Hawthorne," BAL 4:1-36.
886. Browne, Nina E. "Best Editions of Nathaniel Hawthorne," BB 2:138-39 '01.
887. Bruccoli, Matthew J. "A Sophisticated Copy of 'The House of the Seven Gables,'" BSA 59:438-39 '65.
888. Crowley, J. Donald "A False Edition of Hawthorne's 'Twice-Told Tales,'" BSA 59:182-88 '65.
889. "First Editions of Hawthorne," Literary Collector 8:109-16 Ag '04.
890. Jones Buford "A Checklist of Hawthorne Criticism, 1951-1966," Emerson Society Quarterly 52 Supplement pp. 1-90. Reprinted Transcendental Books, 1968.
891. Jones, Gardner M. "Nathaniel Hawthorne," Salem (Mass.) Public Library Bulletin 5:20-24 S 1899; 7:55-56 Je '04.
892. Jones, Gardner M. "Nathaniel Hawthorne: a Complete

HAWTHORNE, Nathaniel (continued)
List of Hawthorne's Writings, with full Contents, and
of Books and Magazine Articles about Hawthorne,"
Salem (Mass.) Public Library Bulletin 1:46-48 O 1891.
893. Paltsits, Victor Hugo "List of Books, etc., by and
Relating to Nathaniel Hawthorne, Prepared as an Exhi-
bition to Commemorate the Centenary of His Birth,"
NYPLB 8:312-22 '04.
894. Phillips, Robert S. "The Scarlet Letter: a Selected
Checklist of Criticism," BB 23:213-16 S-D '62.
895. Phillips, Robert, Jack Kligerman, Robert E. Long,
Robert Hastings "Nathaniel Hawthorne: Criticism of
the Four Major Romances; a Selected Bibliography,"
Thoth 3:39-50 Winter '62.
896. Williamson, G. M. "Bibliography of the Writings of
Nathaniel Hawthorne," Book Buyer 15:218-22, 326-27
O-N 1897.

HAY, John Milton, 1838-1905
897. Blanck, Jacob "John Milton Hay," BAL 4:37-63.
898. Sloane, David E. "John Hay (1838-1905)," ALR 3:178-
88 Spring '70.

HAY, Oliver Perry, 1846-1930
899. Lull, Richard Swann "Memorial of Oliver Perry Hay,"
GSAB 42:30-48 '32.

HAY, Robert, 1835-1895
900. Hill, Robert T. "Memoir of Robert Hay," GSAB 8:370-
74 1897.

HAYDEN, Ferdinand Vandiveer, 1839-1887
901. White, Charles A. "A Partial List of the Published
Writings of Dr. F. V. Hayden," NASBM 3:409-13
1895.

HAYES, Carlton Joseph Huntley, 1882-1964
902. Eagan, J. M. "Contemporary Catholic Authors; C. J.
H. Hayes, Historian, with List of His Publications,"
Catholic Library World 12:130 Jan '41.

HAYES, Charles Willard, 1858-1916
903. Brooks, Alfred H. "Memoir of Charles Willard Hayes,"
GSAB 28:81-123 '17.

HAYFORD, John Fillmore, 1868-1925
904. Burger, William H. "Bibliography," NASBM 16:279-
92 '36.

HAYNE, Paul Hamilton, 1830-1886
905. Blanck, Jacob "Paul Hamilton Hayne," BAL 4:64-74.

HAYNES, Henry Williamson, 1831-1912
906. "Bibliography of Professor Haynes," AA 15:342-46 '13.

HAYWARDE, Richard see COZZENS, Frederic Swartwout.

HEARN, Lafcadio, 1850-1904
907. Blanck, Jacob "Lafcadio Hearn," BAL 4:75-106.
908. Sisson, Martha Howard "A Bibliography of Lafcadio Hearn," BB 15:6-7 My-Ag '33; 15:32-24 S-D '33; 15: 55-56 Jan-Apr '34; 15:73-75 My-Ag '34.
909. Yu, Beongcheon "Lafcadio Hearn (or Koizumi Yakumo, 1850-1904)," ALR #1 pp. 52-55 Fall '67.

HEATON, Ross Leslie, 1890-1950
910. Dobbin, C. E. "Memorial to Ross Leslie Heaton," GSAP pp. 101-03 '50.

HECK, Nicholas Hunter, 1882-1953
911. Willard, Bradford "Memorial to Nicholas Hunter Heck," GSAP pp. 111-17 '54.

HEILAND, Carl August, 1899-1956
912. Van Tuyl, F. M. and J. C. Hollister "Memorial to Carl August Heiland," GSAP pp. 135-38 '58.

HEILPRIN, Angelo, 1853-1907
913. Gregory, Herbert E. "Memoir of Angelo Heilprin," GSAB 19:527-36 '08

HEKTOEN, Ludvig, 1863-1951
914. Cannon, Paul R. "Bibliography," NASBM 18:179-97 '54.

HEMINGWAY, Ernest, 1899-1961
915. Beebe, Maurice "Criticism of Ernest Hemingway: a Selected Checklist with an Index to Studies of Separate Works," MFS 1:36-45 Ag '55.
916. Beebe, Maurice and John Feaster "Criticism of Ernest Hemingway: a Selected Checklist," MFS 14:337-69 Autumn '68.
917. Johnson, Merle "American First Editions: Ernest Hemingway," Publishers' Weekly 121:870 '32.
918. Monteiro, George "The Old Man and the Sea as a German Textbook," BSA 60:89-91 '66.
919. Murray, Donald "Hemingway in Chinese Translation,"

HEMINGWAY, Ernest (continued)
ABC 18:20-21 Mr '68.
920. Orton, Vrest "Some Notes Bibliographical and Other-wise on the Books of Ernest Hemingway," Publishers' Weekly 117:884-86 '30.
921. Perez Gallego, Candido "Aportación española al es-tudio de Hemingway; notas para una bibliográfia," Filologia Moderna (Madrid) 5:57-71 '61.
922. Sister Richard Mary "Addition to the Hemingway Bib-liography," BSA 59:327 '65.
923. Stephens, Robert O. "Some Additions to the Heming-way Checklist," ABC 17:9-11 Apr '67.
924. White, William "Addendum to Hanneman: Hemingway's The Old Man and the Sea," BSA 62:613-14 '68.
925. White William "Hemingway in Korea," BSA 59:189-92 '65.
926. Young, Philip "Our Hemingway Man," Kenyon Review 26:676-707.

HENDERSON, Lawrence Joseph, 1878-1942
927. Cannon, Walter B. "Bibliography," NASBM 23:51-58 '45.

HENNEN, Ray Vernon, 1875-1958
928. Reger, David B. "Memorial to Ray Vernon Hennen," GSAP pp. 139-41 '58.
929. Reger, D. B. "Ray Vernon Hennen," American Associ-ation of Petroleum Geologists. Bulletin 42:2018-19 Ag '58.

HENRY, Joseph, 1797-1878
930. Newcomb, Simon "List of the Scientific Papers of Joseph Henry," NASBM 5:35-45 '05.

HERBERT, Henry William, 1807-1858
931. Blanck, Jacob "Henry William Herbert," BAL 4:107-38.

HERGESHEIMER, Joseph, 1880-1954
932. Napier, James J. "Joseph Hergesheimer: a Selected Bibliography, 1913-1945," BB 24:46-48 S-D '63; 24:52 Jan-Apr '64.
933. Stappenbeck, Herbert L., Jr. "A Catalogue of the Joseph Hergesheimer Collection at the University of Texas," Dissertation, University of Texas, 1969.

HEROLD, Stanley Carrollton, 1883-1958
934. Hook, J. S. "Stanley Carrollton Herold," American

HEROLD, Stanley Carrollton (continued)
Association of Petroleum Geologists, Bulletin 42:2021
Ag '58.

HERRICK, Clarence Luther, 1858-1904
935. Herrick, C. J. "Clarence Luther Herrick, Pioneer
Naturalist, Teacher, and Psychobiologist," American
Philosophical Society. Transactions 45 #1:80-83 '55.

HERRICK, Robert, 1868-1938
936. Genthe, Charles V. "Robert Herrick (1868-1938),"
ALR #1 pp. 56-60 Fall '67.
937. "Robert Herrick: an Addendum," ALR #3 pp. 67-68
Summer '68.

HERSHEY, Oscar H., 1874-1939
938. Lawson, Andrew C. "Memorial to Oscar H. Hershey,"
GSAP pp. 195-200 '40.

HERSKOVITS, Melville Jean, 1895-1963
939. Moneypenny, A. and B. Thorne "Bibliography of Melville Jean Herskovits," AA 66:91-109 F '64.

HERTY, Charles Holmes, 1867-1938
940. "Publications of Charles Holmes Herty," American
Chemical Society. Journal 61:1623-24 Jl '39.

HERTY, Charles Holmes, Jr., 1896-1953
941. Merica, Paul D. "Bibliography," NASBM 31:120-26
'58.

HESSE, Curtis Julian, 1905-1945
942. Turner, F. E. "Memorial to Curtis Julian Hesse,"
GSAP pp. 245-47 '45.

HEWETT, Edgar Lee, 1865-1946
943. Walter, Paul A. F. "Bibliography," AA 49:264-71 '47.

HEWITT, John Napoleon Brinton, 1859-1937
944. Swanton, John R. "Bibliography," AA 40:289-90 '38.

HEYE, George Gustav, 1874-1956
945. Lothrop, S. K. "Bibliography," AAY 23:67 Jl '57.

HIBBERT, Harold, 1877-1945
946. Wolfrom, Melville L. "Bibliography," NASBM 32:159-
80 '58.

HICE, Richard Roberts, 1865-1925
947. Ashley, George H. "Memorial of Richard R. Hice,"
GSAB 37:94-96 '26.

HICKS, Granville, 1901-
948. Bicker, Robert J. "Granville Hicks: an Annotated
Bibliography February, 1927 to June, 1967 with a Supplement to June 1968," Emporia State Research Studies
17:5-160 '68.

HIGGINS, Daniel Franklin, 1882-1930
949. Grant, U. S. , C. H. Behre, Jr. , and J. R. Ball
"Memorial of Daniel Franklin Higgins," GSAP pp. 237-
43 '34.

HIGGINSON, Thomas Wentworth Storrow, 1823-1911
950. Blanck, Jacob "Thomas Wentworth Storrow Higginson,"
BAL 4:139-84.
951. Cary, Richard "More Higginson Letters," CLQ 7:33-
48 Mr '65.

HILGARD, Eugene Woldemar, 1833-1916
952. Loughride, R. H. "Bibliography," NASBM 9:143-55
'19.
953. Smith, Eugene A. "Memorial of Eugene Woldemar
Hilgard," GSAB 28:40-67 '17.

HILL, A. T. , 1871-1953
954. Wedel, Waldo R. "Publications Reporting Fieldwork
Carried on under the Direction of A. T. Hill," AAY 19:
154-55 O '53.

HILL, Frank A. , 1858-1915
955. Halberstadt, Baird "Memorial of Frank A. Hill,"
GSAB 28:67-70 '17.

HILL, George William, 1838-1914
956. Broom, Ernest W. "Bibliography of George William
Hill," NASBM 8:303-09 '19.

HILL, Henry Barker, 1849-1903
957. Jackson, Charles Loring "A List of the Principal
Chemical Papers by Henry Barker Hill," NASBM 5:
264-66 '05.

HILL, Joseph Adna, 1860-1938
958. Goldenweiser, E. A. "Joseph Adna Hill: a Bibliography of His Works," American Statistical Association.

HILL, Joseph Adna (continued)
Journal 34:410-11 Je '39.

HILL, Robert Thomas, 1858-1941
959. Vaughan, Thomas W. "Memorial to Robert Thomas Hill," GSAP pp. 141-68 '43.

HILLEBRAND, William Francis, 1853-1925
960. Clarke, Frank Wigglesworth "List of the More Important Publications of Dr. W. F. Hillebrand," NASBM 12:66-70 '29.

HILLHOUSE, James Abraham, 1789-1841
961. Blanck, Jacob "James Abraham Hillhouse," BAL 4: 185-89.

HILLS, Richard Charles, 1848-1923
962. George, R. D. "Memorial of Richard Charles Hills," GSAB 35:43-46 '24.

HITCHCOCK, Charles Henry, 1836-1919
963. Upham, Warren "Memorial of Charles Henry Hitchcock," GSAB 31:64-80 '20.

HOAGLAND, Dennis Robert, 1884-1949
964. Kelley, Walter P. "Bibliography," NASBM 29:136-43 '56.

HOBBS, William Herbert, 1864-1953
965. Gould, Laurence M. "Memorial to William Herbert Hobbs," GSAP pp. 131-39 '53.

HOFFMAN, Charles Fenno, 1806-1884
966. Blanck, Jacob "Charles Fenno Hoffman," BAL 4:190-203.

HOLBROOK, John Edwards, 1794-1871
967. Gill, Theodore "Bibliography," NASBM 5:67-77 '05.

HOLDEN, Edward Singleton, 1846-1914
968. Campbell, W. W. "Bibliography of Edward Singleton Holden," NASBM 8:358-72 '19.

HOLDEN, Roy Jay, 1870-1945
969. Roberts, Joseph K. "Memorial to Roy Jay Holden," GSAP pp. 167-72 '46.

HOLLAND, Josiah Gilbert, 1819-1881
970. Blanck, Jacob "Josiah Gilbert Holland," BAL 4:204-18.

HOLLAND, William R. , 1928-1964
971. Spicer, Edward H. "William R. Holland," AA 67:80-82 F '65.

HOLLINGWORTH, Leta A. , 1886-1939
972. Hollingworth, H. L. "Bibliography of Leta A. Hollingworth," Teachers College Record 42:188-95 D'40.

HOLMES, John, 1904-1962
973. Erdelyi, Gabor and Mary A. Glavin "John Holmes: a Bibliography of Published and Unpublished Writings in the Special Collections of the Tufts University Library," NYPLB 73:375-97 Je '69.
974. Seaburg, Alan "John Holmes; a Bibliography," NYPLB 71:306-35 My '67.

HOLMES, Joseph Austin, 1859-1915
975. Pratt, Joseph Hyde "Memorial of Joseph Austin Holmes," GSAB 27:22-35 '16.

HOLMES, Mary Jane Hawes, 1825-1907
976. Blanck, Jacob "Mary Jane Hawes Holmes," BAL 4:219-32.

HOLMES, Oliver Wendell, 1809-1894
977. "Bibliography of Writings on Medical and Scientific Subjects," Boston Medical and Surgical Journal 131:379-80 O 11 1894.
978. Blanck, Jacob "Oliver Wendell Holmes," BAL 4:233-39.
979. Tilton, Eleanor M. " 'Literary Bantlings' Addenda to the Holmes Bibliography," BSA 51:1-18 '57.

HOLMES, Oliver Wendell, 1841-1935
980. "Early Writings," Harvard Law Review 44:497-98 Mr '31.
981. "List of Supreme Court Decisions on Constitutional Questions and Other Issues of Public Law January 5, 1903 Through February 24, 1931," Harvard Law Review 44:820-27 Mr '31.
982. "Opinions delivered as Associate Justice and Chief Justice of the Supreme Judicial Court of Massachusetts, January 1883 to December, 1902," Harvard Law Review 44:799-819 Mr '31.

HOLMES, Theodore, 1928-
983. Blackmur, R. P. "A Checklist of the Writings of Theodore Holmes," PULC 25:50-52 Autumn '63.

HOLMES, William Henry, 1846-1933
984. Hough, Walter "Bibliography," AA 35:755-64 '33.
985. Leary, Ella "Bibliography," NASBM 17:238-52 '37.

HONESS, Arthur Pharaoh, 1886-1942
986. Kyrnine, Paul D. "Memorial of Arthur P. Honess," GSAP pp. 195-200 '42.

HONESS, Charles William, 1885-1949
987. Ryniker, Charles "Memorial to Charles William Honess," GSAP pp. 115-16 '51.

HONEYMAN, David, 1814-1889
988. McGregor, J. G. "Geological Writings of David Honeyman," GSAB 5:567-69 1894.

HOOTON, Ernest Albert, 1887-1954
989. "Bibliography," American Journal of Physical Anthropology 12:448-53 S '54.

HOOVER, Herbert Clark, 1874-1964
990. Jeffries, Zay "Selected Bibliography," NASBM 39:290-91 '67.

HOPKINS, Thomas Cramer, 1861-1935
991. Ploger, Louis W. "Memorial of Thomas Cramer Hopkins," GSAP pp. 255-61 '35.

HOPPER, Edward, 1882-1967
992. Haskell, John D., Jr. "Edward Hopper (1882-1967)," BB 26:86 Jl/S '69; 26:111-12 O/D '69.

HORNER, Seward Ellis, 1906-1954
993. Sperry, Arthur B. "Memorial to Seward Ellis Horner," GSAP pp. 119-21 '54.

HOSMER, William Howe Cuyler, 1814-1877
994. Blanck, Jacob "William Howe Cuyler Hosmer," BAL 4:340-44.

HOTCHKISS, William Otis, 1878-1954
995. Bean, E. F. "Memorial to William Otis Hotchkiss," GSAP pp. 133-37 '55.

HOUGH, Emerson, 1857-1923
996. Blanck, Jacob "Emerson, Hough," BAL 4:345-55.

HOVEY, Edmund Otis, 1862-1924
997. Kemp, James F. "Memorial of Edmund Otis Hovey,"
GSAB 36:85-100 '25.

HOVEY, Horace Carter, 1833-1914
998. Clarke, John M. "Memoir of Horace Carter Hovey,"
GSAB 26:21-27 '15.

HOVEY, Richard, 1864-1900
999. Blanck, Jacob "Richard Hovey," BAL 4:356-62.

HOVGAARD, William, 1857-1950
1000. Gibbs, William Francis "Bibliography," NASBM 36:
180-91 '62.

HOWARD, Edgar Billings, 1887-1943
1001. Mason, J. Alden "Bibliography," AAY 9:233-34 O
'43.

HOWARD, Leland Ossian, 1857-1950
1002. Graf, John E. and Dorothy W. Graf "Selected Bibliography," NASBM 33:103-24 '59.

HOWARD, Robert Randolph, 1920-1965
1003. Rouse, Irving "Robert Randolph Howard, 1920-1965,"
AAY 32:223-24 Apr '67.

HOWE, Edgar Watson, 1853-1937
1004. Eichelberger, Clayton L. "Edgar Watson Howe (1852-
1937): a Critical Bibliography of Secondary Comment,"
ALR 2:1-49 Spring '69.

HOWE, Ernest, 1875-1932
1005. Cross, Whitman and Charles H. Warren "Memorial
of Ernest Howe," GSAP pp. 211-25 '33.

HOWE, Henry Marion, 1848-1922
1006. Burgess, George K. "Publications," NASBM 11:8-11
'22.

HOWE, Julia Ward, 1819-1910
1007. Blanck, Jacob "Julia Ward Howe," BAL 4:363-83.

HOWE, Marshall Avery, 1867-1936
1008. Barnhart, John Hendley "Bibliography," NASBM 19:

HOWE, Marshall Avery (continued)
    259-69 '38.

HOWELL, William Henry, 1860-1945
1009. Erlanger, Joseph "Bibliography," NASBM 26:175-80
    '51.

HOWELLS, William Dean, 1837-1920
1010. Anderson, Stanley P. "A Bibliography of Writing a-
    bout William Dean Howells, 1920-Present," ALR 2:33-
    139 Special Number '69.
1011. Bennett, Scott "A Concealed Printing in W. D.
    Howells," BSA 61:56-60 '67.
1012. Blanck, Jacob "William Dean Howells," BAL 4:384-
    448.
1013. Carpenter, Kenneth E. "Copyright Deposit Copies,"
    BSA 60:473-74 '66.
1014. Gibson, William M. and George Arms "A Bibliogra-
    phy of William Dean Howells," NYPLB 50:675-98 S '46;
    50:857-68 N '46; 50:909-28 D '46; 51:49-56 Jan '47; 51:
    91-105 F '47; 51:213-48 Apr '47; 51:341-45 My '47; 51:
    384-88 Je '47; 51:431-57 Jl '47; 51:486-512 Ag '47.
1015. Graham, Philip "American First Editions at TxU XI
    William Dean Howells (1837-1920)," TLC 6:17-21 Spring
    '58.
1016. Monteiro, George "William Dean Howells: a Biblio-
    graphical Amendment," BSA 58:468-69 '64.
1017. Monteiro, George "William Dean Howells: Two Mis-
    taken Attributions," BSA 56:254-57 '62.
1018. Reeves, John K. "The Literary Manuscripts of Wil-
    liam Dean Howells," NYPLB 62:267-78 Je '58; 62:350-
    63 Jl '58.
1019. Stafford, William T. "The Two Henry Jameses and
    Howells: a Bibliographical Mix-up," BB 21:135 Jan-
    Apr '55.
1020. Walts, Robert W. "Howells's Plans for 2 Travel
    Books," BSA 57:453-59 '63.
1021. Woodress, James "A Bibliography of Writing About
    William Dean Howells: 1860-1919," ALR 2:1-31 Special
    Number '69.

HRDLIČKA, Aleš, 1869-1943
1022. Schultz, Adolf H. "Bibliography," NASBM 23:317-38
    '45.

HUBBARD, Bela, 1890-1959
1023. Weeks, Lewis G. "Memorial to Bela Hubbard,"
    GSAP pp. 107-11 '60.

HUBBARD, George David, 1875-1958
1024. Holmes, Chauncey D. "Memorial to George David Hubbard," GSAP pp. 143-46 '58.

HUBBLE, Edwin Powell, 1889-1953
1025. Mayall, N. U. "Bibliography," NASBM 41:208-14 '70.

HUDSON, Claude Silbert, 1881-1952
1026. Small, Lyndon F. and Melville J. Wolfram "Bibliography," NASBM 32:198-220 '58.

HUDSON, George Henry, 1855-1934
1027. Ruedemann, Rudolf "Memorial of George Henry Hudson," GSAP pp. 245-50 '34.

HUGHES, Langston, 1902-1967
1028. O'Daniel, Therman B. "Langston Hughes: a Selected Classified Bibliography," CLA 11:349-66 Je '68.
1029. O'Daniel, Therman B. "A Langston Hughes Bibliography," CLA Bulletin 7:12-13 Spring '51. Reprinted CLA Journal 11:349 Je '68.

HULETT, George Augustus, 1867-1955
1030. Sullivan, E. C. "Bibliography," NASBM 34:100-05 '60.

HULL, Albert Wallace L. , 1880-1961
1031. Suits, C. G. and J. M. Lafferty "Bibliography," NASBM 41:228-33 '70.

HULL, Clark Leonard, 1884-1952
1032. Beach, Frank A. "Bibliography," NASBM 33:136-41 '59.

HUNEKER, James Gibbons, 1857-1921
1033. Blanck, Jacob "James Gibbons Huneker," BAL 4:449-58.

HUNG, William, 1893-
1034. "Annotated Partial List of the Publications of William Hung," Harvard Journal of Asiatic Studies 24:7-16 '62-'63.

HUNT, Reid, 1870-1948
1035. Marshall, E. K. , Jr. "Bibliography of Reid Hunt," NASBM 26:38-44 '51.

HUNT, Thomas Sperry, 1826-1892
1036. Adams, Frank Dawson "Bibliography," NASBM 15: 221-38 '34.
1037. Pumpelly, Ralph "Memorial of Thomas Sperry Hunt," GSAB 4:379-93 1893.

HUNTER, Albert Clayton, 1893-1946
1038. "Albert Clayton Hunter," Food Research 11:459-60 N '46.

HUNTER, Walter Samuel, 1889-1954
1039. Graham, Clarence H. "Bibliography," NASBM 31:147-55 '58.

HUNTINGTON, George Sumner, 1861-1927
1040. Hrdlička, Aleš "Bibliography," NASBM 18:277-84 '38.

HUREWICZ, Witold, 1904-1956
1041. Lefschetz, S. "Witold Hurewicz, In Memoriam," American Mathematical Society. Bulletin 63:80-82 Mr '57.

HURST, Clarence T., 1895-1949
1042. "Bibliography," Southwestern Lore 14:83-88.

HUTCHINS, Robert Maynard, 1899-
1043. Frodin, R. "Bibliography of Robert M. Hutchins, 1925-1950," Journal of General Education 4:303-24 Jl '50.

HYATT, Alpheus, 1838-1902
1044. Brooks, William K. "Bibliography," NASBM 6:322-25 '09.
1045. Crosby, W. O. "Memoir of Alpheus Hyatt," GSAB 14:504-12 '03.

HYDE, Jesse Earl, 1884-1936
1046. Morris, Frederick K. "Memorial of Jesse Earl Hyde," GSAP pp. 163-73 '36.

I

INGE, William, 1913-
1047. Manley, Frances "William Inge: a Bibliography," ABC 16:13-21 O '65.

INGRAHAM, Joseph Holt, 1809-1860
1048. Blanck, Jacob "Joseph Holt Ingraham," BAL 4:459-91.

IRVING, John Duer, 1874-1918
1049. Kemp, James F. "Memorial of John Duer Irving," GSAB 30:37-42 '19.

IRVING, Washington, 1783-1859
1050. Blanck, Jacob "Washington Irving," BAL 5:1-96.
1051. Bowden, Edwin T. "American First Editions at TxU XII Washington Irving (1783-1859)," TLC 6:20-23 Spring '59.
1052. "Catalogue of the Hellman Collection of Irvingiana," NYPLB 33:209-19 Apr '29.
1053. "Catalogue of the Seligman Collection of Irvingiana," NYPLB 30:83-109 F '26.
1054. Langfeld, William R. "Washington Irving: a Bibliography," NYPLB 36:415-22, 487-94, 561-71, 627-36, 683-89, 755-78, 828-41 '32.
1055. Reichart, Walter A. "The Earliest German Translations of Washington Irving's Writings," NYPLB 61:491-98 O '57.
1056. "Washington Irving," Critic (New York) Mr 31 1883.

IVES, Herbert Eugene, 1882-1953
1057. Buckley, Oliver E. and Karl K. Darrow "Bibliography," NASBM 29:173-89 '56.

J

JACKSON, Abraham Valentine Williams, 1862-1937
1058. Haas, G. C. O. "Bibliography of A. V. Williams Jackson," American Oriental Society Journal 58:243-57 Je '38.

JACKSON, Charles Loring, 1847-1935
1059. Forbes, George Shannon "Bibliography," NASBM 37: 118-28 '64.

JACKSON, Dunham, 1888-1946
1060. Hart, William L. "Bibliography," NASBM 33:172-79 '59.
1061. Hart, William L. "Dunham Jackson, 1888-1946," American Mathematical Society. Bulletin 54:858-60 S '48.

JACKSON, Helen Maria Fiske Hunt, 1830-1885
1062. Blanck, Jacob "Helen Maria Fiske Hunt Jackson,"
BAL 5:97-116.
1063. Byers, John R., Jr. "Helen Hunt Jackson (1830-
1885)," ALR 2:143-48 Summer '69.

JACKSON, Robert Tracy, 1861-1948
1064. Diechmann, Elisabeth "Memorial to Robert Tracy
Jackson," GSAP pp. 117-20 '51.

JACKSON, Shirley, 1919-1965
1065. Phillips, Robert S. "Shirley Jackson: a Checklist,"
BSA 56:110-13 '62.
1066. Phillips, Robert S. "Shirley Jackson: a Chronology
and a Supplementary Checklist," BSA 60:203-13 '66.

JACOBS, Elbridge Churchill, 1873-1957
1067. Dolton, R. K. "Memorial to Elbridge Churchill
Jacobs," American Mineralogist 44:378-79 Mr '59.

JACOBS, Melville, 1902-
1068. Connors, Maureen E. "A Selected Bibliography of
Melville Jacobs Through Early 1966," International
Journal of American Linguistics 32:388-89 O '66.

JAMES, Henry, 1843-1916
1069. Beebe, Maurice and William T. Stafford   "Criticism
of Henry James: a Selected Checklist," MFS 12:117-
77 Spring '66.
1070. Beebe, Maurice and William T. Stafford   "Criticism
of Henry James: a Selected Checklist with an Index to
Studies of Separate Works," MFS 3:73-96 Spring '57.
1071. Blanck, Jacob "Henry James," BAL 5:117-81.
1072. Bowden, Edwin T. "Henry James and the Struggle for
International Copyright; an Unnoticed item on the James
Bibliography," AL 24:537-39 '52-'53.
1073. Bowden, Edwin T. "In Defense of a Henry James
Collection," TLC 6:7-12 Winter '60.
1074. Dunbar, Viola R. "Addenda to 'Biographical and
Critical Studies of Henry James 1941-1948,'" AL 22:
56-61 '50-'51.
1075. Ferguson, Alfred R. "Some Bibliographical Notes on
the Short Stories of Henry James," AL 21:292-97 '49-
'50.
1076. Hagemann, E. R. "Life Buffets (and Comforts) Henry
James, 1883-1916: an Introduction and Annotated
Checklist," BSA 62:207-25 '68.
1077. Hamilton, Eunice C. "Biographical and Critical Stud-

JAMES, Henry (continued)
    ies of Henry James, 1941-1948," AL 20:424-35 '48-
    '49.
1078. McElderry, B. R. "The Published Letters of Henry
    James: a Survey," BB 20:165-71 Jan-Apr '52; 20:187
    My-Ag '52.
1079. Monteiro, George "Addendum to Edel and Laurence:
    Henry James's 'Future of the Novel,'" BSA 63:130 '69.
1080. Monteiro, George "Henry James and His Reviewers:
    Some Identifications," BSA 63:300-04 '69.
1081. Russell, John R. "The Henry James Collection,"
    University of Rochester Library Bulletin 11:50-52 '56.
1082. "Some Bibliographical Notes of Henry James," Hound
    and Horn 7:535-40 '34.
1083. Stafford, William T. "The Two Henry Jameses and
    Howells: a Bibliographical Mix-up," BB 21:135 Jan-
    Apr '55.

JAMES, Joseph Francis, 1857-1897
1084. Stanton, Timothy W. "Memoir of Joseph Francis
    James," GSAB 9:408-13 1898.

JAMES, William, 1842-1910
1085. "List of the Published Writings of William James,"
    Psychological Review 18:157-65 Mr '11.
1086. Perry, Ralph Barton "Annotated Bibliography of the
    Writings of William James," Journal of Philosophy 18:
    615-16 '21.

JANEWAY, Theodore Caldwell, 1872-1917
1087. Flaxman, N. "Janeway on Hypertension: Theodore
    Caldwell Janeway (1872-1917)," Bulletin of the History
    of Medicine 9:585-86 My '41.

JANVIER, Thomas Allibone, 1849-1913
1088. Blanck, Jacob "Thomas Allibone Janvier," BAL 5:
    182-88.

JARRELL, Randall, 1914-1965
1089. Kisslinger, Margaret V. "A Bibliography of Randall
    Jarrell," BB 24:243-47 My-Ag '66.

JASTROW, Morris, Jr., 1861-1921
1090. Clay, A. T. and J. A. Montgomery "Bibliography of
    Morris Jastrow, Jr.," American Oriental Society Jour-
    nal 41:337-44 D '21.

JEFFERS, Robinson, 1887-1962
1091. White, William "Robinson Jeffers: a Checklist, 1959-1965," Serif 3:36-39.

JEFFERSON, Mark, 1863-1949
1092. Visher, S. S. "Mark Jefferson, 1863-1949," Association of American Geographers. Annals 39:310-12 D '49.
1093. Visher, Stephen S. "Memorial to Mark Jefferson," GSAP pp. 175-76 '49.

JEFFERSON, Thomas, 1743-1826
1094. "Suggestions for April Reading," NEA Journal 39:306 Apr '50.

JENNISON, Harry Milliken, 1885-1940
1095. Cain, S. A. and L. R. Hesler "Harry Milliken Jennison, 1885-1940," Tennessee Academy of Sciences. Journal 15:175-76 Apr '40.

JEWETT, Frank Baldwin, 1879-1949
1096. Buckley, Oliver E. "Bibliography," NASBM 27:261-64 '52.

JEWETT, Sarah Orne, 1849-1909
1097. Blanck, Jacob "Sarah Orne Jewett," BAL 5:189-205.
1098. Cary, Richard "Sarah Orne Jewett (1849-1909)," ALR #1 pp. 61-66 Fall '67.
1099. Cary, Richard "Some Bibliographical Ghosts of Sarah Orne Jewett," CLQ 8:139-45 S '68.
1100. Eichelberger, Clayton L. "Sarah Orne Jewett (1849-1909): a Critical Bibliography of Secondary Comment," ALR 2:189-262 Fall '69.
1101. Frost, John E. "Sarah Orne Jewett Bibliography: 1949-1963," CLQ 6:405-17 Je '64.
1102. Green, David B. "The Sarah Orne Jewett Canon: Additions and a Correction," BSA 55:141-42 '61.

JOHNSON, Douglas Wilson, 1878-1944
1103. Bucher, Walter H. "Bibliography," NASBM 24:221-30 '47.
1104. Wright, Frank J. and Anna Z. Wright "Memorial to Douglas Johnson," GSAP pp. 223-39 '44.

JOHNSON, Paul Emanuel, 1898-
1105. "Bibliography of Paul E. Johnson (1921-1968)," Pastoral Psychology 20:47-56 Jan '69.

JOHNSON, Samuel William, 1830-1901
1106. Osborne, Thomas B. "Bibliography," NASBM 7:215-22 '13.

JOHNSON, Treat Baldwin, 1875-1947
1107. Vickery, Hubert Bradford "Bibliography," NASBM 27: 96-119 '52.

JOHNSTON, Richard Malcolm, 1822-1898
1108. Blanck, Jacob "Richard Malcolm Johnston," BAL 5: 206-13.

JONES, Grinnell, 1884-1947
1109. Dole, M. "Scientific Contributions of Grinnell Jones," New York Academy of Science. Annals 51:no. 4; 723-26 '49.

JONES, John Beauchamp, 1810-1866
1110. Blanck, Jacob "John Beauchamp Jones," BAL 5:214-20.

JONES, Lewis Ralph, 1864-1945
1111. Walker, J. C. and A. J. Riker "Bibliography," NASBM 31:168-79 '58.

JONES, Walter Jennings, 1865-1935
1112. Clark, William Mansfield "Bibliography of Walter Jennings Jones," NASBM 20:134-39 '39.

JORDAN, Edwin Oakes, 1866-1936
1113. Burrows, William "Bibliography of Edwin Oakes Jordan," NASBM 20:219-28 '39.

JUDAH, Samuel Benjamin Helbert, 1804-1876
1114. Blanck, Jacob "Samuel Benjamin Helbert Judah," BAL 5:221-23.

JUDD, Sylvester, 1813-1853
1115. Blanck, Jacob "Sylvester Judd," BAL 5:224-27.

JUDD, Sylvester Dwight, 1870-1903
1116. McAtee, W. L. "Sylvester Dwight Judd: with List of His Publications," Auk n. s. 59:466-67 Jl '42.

JULIEN, Alexis Anastay, 1840-1919
1117. Kemp, James F. "Memorial of Alexis Anastay Julien," GSAB 31:81-88 '20.

K

KAHANE, Henry Romanos, 1902-
1118. Pietrangeli, A. "Analytical Bibliography of the Writings of Henry and Reneé Kahane," Romance Philology 15:207-20 F '62.

KAHANE, Reneé Toole
1119. Pietrangeli, A. "Analytical Bibliography of the Writings of Henry and Reneé Kahane," Romance Philology 15:207-20 F '62.

KALLEN, Horace Meyer, 1882-
1120. Kallen, H. M. "Kallan Bibliography in Aesthetics," Journal of Aesthetics 11:303-05 Mr '53.

KASER, Arthur L.
1121. Kaser, David "Arthur L. Kaser: Gag Man for the Amateur," Books at Brown 18:94-115.

KASNER, Edward, 1878-1955
1122. Douglas, Jesse "Bibliography," NASBM 31:198-209 '58.

KATZ, Frank James, 1883-1930
1123. Smith, George Otis "Memorial of Frank James Katz," GSAB 42:49-51 '32.

KAY, George Frederick, 1873-1943
1124. Trowbridge, A. C. "Memorial to George Frederick Kay," GSAP pp. 169-76 '43.

KEELER, James Edward, 1857-1900
1125. Hastings, Charles S. "Published Writings of James Edward Keeler," NASBM 5:241-46 '05.

KEESING, Felix Maxwell, 1902-1961
1126. Siegel, Bernard J. and George D. Spindler "Felix Maxwell Keesing," AA 64:351-55 Apr '62.

KEITH, Arthur, 1864-1944
1127. Larsen, Esper S., Jr. "Memorial to Arthur Keith," GSAP pp. 241-45 '44.
1128. Longwell, Chester R. "Bibliography," NASBM 29:197-200 '56.

KELLEY, Walter Pearson, 1878-1965
1129. Chapman, Homer D. "Bibliography," NASBM 40:167-75 '69.

KELLOGG, Vernon Lyman, 1867-1937
1130. "List of Publications in the Field of Entomology by V. L. Kellogg," Entomology Society of America. Annals 33:601-07 D '40.
1131. McClung, C. E. "Bibliography," NASBM 20:253-57 '39.

KELLY, George, 1887-
1132. Doyle, Paul A. "George Kelly: an Eclectic Bibliography," BB 24:173-74 S-D '65.

KELLY, George Alexander, 1905-1967
1133. Thompson, George D. "George Alexander Kelly (1905-1967)," Journal of General Psychology 79:19-24 '68.

KELSER, Raymond Alexander, 1892-1952
1134. Shope, Richard E. "Bibliography," NASBM 28:218-21 '54.

KEMP, James Furman, 1859-1926
1135. Adams, Frank Dawson "Bibliography," NASBM 16: 9-18 '36

KENNEDY, John Fitzgerald, 1917-1963
1136. Gropp, Arthur E. "A Kennedy Bibliography," Americás pp. 40-41 Jan '64.
1137. "John Fitzgerald Kennedy (Bibliografia Brasilera)," Brazil. Camara dos Deputados. Biblioteca. Boletin 12:691-700 Jl '63.
1138. McDade, Thomas M. "The Assassination Industry: a Tentative Checklist of Publications on the Murder of President John F. Kennedy," ABC 18:8-14 Summer '68.

KENNEDY, John Pendleton, 1795-1870
1139. Blanck, Jacob "John Pendleton Kennedy," BAL 5: 228-42.
1140. Johnson, Merle "American First Editions: John Pendleton Kennedy," Publishers' Weekly 122:589 '32.

KENNEDY, William, d. 1927
1141. Wrather, W. E. "Memorial of William Kennedy," GSAB 39:29-34 '28.

KENNELLY, Arthur Edwin, 1861-1939
1142. Bush, Vannevar "Bibliography of Arthur Edwin Kennelly," NASBM 22:95-119.

KENT, Rockwell, 1882-
1143. Jones, Dan Burne "A Descriptive Checklist of the Written and Illustrated Work of Rockwell Kent," ABC 14:21-24 Summer '64.

KERR, Forrest Alexander, 1896-1938
1144. Mawdsley, J. B. "Memorial to Forrest Alexander Kerr," GSAP pp. 147-52 '38.

KETTERING, Charles Franklin, 1876-1958
1145. Jeffries, Zay "Selected Bibliography," NASBM 34: 117-22 '60.

KEY, Francis Scott, 1779-1843
1146. Blanck, Jacob "The Star Spangled Banner," BSA 60: 176-84 '66.
1147. Blanck, Jacob "Francis Scott Key," BAL 5:243-51.

KHARASCH, Morris Selig, 1895-1957
1148. Westheimer, Frank H. "Bibliography," NASBM 34: 133-52 '60.

KIDDER, Alfred Vincent, 1885-1963
1149. Wauchope, Robert "Alfred Vincent Kidder, 1885-1963," AAY 31:149-71 O '65.
1150. Willey, Gordon R. "Bibliography," NASBM 39:309-22 '67.

KILDALE, Malcolm B. , 1899-1959
1151. Perry, Vincent D. "Memorial to Malcolm B. Kildale," GSAP pp. 113-14 '60.

KILMER, Alfred Joyce, 1886-1918
1152. Blanck, Jacob "Alfred Joyce Kilmer," BAL 5:252-59.

KING, Clarence, 1842-1901
1153. Emmons, Samuel Franklin "Bibliography," NASBM 6:55 '09.

KING, Grace Elizabeth, 1852-1932
1154. Vaughan, Bess "A Bio-bibliography of Grace Elizabeth King," Louisiana Historical Quarterly 17:752-70 '34.

KING, Martin Luther, Jr., 1929-1968
1155. Pagenstecher, Ann "Martin Luther King, Jr.: an Annotated Checklist," BB 24:201-07 Jan-Apr '66.

KINNELL, Galway, 1927-
1156. Hawkins, Sherman "A Checklist of the Writings of Galway Kinnell," PULC 25:65-70 Autumn '63.

KIRK, Charles Townsend, 1876-1945
1157. Gould, Charles N. "Memorial to Charles Townsend Kirk," GSAP pp. 249-51 '45.

KIRK, Edwin, 1884-1955
1158. Cooper, G. Arthur "Memorial to Edwin Kirk," GSAP pp. 141-46 '56.

KIRKLAND, Caroline Matilda Stansbury, 1801-1864
1159. Blanck, Jacob "Caroline Matilda Stansbury Kirkland," BAL 5:260-69.

KIRKLAND, Joseph, 1830-1894
1160. Blanck, Jacob "Joseph Kirkland," BAL 5:270-73.
1161. Eichelberger, Clayton, L. "Joseph Kirkland (1830-1893): A Critical Bibliography of Secondary Comment," ALR 2:52-69 Spring '69.
1162. Henson, Clyde E. "Joseph Kirkland (1830-1894)," ALR #1 pp. 67-70 Fall '67.

KLINE, Virginia Harriett, 1910-1959
1163. Oros, Margaret O. "Memorial to Virginia Harriett Kline," GSAP pp. 115-17 '60.

KLINGBERG, Frank Joseph 1883-
1164. "Frank J. Klingberg: a Selected List of Publications," Negro History Bulletin 21:52-57 D '57

KLUCKHOHN, Clyde Kay Maben, 1905-1960
1165. Herskovits, Melville J. "Bibliography," NASBM 37: 139-59 '64.
1166. Wales, Lucy "A Bibliography of the Publications of Clyde Kluckhohn," AA 64:148-61 F '62.

KNIGHT, James Brookes, 1888-1960
1167. Dunbar, Carl O. "Memorial to James Brookes Knight," GSAP pp. 119-22 '60.

KNIGHT, Wilbur Clinton, 1858-1903
1168. Barbour, Erwin H. "Memoir of Wilbur Clinton

KNIGHT, Wilbur Clinton (continued)
Knight," GSAB 51:544-49 '04.

KNOPF, Adolph, 1882-1966
1169. Longwell, Chester R. "Bibliography," NASBM 41:
242-49 '70.

KNOWLTON, Frank Hall, 1860-1926
1170. White, David "Memorial of Frank Hall Knowlton,"
GSAB 38:52-70 '27

KOBER, Alice Elizabeth, 1906-1950
1171. Dow, S. "Bibliography of Alice Elizabeth Kober,"
American Journal of Archaeology 58:83-85 Apr '54.

KOFOID, Charles Atwood, 1865-1947
1172. Goldschmidt, Richard B. "Bibliography of C. A.
Kofoid," NASBM 26:134-51 '51.

KOHLER, Elmer Peter, 1865-1938
1173. Conant, James B. "Bibliography of Elmer P. Kohler,"
NASBM 27:285-91 '52.

KORZYBSKI, Alfred, 1879-1950
1174. "Bibliography of the Writings of Alfred Korzybski,"
General Semantics Bulletin #3:i-iii Spring '50.

KRIEGER, Philip, 1900-1940
1175. Berkey, Charles P. "Memorial to Philip Krieger,"
GSAP pp. 177-81 '43.

KROEBER, Alfred Louis, 1876-1960
1176. Gibson, Judith Ann and John Howland Rowe "Bibliography," NASBM 36:216-53 '62.
1177. Gibson, Anna J. and John H. Rowe "A Bibliography
of the Publications of Alfred Louis Kroeber," AA 63:
1060-87 O '61.
1178. Rowe, John Howland "Archeological Publications of
A. L. Kroeber," AAY 27:410-15 Jan '62.

KUENEN, Philip Henry, 1902-
1179. "List of Publications of P. H. Kuenen, 1925-1956,"
Journal of Paleontology 31:818-19 Jl '57.

KUMMEL, Henry Barnard, 1867-1945
1180. Johnson, Meredith E. "Memorial to Henry Barnard
Kummel," GSAP pp. 253-58 '45.

KUNKEL, Louis Otto, 1884-1960
1181. Stanley, Wendell M. "Bibliography," NASBM 38:152-
60 '65.

L

LACOE, Ralph Dupuy d. 1901
1182. White, David "Memoir of Ralph Dupuy Lacoe," GSAB
13:509-15 '02.

LA FARGE, Oliver, 1901-1963
1183. Byers, Douglas S. "Oliver La Farge, 1901-1963,"
AAY 31:408-09 Jan '66.

LAFITTE, Jean
1184. Oreans, G. Harrison "Lafitte, a Bibliographical
Note," AL 9:351-53 N '37.

LA FLESCHE, Francis, 1857-1932
1185. Alexander, Hartley B. "Bibliography," AA 35:330-31
'33.

LAMB, Arthur Becket, 1880-1952
1186. Keyes, Frederick G. "Bibliography," NASBM 29:
320-34 '56.

LANDES, Henry, 1867-1936
1187. Goodspeed, G. E. "Memorial of Henry Landes,"
GSAP pp. 207-13 '36.

LANDON, Melville de Lancey, 1839-1910
1188. Blanck, Jacob "Melville de Lancey Landon," BAL
5:274-79.

LANDSTEINER, Karl, 1868-1943
1189. Heidelberger, Michael "Bibliography," NASBM 40:
187-210 '69.

LANE, Alfred Church, 1863-1948
1190. Larsen, E. S. "Memorial to Alfred Church Lane,"
American Mineralogist 34:252 Mr '49.
1191. Nichols, Robert L. "Memorial to Alfred Church
Lane," GSAP pp. 107-18 '52.

LANE, Jonathan Homer, 1819-1880
1192. Abbe, Cleveland "Publications of J. Homer Lane,"
NASBM 3:263-64 1895.

LANGLEY, Samuel Pierpont, 1834-1906
1193. Walcott, Charles D. "Bibliography," NASBM 7:258-68 '13.

LANGTON, Daniel W., Jr., 1864-1909
1194. Smith, Eugene A. "Memoir of Daniel W. Langton, Jr.," GSAB 21:12-16 '10.

LANIER, Sidney Clopton, 1842-1881
1195. Blanck, Jacob "Sidney Clopton Lanier," BAL 5:280-98.

LARCOM, Lucy, 1824-1893
1196. Blanck, Jacob "Lucy Larcom," BAL 5:299-325.

LARDNER, Ring, 1885-1933
1197. Bruccoli, Matthew J. "Five Notes on Ring Lardner," BSA 58:297-98 '64.
1198. Bruccoli, Matthew J. "A Further Note on Lardner's 'What of It?'" BSA 57:377 '63.
1199. Bruccoli, Matthew J. "Notes on Ring Lardner's 'What of It?'" BSA 57:88-90 '63.
1200. Bruccoli, Matthew J. "Ring Lardner's First Book," BSA 58:34-35 '64.
1201. Goldsmith, Robert H. "Ring W. Lardner: a Checklist of His Published Work," BB 21:104-06 S-D '54.

LARSEN, Espersignius, Jr., 1879-1961
1202. Buddington, A. F. "Bibliography," NASBM 37:172-84 '64.

LASHLEY, Karl Spencer, 1890-1958
1203. Beach, Frank A. "Bibliography," NASBM 35:196-204 '61.

LAST, Hugh MacIlwain, 1894?-1957
1204. "Bibliography of the Published Writings of H. M. Last," Journal of Roman Studies 47:3-8 '57.

LATHROP, Dorothy Pulis, 1891-
1205. Bechtel, L. S. "Bibliography of Dorothy Pulis Lathrop," Library Journal 63:487 Je 15 '38.

LATHROP, George Parsons, 1851-1898
1206. Blanck, Jacob "George Parsons Lathrop," BAL 5: 326-39.

LATIMER, Wendell Mitchell, 1893-1955
1207. Hildebrand, Joel H. "Bibliography," NASBM 32:230-39 '58.

LAUFER, Berthold, 1874-1934
1208. Latourette, K. S. "Bibliography of Berthold Laufer, 1895-1934," NASBM 18:57-68 '38.
1209. Martin, Paul S. "Bibliography," AA 38:103-11 '36.

LAVIN, Mary
1210. Doyle, Paul A. "Mary Lavin: a Checklist," BSA 63:317-21 '69.

LAWRENCE, Ernest Orlando, 1901-1958
1211. Alvarez, Luis W. "Bibliography," NASBM 41:288-94 '70.

LAWSON, Andrew Cowper, 1861-1952
1212. Byerly, Perry and George D. Louderback "Bibliography," NASBM 37:198-204 '64.
1213. Byerly, Perry and George D. Louderback "Memorial to Andrew Cowper Lawson," GSAP pp. 141-47 '53.

LAZARUS, Emma, 1849-1887
1214. Blanck, Jacob "Emma Lazarus," BAL 5:340-46.

LEA, Matthew Carey, 1823-1897
1215. Barker, George F. "A List of the More Important Scientific Papers of Matthew Carey Lea," NASBM 5:204-08 '05.

LE CONTE, John, 1818-1891
1216. Le Conte, Joseph "A Partial List of His Scientific Papers," NASBM 3:390-93 1895.

LE CONTE, Joseph, 1823-1901
1217. Fairchild, Herman L. "Memoir of Joseph Le Conte," GSAB 26:47-57 '15.
1218. Hilgard, Eugene W. "Writings of Joseph Le Conte," NASBM 6:212-18 '09.

LEE, Willis Thomas, 1864-1926
1219. Alden, William C. "Memorial of Willis Thomas Lee," GSAB 38:70-93 '27.

LEES, James Henry, 1875-1935
1220. Kay, George F. "Memorial of James Henry Lees," GSAP pp. 125-19 '36.

LEHMANN, Walter 1878-
1221. "Bibliografías de antropólogos: Walter Lehmann,"
Boletín Bibliográfico de antropología Americana 3:86-
89 Jan '39.

LEIDY, Joseph, 1823-1891
1222. Osborn, Henry Fairfield "Bibliography," NASBM 7:
370-96 '13.

LEIGHTON, Alexander Hamilton, 1908-
1223. "Alexander Hamilton Leighton," Psychiatry 4:660 N
'41.

LEITH, Charles Kenneth, 1875-1956
1224. Hewett, D. F. "Bibliography," NASBM 33:196-204
'59.
1225. Lund, Richard J. "Memorial to Charles Kenneth
Leith," GSAP pp. 147-58 '56.

LELAND, Charles Godfrey, 1824-1903
1226. Blanck, Jacob "Charles Godfrey Leland," BAL 5:347-
98

LEONARD, Raymond Jackson, 1887-1937
1227. Butler, B. S. "Memorial to Raymond Jackson Leonard," GSAP pp. 153-55 '38.

LESLEY, J. Peter, 1819-1903
1228. Stevenson, John J. "Memoir of J. Peter Lesley,"
GSAB 15:532-41 '04.

LEVENE, Phoebus Aaron Theodor, 1869-1940
1229. Van Slyke, Donald D. and Walter A. Jacobs "Bibliography of Phoebus Aaron Theodor Levene," NASBM 23:
87-126 '45.

LEVERETT, Frank, 1859-1943
1230. Hobbs, William H. "Bibliography of Frank Leverett,"
NASBM 23:209-15 '45.
1231. Hobbs, William H. "Memorial to Frank Leverett,"
GSAP pp. 183-93 '43.

LEWENT, Kurt
1232. Woodbridge, Benjamin M., Jr. "Analytical Bibliography of the Writings of Kurt Lewent," Romand Philology
20:391-403 My '67.

LEWIN, Bertram D. , 1896–
1233. "Bibliography of Bertram D. Lewin (1926-1966),"
Psychoanalytical Quarterly 35:488-96 O '66.

LEWIS, Alfred Henry, 1857-1914
1234. Blanck, Jacob "Alfred Henry Lewis," BAL 5:399-404.

LEWIS, George William, 1882-1948
1235. Durand, William F. "Bibliography," NASBM 25:312
'49.

LEWIS, Gilbert Newton, 1875-1946
1236. Hildebrand, Joel H. "Bibliography," NASBM 31:225-
35 '58.

LEWIS, Warren Harmon, 1870-1964
1237. Corner, George W. "Bibliography," NASBM 39:345-
58 '67.

LIBBEY, Donald Smith, 1892-1959
1238. Libbey, Donald L. "Memorial to Donald Smith Libbey," GSAP pp. 123-24 '60.

LILLIE, Frank Rattray, 1870-1947
1239. Willier, B. H "Bibliography," NASBM 30:229-36 '57.

LINCOLN, Abraham, 1809-1865
1240. "Books About Abraham Lincoln for Children," ALA
Bulletin 53:308 Apr '59.
1241. Griffith, A. H. "Lincoln Literature, Lincoln Collections, and Lincoln Collectors," Wisconsin Magazine of
History 15:148-67 D '31.
1242. Gunderson, R. G. "Another Shelf of Lincoln Books,"
Quarterly Journal of Speech 48:308-13 O '62.
1243. "Lincoln Bookshelf," Our World Weekly 2:25 F 9 '25.
1244. "Lincoln Collection in the St. Procopius Library,"
Illinois Libraries 47:588-92 Je '65.
1245. Mearns, David C. "Lincoln Collections in the Library
of Congress," Abraham Lincoln Quarterly D '41.
1246. Pratt, H. E. "Lincoln Literature," Illinois Libraries
24:34-37 F '42.
1247. Taylor, William E. "The Lincoln Collection," Lincoln Herald 59:27-31 Spring '57.
1248. Wheeler, B. E. "Lincolniana in 1952 (etc.)," Hob-
bies 57:125-30 F '53; 60:24-27 F '56; 61:26-28 F '57;
62:22-25 F '58; 63:26-27 F '58; 64:108-09 Apr '59;
64:27-30 F '60; 65:28-29 F '61; 65:28-29 Mr '61; 67:
24-25 F '63; 68:24-25 F '64; 69:28-29 F '65; 70:28-29

LINCOLN, Abraham (continued)
F '66; 70:28-29 F '66; 71:35 F '67; 72:114-15 Mr '67;
72:32-33 F '68.

LINDERMAN, Frank Bird, 1868-1938
1249. White, C. "Bibliography of the Writings of Frank
Bird Linderman," Frontier and Midland 19:147-48
Spring '39.

LINDGREN, Waldemar, 1860-1939
1250. Butler, B. S. "Memorial to Waldemar Lindgren,"
GSAP pp. 177-96 '49.

LINDSAY, Vachel, 1879-1931
1251. Byrd, Cecil K. "Checklist of the Melcher Lindsay
Collections," Indiana University Bookman #5 pp. 64-
106 '60.

LINN, John Blair, 1777-1804
1252. Leary, Lewis "The Writings of John Blair Linn
(1777-1804)," BB 19:18-19 S-D '46.

LINTON, Ralph, 1893-1953
1253. Gillin, John "Bibliography," AA 56:274-81 '54.
1254. Kluckhohn, Clyde "Bibliography," NASBM 31:248-53
'58.
1255. McKern, William C. "Bibliography," AAY 19:410 Apr
'54.

LIPPARD, George, 1822-1854
1256. Blanck, Jacob "George Lippard," BAL 5:405-418.

LIVINGSTON, Luther Samuel, 1864-1914
1257. Winship, George Parker "Bibliography of the Separate Publications of Luther S. Livingston," BSA 8:121-
42 '14.

LIVINGSTON, Robert R., 1746-1813
1258. "List of Works in the New York Public Library Relating to Henry Hudson, the Hudson River, Robert Fulton, Early Steam Navigation, etc." NYPLB 13:585-
613 '09.

LLOYD, Edwin Russell, 1882-1955
1259. Adams, John Emery "Memorial to Edwin Russell
Lloyd," GSAP pp. 139-41 '55.

LOBECK, Armin Kohl, 1886-1958
1260. Miller, Ralph L. "Memorial to Armin Kohl Lobeck,"
GSAP pp. 147-55 '58.
1261. Smith, G. H. "Armin Kohl Lobeck, Geomorphologist
and Landscape Artist, 1886-1958," Association of
American Geographers. Annals 49:85-87 Mr '59.

LOCKE, David Ross, 1833-1888
1262. Blanck, Jacob "David Ross Locke," BAL 5:419-30.

LOEB, Jacques, 1859-1924
1263. Kohelt, Nina "Bibliography," NASBM 13:372-401 '30.

LOEB, Leo, 1869-1959
1264. Goodpasture, Ernest W. "Bibliography," NASBM 35:
220-51 '61.

LOGAN, William Newton, 1869-1941
1265. Cumings, E. R. "Memorial to William Newton Logan," GSAP pp. 177-86 '41.

LONDON, Jack, 1876-1916
1266. Blanck, Jacob "Jack London," BAL 5:431-67.
1267. Chomet, Otto "Jack London: Works, Reviews, and
Criticism Published in German," BB 19:211-15 Jan-
Apr '49; 19:239-40 My-Ag '49.
1268. Haydock, James "Jack London: a Bibliography of
Criticism," BB 23:42-46 My-Ag '60.
1269. "Jack London: a Bibliography - a Supplement," Jack
London Newsletter 2:5-25.
1270. "Jack London: an Addendum," ALR 2 pp. 91-93
Spring '68.
1271. Nichol, John W. "Jack London: a Bibliography, Addenda I," Jack London Newsletter 2:84-87.
1272. Schubert, Renate "Jack London Auswaklbibliographie,"
Jahrbuch für Amerikastudien 12:94-108 '64.
1273. Walker, Dale L. "Jack London (1876-1916)," ALR
#1 pp. 71-78 Fall '67.
1274. Woodbridge, Hensley "Jack London: a Bibliography:
a Supplement," ABC 17:32-35 N '66.
1275. Woodward, Robert H. "Jack London: a Bibliography,
Addenda II," Jack London Newsletter 2:88-90.

LONG, Stanley V., 1937-1967
1276. Meighan, Clement W. "Stanley V. Long 1937-1967,"
AAY 34:72 Jan '69.

LONGCOPE, Warfield Theobald, 1877-1953
1277. Tillett, William S. "Bibliography," NASBM 33:215-
25 '59.

LONGFELLOW, Henry Wadsworth, 1807-1882
1278. Blanck, Jacob "Henry Wadsworth Longfellow," BAL
5:468-640.
1279. Gohdes, Clarence "A Checklist of Volumes by Longfellow Published in the British Isles During the Nine-
teenth Century," BB 17:46 S-D '40; 17:67-69 Jan-Apr
'41; 17:93-96 My-Ag '41.
1280. Walsh, James E. "American Printings of Longfellow's 'The Golden Legend,' 1851-1855," BSA 57:81-88
'63.

LOOMIS, Elias, 1811-1889
1281. Newton, H. A. "Publications of Elias Loomis,"
NASBM 3:241-52 1895.

LOOMIS, Frederick Brewster, 1873-1937
1282. Granger, Walter "Memorial to Frederick Brewster
Loomis," GSAP pp. 173-81 '37.

LOTHROP, Samuel Kirkland, 1892-1965
1283. "Bibliografías de antropólogos: Samuel Kirkland Lothrop," Boletín bibliográfica de antropólogos Americana
3:188-91 My '39.
1284. Easby, Dudley T., Jr. "Samuel Kirkland Lothrop,
1892-1965," AAY 31:256-61 O '65.

LOTKA, Alfred James, 1880-1949
1285. Notestein, F. W. "Alfred James Loka, 1880-1949,"
Population Index 16:23-29 Jan '50.

LOUDERBACK, George Davis, 1874-1957
1286. Byerly, Perry and N. L. Taliaferro "Memorial to
George Davis Louderback," GSAP pp. 137-42 '59.

LOUGHLIN, Gerald Francis, 1880-1946
1287. Burchard, Ernest F. "Memorial to Gerald Francis
Loughlin," GSAP pp. 173-82 '46.

LOUGHRIDGE, Robert Hills, 1843-1917
1288. Smith, Eugene Allen "Memorial of Robert Hills
Loughridge," GSAB 29:48-55 '18.

LOVECRAFT, H. P., 1890-1937
1289. Emmons, Winfred S., Jr. "A Bibliography of H. P.

LOVECRAFT, H. P. (continued)
Lovecraft," Extrapolation 3:2-25.

LOVEJOY, Ellis, 1860-
1290. "Publications of Ellis Lovejoy," American Ceramic
Society. Bulletin 16:261-62 Je '37.

LOVERING, Joseph, 1813-1892
1291. Peirce, B. Osgood "Bibliography," NASBM 6:339-44
'09.

LOWELL, Amy, 1874-1925
1292. Kemp, Frances "Bibliography of Amy Lowell," BB
15:8-9 My-Ag '33; 15:25-26 S-D '33; 15:50-53 Jan-Apr
'34.

LOWELL, James Russell, 1819-1891
1293. Campbell, Killis "Bibliographical Notes on Lowell,"
Texas Studies in English #4 pp. 115-19 '24.
1294. Joyce, H. E. "A Bibliographical Note on James Russell Lowell," Modern Language Notes 35:249-50 '20.
1295. Wheeler, Martha Thorne "Best Editions of James
Russell Lowell," BB 3:42-43 '02.

LOWELL, Robert, 1917-
1296. Staples, Hugh B. "Robert Lowell: Bibliography 1939-
1959, with An Illustrative Critique," HLB 13:292-318
'59.

LOWERY, Janette Sebring, 1892-
1297. Johnston, L. C. "Texas Author: Janette Sebring
Lowery," Horn Book 23:66 Jan '47.

LOWIE, Robert H., 1883-1957
1298. Lowie, Robert H., Louella Cole Lowie, and Madge D.
Richardson "Bibliography of Robert H. Lowie," AA
60:362-75 Apr '58.

LUDLOW, Fitz Hugh, 1836-1870
1299. "Books and Articles By and About Fitz Hugh Ludlow,"
Union Worthies (Union College) 8:28.

LULL, Richard Swann, 1867-1957
1300. Simpson, George Gaylor "Memorial to Richard Swann
Lull," GSAP pp. 127-33 '57.

LUNIN, Nicolai I., 1853-1937
1301. Voss, H. E. "Nicolai I. Lunin - 1853-1937," Ameri-

LUNIN, Nicolai I. (continued)
can Dietetic Association. Journal 32:319-20 Apr '56.

LUPTON, Charles Thomas, 1878-1935
1302. Ball, Max W. "Memorial of Charles Thomas Lupton,"
GSAP pp. 273-81 '35.

LUSK, Graham, 1866-1932
1303. Du Bois, Eugene F. "Bibliography," NASBM 21:131-
42 '41.

LUSKA, Sidney see HARLAND, Henry.

LYDENBERG, Harry Miller, 1874-1960
1304. McKay, George L. "A Bibliography of the Published
Writings of Harry Miller Lydenberg," Bookmen's Holi-
day pp. 5-26 '43.
1305. Stam, David H. "A Bibliography of the Published
Writings of Harry Miller Lydenberg, 1942-1960,"
NYPLB 64:298-302 Je '60.

LYMAN, Theodore, 1833-1897
1306. Bowditch, H. P. "List of Publications by Theodore
Lyman," NASBM 5:151-53 '05.

LYMAN, Theodore, 1874-1954
1307. Bridgman, P. W. "Bibliography," NASBM 30:253-56
'57.

LYON, Harris Merton, 1883-1916
1308. Eichelberger, Clayton, L. and Zoë Lyon "A Partial
Listing of the Published Work of Harris Merton Lyon,"
ALR 3:41-52 Winter '70.

LYON, Marcus Ward, 1875-1942
1309. "Marcus Ward Lyon, Jr.," American Midland Naturalist 27:vii-xv My '42.

M

McCALLEY, Henry, 1852-1904
1310. Smith, Eugene A. "Memoir of Henry McCalley,"
GSAB 16:555-58 '05.

McCALLIE, Samuel Washington, 1856-1933
1311. Bayley, W. S. "Memorial of Samuel Washington Mc
Dallie," GSAP pp. 227-33 '33.

MacCALLUM, William George, 1874-1944
1312. Longcope, W. T. "Bibliography," NASBM 23:354-64
'45.

McCAUGHEY, William John, 1882-1962
1313. Foster, W. R. "Publications and Patents of William
John McCaughey," GSAB 73: Supplement 93-94 Ag '62.

McCORRY, Vincent Patrick, 1909-
1314. Gardiner, H. C. "McCorry Checklist," America 104:
389 D '60.

McCOURT, Walter Edward, 1884-1943
1315. Buehler, Henry A. "Memorial to Walter Edward Mc-
Court," GSAP pp. 201-04 '43.

McCOY, Alex Watts, d. 1944
1316. Wilson, W. B. "Memorial to Alex Watts McCoy,"
GSAP pp. 271-76 '44.

McCULLERS, Carson, 1917-1967
1317. Phillips, Robert S. "Carson McCullers; 1956-1964,"
BB 24:113-16 S-D '64.
1318. Stewart, Stanley "Carson McCullers, 1940-1956; a
Selected Checklist," BB 22:182-85 Jan-Apr '59.

MacCURDY, George Grant, 1863-1947
1319. McCown, Theodore D. "Bibliography," AA 50:520-24
'48.

MacDONALD, Donald Francis, 1875-1942
1320. Wrather, W. E. "Memorial to Donald Francis Mac-
Donald," GSAP pp. 197-200 '49.

MacDONALD, Gilmour Byers, 1883-
1321. Getty, R. E. et al. "Professor G. B. MacDonald,"
Iowa State College. Journal of Science 22:321 Jl '48.

MacDOUGAL, Daniel Trembly, 1892-1938
1322. "Selected List of Publications," Plant Physiology 14:
198-202 Apr '39.

MACELWANE, James B., S. J., 1883-1956
1323. Byerly, Perry and William V. Stauder, S. J. "Bibliography," NASBM 31:276-81 '58.
1324. Byerly, Perry and William V. Stauder, S. J. "Memorial to James Bernard Macelwane, S. J.," GSAP pp.
159-63 '56.

McGEE, William John, 1853-1912
1325. Knowlton, F. H. "Memoir of W. J. McGee," GSAB 24:18-29 '13.

MacINNES, Duncan Arthur, 1885-1965
1326. Longworth, Lewis G. and Theodore Shedlovsky "Bibliography," NASBM 41:308-17 '70.

MacINNES, William, 1858-1925
1327. Alcock, Frederick J. "Memorial of William Mac Innes," GSAB 37:96-99 '26.

McKELLAR, Peter, 1838-1929
1328. Tanton, T. L. "Memorial of Peter McKellar," GSAB 42:52-55 '32.

McKENZIE, Roderick Duncan, 1885-1940
1329. Eubank, E. "Selected and Partial Bibliography of the Sociological Writings of R. D. McKenzie," Sociology and Social Research 25:73 S '40.

McKIE, Douglas, 1896-1967
1330. Robinson, E. H. "Douglas McKie," Isis 59:321-27 Fall '68.

MacLEISH, Archibald, 1892-
1331. Frederic, G. "Check List of Archibald MacLeish," Publishers' Weekly 124:180 '33.
1332. Thurber, Gerrish "MacLeish Published Books," Library Journal 64:864, 866 '39.

MacNAIR, Harley Fransworth, 1891-1947
1333. Price, M. T. "Harley Farnsworth MacNair (July 22, 1891-June 22, 1947)," Far Eastern Quarterly 8:59-63 N '48.

MacNIDER, William deBerniere, 1881-1951
1334. Richards, A. N. "Bibliography," NASBM 32:262-72 '58.

MADELEVA, Sister Mary (Wolff, Mary Evaline), 1887-1964
1335. Kilmer, K. "Contemporary Catholic Authors; Sister Mary Madeleva, C. S. C. , Pioneer Poet," Catholic Library World 12:89 D '40.

MALINOWSKI, Bronislaw, 1884-1942
1336. Murdock, George Peter "Bibliography," AA 45:445-51 '43.

MALL, Franklin Paine, 1862-1917
1337. Sabin, Florence R. "Publications of Franklin Paine Mall," NASBM 16:117-22 '36.

MALOTT, Clyde Arnett, 1887-1950
1338. Shrock, Robert R. "Memorial to Clyde Arnett Malott," GSAP pp. 105-09 '50.

MANFRED, Frederick, 1912-
1339. Kellogg, George "Frederick Manfred: a Bibliography," TCL 11:30-35 Apr '65.

MANN, Frank Charles, 1887-1962
1340. Visscher, Maurice B. "Bibliography," NASBM 38: 174-204 '65.

MANN, Horace, 1796-1859
1341. "Horace Mann Bibliography," Instructor 46:66 My '37.

MANSFIELD, George Rogers, 1875-1947
1342. King, Philip B. "Memorial to George Rogers Mansfield," GSAP pp. 187-96 '48.

MANSFIELD, Wendell Clay, 1874-1939
1343. Reeside, John B., Jr. "Memorial to Wendell Clay Mansfield," GSAP pp. 213-17 '39.

MARBLE, John Putnam, 1897-1955
1344. Foshag, William F. "Memorial to John Putnam Marble," American Mineralogist 41:304-05 Mr '56.
1345. Ingerson, Earl "Memorial to John Putnam Marble," GSAP pp. 143-46 '55.

MARBUT, Curtis Fletcher, 1863-1935
1346. Darton, N. H. "Memorial of Crutis Fletcher Marbut," GSAP pp. 221-27 '36.

MARQUAND, John P., 1893-1960
1347. White, William "John P. Marquand; a Preliminary Checklist," BB 19:268-71 S-D '49.
1348. White, William "John P. Marquand Since 1950," BB 21:230-34 My-Ag '56.
1349. White, William "Marquandiana," BB 20:8-12 Jan-Apr '50.

MARSH, Charles Dwight, 1855-1932
1350. Marsh, F. W. "List of Papers on Lakes and on Crustacea by C. D. Marsh," Wisconsin Academy of

MARSH, Charles Dwight (continued)
Sciences, Arts and Letters. Transactions 31:538-41
'38.

MARSH, Othneil Charles, 1831-1899
1351. Schuchert, Charles "Bibliography of Othniel Charles
Marsh 1831-1899," NASBM 20:59-78 '39.

MARTIN, George Curtis, 1875-1943
1352. Smith, Philip S. "Memorial to George Curtis Martin,"
GSAP pp. 247-57 '44.

MARTIN, Lawrence, 1880-1955
1353. Thwaites, F. T. and Kenneth Bertrand "Memorial to
Lawrence Martin," GSAP pp. 147-51 '55.
1354. Williams, F. E. "Lawrence Martin, 1880-1955,"
Association of American Geographers. Annals 46:360-
64 S '56.

MASON, John Alden, 1885-
1355. Bibliografías de Antropólogos: John Alden Mason,"
Boletín Bibliográfica Antropólogos Americana 4:84-90
Jan '40.
1356. Satterthwaite, Linton "John Alden Mason," AA 71:871-
79 O '69.

MASON, Lowell, 1792-1872
1357. Rich, A. L. "Lowell Mason, Modern Music Teacher:
with a List of His Publications on the Teaching of
Music," Music Educators Journal 28:23 Jan '42.

1358. Weaver, Warren "Bibliography," NASBM 37:233-36
'64.

MASON, Otis Tufton, 1838-1908
1359. Hough, Walter "A Selected List of Professor Mason's
Writings," AA 10:666-67 '08.

MASON, Warren P. , 1900-
1360. "Publications of Warren P. Mason, 1921-   ," Acousti-
cal Society of America. Journal 41:907-11 Apr '65.

MASTERS, Edgar Lee, 1868-1950
1361. Robinson, F. K. "Edgar Lee Masters; an Exhibition
in Commemoration of the Centenary of his Birth; Catalogue and Checklist of Books," Texas Quarterly 12:4-68
Spring '69.

MATHER, Cotton, 1663-1728
1362. Holmes, Thomas J. "Cotton Mather and His Writings on Witchcraft," BSA 18:31-59 '24.

MATHEWS, Edward Bennett, 1869-1944
1363. Swartz, Charles K. "Memorial to Edward Bennett Mathews," GSAP pp. 259-64 '44.

MATSON, George Charlton, 1873-1940
1364. Levorsen, A. I. "Bibliography of Works by George C. Matson," American Association of Petroleum Geologists Bulletin 24:608-09 Mr '40. Reprinted GSAP pp. 231-32 '40.

MATTHES, Francois Emile, 1874-1948
1365. Fryxell, Fritiof "Memorial to Francois Emile Matthes," GSAP pp. 153-68 '55.

MATTHEW, William Diller, 1871-1930
1366. Osborn, Henry Fairfield "Memorial William Diller Matthew," GSAB 42:55-95 '32.

MAUDSLEY, Alfred Percival, 1850-1931
1367. Tozzer, Alfred M. "Bibliography," AA 33:411-12 '31.

MAURY, Carlotta Joaquina, 1874-1938
1368. Reeds, Chester A. "Memorial to Carlotta Joaquina Maury," GSAP pp. 157-68 '38.

MAYER, Alfred Marshall, 1836-1897
1369. Mayer, Alfred G. and Robert S. Woodward "Bibliography of Scientific Papers by Alfred M. Mayer," NASBM 8:266-72 '19.

MAYNARD, Theodore, 1890-1956
1370. Sister Miriam "Contemporary Catholic Authors: Theodore Maynard, Divine Adventurer," Catholic Library World 12:146, 168 F '41.

MAYNARD, Thomas Poole, 1883-1952
1371. Lester, J. G. and A. S. Furcon "Memorial to Thomas Poole Maynard," GSAP pp. 119-20 '52.

MAYOR, Alfred Goldsborough, 1868-1922
1372. Davenport, Charles B. "Scientific Papers by Alfred G. Mayor," NASBM 11:11-14 '22.

MAYO-SMITH, Richmond, 1854-1901
1373. Seligman, R. "Bibliography," NASBM 10:77 '19.

MEAD, George Herbert, 1863-1931
1374. Stevens, E. "Bibliographical Note," American Journal of Sociology 72:551-57 Mr '67.

MEAD, Warren Judson, 1883-1960
1375. Shrock, Robert R. "Bibliography," NASBM 35:269-71 '61.
1376. Shrock, Robert R. "Memorial to Warren Judson Mead," GSAP pp. 125-36 '60.

MEANS, Philip Ainsworth, 1892-1944
1377. Lothrop, S. K. "Bibliography," AAY 11:110-12 O '45.

MEEK, Fielding Bradford, 1817-1876
1378. White, Charles A. "Bibliography," NASBM 4:80-91 '02.

MEGGERS, William Frederick, 1888-1966
1379. Foote, Paul D. "Bibliography," NASBM 41:324-40 '70.

MEINZER, Oscar Edward, 1876-1948
1380. Sayre, Nelson "Memorial to Oscar Edward Meinzer," GSAP pp. 197-206 '48.

MEKEEL, H. Scudder, 1902-1947
1381. MacGregor, Gordon "Bibliography," AA 50:99-100 '48.

MELL, Patrick Hues, 1850-1918
1382. Calhoun, Fred H. H. "Memorial of Patrick Hues Mell," GSAB 30:43-47 '19.

MELTZER, Samuel James, 1851-1920
1382. Howell, William H. "Bibliography of Dr. S. J. Meltzer," NASBM 11:15-23 '22.

MELVILLE, Herman, 1819-1891
1383. Beebe, Maurice and others "Criticism of Herman Melville; a Selected Checklist," MFS 8:312-46 Autumn '62.
1384. "Bibliography," Melville Society Newsletter Mr '45.
1385. Cahoon, Herbert "Herman Melville: A Check List of Books and Manuscripts in the Collections of the New York Public Library," NYPLB 55:325-38 Jl '51.
1386. Ives, Sidney "A Melville Ghost," BSA 59:318 '65.

MELVILLE, Herman (continued)
1387. Mills, Gordon H. "American First Editions at TxU VII Herman Melville (1819-1891)," University of Texas Library Chronicle 4:89-92 '51.
1388. Vann, J. Don "A Checklist of Melville Criticism, 1958-1968," Studies in the Novel 1:507-30.
1389. Zimmerman, Michael "Herman Melville in the 1920's; an Annotated Bibliography," BB 24:117-20 S-D '64; 24:139-44 Jan-Apr '65.

MENCKEN, H. L., 1880-1956
1390. Porter, Bernard H. "H. L. Mencken; a Bibliography," TCL 4:100-07 O '58.

MENDEL, Lafayette Benedict, 1872-1935
1391. Chittenden, Russell H. "Bibliography of Lafayette Benedict Mendel," NASBM 18:138-55 '38.

MENDENHALL, Charles Elwood, 1872-1935
1392. Van Vleck, J. H. "Bibliography," NASBM 18:21-22 '38.

MENDENHALL, Thomas Corwin, 1841-1924
1393. Crew, Henry "Bibliography of Thomas C. Mendenhall," NASBM 16:347-51 '36.

MERA, Harry P., 1875-1951
1394. Chapman, Kenneth "Bibliography," AAY 17:48 Jl '51.

MEREDITH, William, 1919-
1395. Ludwig, Richard M. "A Checklist of the Writings of William Meredith," PULC 25:79-85 Autumn '63.

MERICA, Paul Dyer, 1889-1957
1396. Jeffries, Zay "Bibliography," NASBM 33:235-40 '59.

MERRIAM, Clinton Hart, 1855-1942
1397. Grinnell, Hilda W. "Bibliography of Clinton Hart Merriam," Journal of Mammalogy 24:436-57 N '43; Reprinted NASBM 24:27-57 '47.

MERRIAM, John Campbell, 1869-1945
1398. Stock, Chester "Bibliography, NASBM 26:218-32 '51.
1399. Stock, Chester "Memorial to John Campbell Merriam," GSAP pp. 183-97 '46.

MERRILL, Elmer Drew, 1876-1956
1400. Schwarten, Lazella and Elmer D. Merrill "Bibliog-

MERRILL, Elmer Drew (continued)
raphy," NASBM 32:302-33 '58.

MERRILL, Frederick James Hamilton, 1861-1916
1401. Berkey, Charles P. "Memorial of Frederick James
Hamilton Merrill," GSAB 42:165-71 '32.

MERRILL, George Perkins, 1854-1929
1402. Moodey, Margaret W. "Bibliography of George Perkins Merrill, 1879-1930," NASBM 17:42-53 '37.
1403. Schuchert, Charles "Memorial of George Perkins
Merrill," GSAB 42:95-122 '32.

MERRILL, Paul Willard, 1887-1961
1404. Wilson, Olin C. "Bibliography," NASBM 37:247-66
'64.

MERTON, Robert King, 1910-
1405. "Writings of Merton," Psychiatry 4:503-04 Ag '41.

MERTON, Thomas, 1915-1968
1406. Dell'Isola, Frank "A Bibliography of Thomas Merton,"
Thought 29:574-96 '54.

MERWIN, William Stanley, 1927-
1407. Roche, Thomas P., Jr. "A Checklist of the Writings
of William Stanley Merwin," PULC 25:94-104 Autumn
'63.

METCALF, Haven, 1875-1940
1408. Meinecke, E. P. "Haven Metcalf (1875-1940) with
List of His Published Papers," Phytopathology 31:294-
95 Apr '41.

METCALF, Keyes D., 1889-
1409. Williams, Edwin E. "Keyes D. Metcalf: A Bibliography of Published Writings," HLB 17:131-42 Apr '69.

MEYERHOF, Otto, 1884-1951
1410. Peters, Sir Rudolph A. "Bibliography," NASBM 34:
164-82 '60.

MICHAELIS, Leonor, 1875-1949
1411. MacInnes, D. A. and S. Granick "Bibliography,"
NASBM 31:293-321 '58.

MICHELSON, Albert Abraham, 1852-1931
1412. Millikan, Robert A. "Bibliography of Publications of
116

MICHELSON, Albert Abraham (continued)
Albert Abraham Michelson," NASBM 19:142-46 '38.

MICHELSON, Truman, 1879-1939?
1413. Cooper, J. M. "Truman Michelson, Bibliography of
His Works," AA 31:282-85 Apr '39.

MIDGLEY, Thomas, Jr., 1889-1944
1414. Kettering, Charles F. "Bibliography of Thomas Midgley, Jr.," NASBM 24:377-80 '47.

MILES, Lee Ellis, 1890- 1941
1415. Neal, D. C. "Lee Ellis Miles, September 25, 1890-
May 10, 1941: with List of His Publications," Phytopathology 32:269-70 Apr '42.

MILES, Suzanna Whitelaw, 1922-1966
1416. Proskouriakoff, Tatiana "Bibliography," AA 70:753-54
Ag '68.

MILLAY, Edna St. Vincent, 1892-1950
1417. Brenni, Vito J. and John E. James "Edna St. Vincent Millay: Selected Criticism," BB 23:177-78 My-
Ag '62.
1418. Kohn, John S. and Van E. Kohn "Some undergradu-
ate Printings of Edna St. Vincent Millay," Publishers'
Weekly 138:2026-29 N 30 '40.
1419. Patton, John J. "Comprehensive Bibliography of
Criticism of Edna St. Vincent Millay," Serif 5:10-32
S '68.

MILLER, Arthur, 1915-
1420. Eissenstat, Martha Turnquist "Arthur Miller: a
Bibliography," Modern Drama 5:93-106 My '62.
1421. Hayashi, Tetsumaro "Arthur Miller; the Dimension
of His Art and a Checklist of His Published Work,"
Serif 11:26-32.
1422. Ungar, Harriet "The Writings By and About Arthur
Miller: a Checklist 1936-1967," NYPLB 74:107-37 F
'70.

MILLER, Arthur McQuiston, 1861-1929
1423. McFarlan, Arthur C. "Memorial of Arthur McQuiston Miller," GSAP pp. 283-87 '35.

MILLER, Benjamin LeRoy, 1874-1944
1424. Ashley, George H. "Memorial to Benjamin LeRoy
Miller," GSAP pp. 277-85 '44.

MILLER, Dayton Clarence, 1866-1941
1425. Fletcher, Harvey "Bibliography," NASBM 23:67-74 '45.
1426. Shankland, R. S. "Dayton Clarence Miller: Physics Across Fifty Years; with List of His Publications," American Journal of Physics 9:281-83 O '41.

MILLER, George Abram, 1863-1951
1427. Brahana, H. R. "Bibliography," NASBM 30:277-312 '57.

MILLER, Henry, 1891-
1428. Renken, Maxime "Bibliography of Henry Miller: 1945-1961," TCL 7:180-90 Jan '62.

MILLER, Joaquin, 1841?-1913
1429. De Gruson, Gene "An Unlocated Bret Harte - Joaquin Miller Book," BSA 61:60 '67.

MILLER, Perry, 1905-1963
1430. Kinnamon, Keneth "A Bibliography of Perry Miller," BB 26:45-51 Apr-Je '69.

MILLER, Willet Green, d. 1925
1431. Tyrrell, Joseph B. "Memorial of Willet Green Miller," GSAB 37:99-110 '26.

MILLIKAN, Clark Blanchard, 1903-1966
1432. Sechler, E. E. "Bibliography," NASBM 40:222-25 '69.

MILLIKAN, Robert Andrews, 1868-1953
1433. DuBridge, Lee A. and Paul S. Epstein "Bibliography," NASBM 33:271-82 '59.

MILLS, James Ellison, 1834-1901
1434. Branner, J. C. "Memoir of James E. Mills," GSAB 14:512-17 '03.

MINER, Neil Alden, 1898-1947
1435. Fryxell, F. M. "Memorial to Neil Alden Miner," GSAP pp. 201-07 '49.

MINOT, Charles Sedgwick, 1852-1914
1436. Morse, Edward S. "Bibliography," NASBM 9:276-85 '19.

MISHKIN, Bernard, 1913-1954
1437. Wagley, Charles "Bernard Mishkin, 1913-1954,"

MISHKIN, Bernard (continued)
AA 57:1033-35 '55.

MITCHELL, Henry, 1830-1902
1438. Marmer, H. A. "Bibliography," NASBM 20:148-50
'39.

MITCHELL, Samuel Alfred, 1874-1960
1439. Abbot, C. G. "Bibliography," NASBM 36:270-76 '62.

MITCHELL, Silas Weir, 1829-1914
1440. Bailey, Percival "Scientific Bibliography," NASBM
32:341-53 '58.
1441. Haynes, Barrie "S. Weir Mitchell (1892-1914),"
ALR 2:149-55 Summer '69.

MODJESKI, Ralph, 1861-1940
1442. Durand, W. F. "Appendices," NASBM 23:256-61 '45.

MOFFIT, Fred Howard, 1874-1958
1443. Mertie, John B., Jr. "Memorial to Fred Howard
Moffit," GSAB pp. 157-59 '58.

MONTAGUE, Margaret Prescott, 1878-1955
1444. Stemple, Ruth M. "Margaret Prescott Montague,
1878-1955: a Checklist," BB 22:62-64 My-Ag '57.

MONTGOMERY, Edmund Duncan, 1835-1911
1445. Keeton, M. T. "Bibliography of Articles, Books, and
Monographs by Edmund Duncan Montgomery," Journal
of the History of Ideas 8:338-41 Je '47.

MONTGOMERY, James Alan, 1866-1949
1446. Speiser, E. A. "Bibliography of James Alan Montgomery," American School of Oriental Research. Bulletin #117:8-13 F '50.

MOONEY, James, 1861-1921
1447. Mooney, Ione Lee Gaut "Bibliography," AA 24:212-
14 '22.

MOORE, Anne Carroll, 1871-1961
1448. Mahony, B. E. "Anne Carroll Moore, Doctor of Hu-
mane Letters," Horn Book 18:17-18 Jan '42.
1449. Weeks, Elizabeth Harriet and Francis Lander Spain
"Anne Carroll Moore: a Contribution Toward a Bibliography," NYPLB 60:629-36 N-D '56.

MOORE, Eliakim Hastings, 1862-1932
1450. Bliss, G. A. and L. E. Dickson "Bibliography,"
NASBM 17:99-102 '37

MOORE, Joseph Haines, 1878-1949
1451. Wright, William H. "Bibliography," NASBM 29:243-51 '56.

MOORE, Marianne, 1887-
1452. Sheehy, Eugene P. and Kenneth A. Lohf "The Achievement of Marianne Moore: a Bibliography," NYPLB 62:132-49 Mr '58; 62:183-90 Apr '58; 62:249-59 My '58.

MOOREHEAD, Warren King, 1866-1939
1453. Byers, D. S. "Warren King Moorehead: Bibliography of His Works," AA 41:289-94 Apr '39.

MOREY, Charles Rufus, 1877-1955
1454. Martin, J. R. "Bibliography of the Principal Publications of Charles Rufus Morey," Art Bulletin 32:345-49 D '50.

MORGAN, George Dillon, 1894-1950
1455. Bybee, Hal P. and Fred M. Bullard "Memorial to George Dillon Morgan," GSAP pp. 121-23 '51.

MORGAN, Lewis Henry 1818-1881
1456. Holmes, W. H. "Bibliography," NASBM 6:237-29 '09.

MORGAN, Richard G., 1903-1968
1457. Griffen, James B. "Richard G. Morgan 1903-1968," AAY 34:467-70 O '69.

MORGAN, Thomas Hunt, 1866-1945
1458. Wallace, Edith M. and Oliver C. Dunn "Bibliography," NASBM 33:300-25 '59.

MORLEY, Christopher, 1890-1957
1459. Bracker, Jon "The Christopher Morley Collection," TLC 7:19-35.

MORLEY, Edward Williams, 1838-1923
1460. Clarke, Frank Wigglesworth "Bibliography," NASBM 11:7-8 '22.

MORLEY, Sylvanus Griswold, 1883-1948
1461. Harrison, Margaret W. "Bibliography," AAY 14:

MORLEY, Sylvanus Griswold (continued)
219-21 Jan '49.

MORRIS, Earl Halstead, 1889-1956
1462. Morris, Elizabeth Ann "Bibliography," AAY 22:395-97 Apr '57.

MORRIS, Wright, 1910-
1463. Linden, Stanton J. and David Madden "A Wright Morris Bibliography," C 4:77-87 Winter '61-'62.

MORSE, Edward Sylvester, 1838-1925
1464. Howard, L. O. "Bibliography," NASBM 17:20-29 '37.

MORSE, Harmon Northrop, 1848-1920
1465. Remsen, Ira "Investigations Carried Out Under the Direction of H. N. Morse," NASBM 11:13-14 '22.

MORSE, William Clifford, 1874-
1466. "Publications of W. C. Morse," American Ceramic Society. Bulletin 16:453-54 N '37.

MORTON, David, 1886-1957
1467. Kiley, Mark "David Morton - a Bibliography," BB 13:202 S-D '29; 14:25-28 My-Ag '30.

MOSELEY, John Reed, 1900-1959
1468. Sanford, John T. "Memorial to John Reed Moseley," GSAP pp. 137-38 '60.

MOULTON, Forest Ray, 1872-1952
1469. Gasteyer, Charles E. "Bibliography," NASBM 41:349-55 '70.

MUMFORD, Lewis, 1895-
1470. "Books by Lewis Mumford," Southern Packet 5:5 Apr '49.

MUNRO, Thomas, 1897-
1471. "Bibliography of Thomas Munro from 1922 to 1964," Journal of Aesthetics 23:7-11 Fall '64.

MURFREE, Mary Noailles, 1850-1922
1472. Cary, Richard "Mary Noailles Murfree (1850-1922)," ALR #1 pp. 79-83 Fall '67.

MURPHREE, Edgar Vaughan, 1898-1962
1473. Gilliland, Edwin R. "Bibliography," NASBM 40:235-
121

MURPHREE, Edgar Vaughan (continued)
37 '69.

MURPHY, James Baumgardner, 1884-1950
1474. Little, C. C. "Bibliography," NASBM 34:193-203 '60.

MURRAY, Harold Watson, 1906-1948
1475. Jordan, George F. "Memorial to Harold Watson Murray," GSAP pp. 209-10 '49.

MURSELL, James L., 1893-1963
1476. Simutis, Leonard J. "James L. Mursell: an Annotated Bibliography," Journal of Research in Music Education 16:254-66 Fall '68; 17:248-51 Summer '69.

MYERS, George Edmund, 1871-1946
1477. "What is Guidance," University of Michigan School of Education. Bulletin 13:79-80 F '42.

N

NABOKOV, Vladimir V., 1899-
1478. "Selected Bibliography of Nabokov's Work," Wisconsin Studies in Contemporary Literature 8:310-11 Spring '67.

NASBY, Petroleum V. see LOCKE, David Ross.

NASH, Charles H., 1908-1968
1479. McNutt, Charles H. "Charles H. Nash 1908-1968," AAY 34:172-74 Apr '69.

NASON, Frank Lewis, 1856-1928
1480. Newland, D. H. "Memorial of Frank Lewis Nason," GSAB 40:45-50 '30.

NEAL, John 1793-1876
1481. Richards, Irving T. "John Neal: a Bibliography," Jahrbuch für Amerikastudien 7:296-319 '62.

NEEDHAM, Claude Ervin, 1894-1951
1482. Lasky, S. G. and Evan Just "Memorial to Claude Ervin Needham," GSAP pp. 125-26 '51.

NEF, John Ulric, 1862-1915
1483. Wolfrom, Melville L. "Bibliography," NASBM 34: 221-27 '60.

NELSON, Edward William, 1855-1934
1484. Lantis, M. "Edward William Nelson," University of
Alaska. Anthropological Papers 3:15-16 D '54.

NELSON, Nels Christian, 1875-1964
1485. Mason, J. Alden "Nels Christian Nelson, 1875-1964,"
AAY 31:393-97 Jan '66.

NEUMANN, John von see von Neumann, John.

NEWBERRY, John Strong, 1822-1892
1486. Kemp, J. F. "Memorial of J. S. Newberry," GSAB
4:393-406 1893.
1487. White, Charles A. "List of Publications of Professor
John S. Newberry," NASBM 6:15-24 '09.

NEWCOMB, Simon, 1835-1909
1488. Archibald, Raymond Clare "Bibliography of His Life
and Work," NASBM 10:23-69 '19.

NEWELL, Edward Theodore, 1886-1941
1489. "Bibliography," Coin Collectors Journal 8:xvi-xviii
Apr '41.
1490. Clement, P. A. "Bibliography of the Writings of
Edward T. Newell," American Journal of Philology 68:
427-32 O '47.

NEWLAND, David H. , 1872-1943
1491. Ruedemann, Rudolf and Winifred Goldring "Memorial
to David H. Newland," GSAP pp. 209-16 '43.

NEWSOM, John Flesher, 1869-1928
1492. Blackwelder, Eliot "Memorial of John Flesher Newsom," GSAB 41:30-33 '31.

NEWSTEAD, Helaine, 1906-
1493. Brodey, H. and B. M. Woodbridge "Analytical Bibliography of the Writings of Helaine Newstead," Romance Philology 17:527-34 F '64.

NEWTON, Hubert Anson, 1830-1896
1494. Gibbs, J. Willard "Published Writings of Hubert A.
Newton," NASBM 4:120-24 '02.

NICHOLAS, John Spangler, 1895-1963
1495. Oppenheimer, Jane M. "Bibliography," NASBM 40:
279-89 '69.

NICHOLS, Edward Leamington, 1854-1937
1496. Merritt, Ernest "Bibliography," NASBM 21:355-66 '41.

NICHOLS, Ernest Fox, 1869-1924
1497. Nichols, E. L. "Bibliography," NASBM 12:130 '29.

NICHOLSON, Meredith, 1866-1947
1498. Tanselle, G. Thomas "The ABA Issue of Meredith's 'A Hoosier Chronicle' (1912)," BSA 60:223-24 '66.

NIEMANN, Carl, 1908-1964
1499. Roberts, John D. "Bibliography," NASBM 40:301-19 '69.

NILES, William Harmon, 1838-1910
1500. Barton, George H. "Bibliography of W. H. Niles," GSAB 23:34-35 '12.

NISSEN, Henry Wieghorst, 1901-1958
1501. Carmichael, Leonard "Bibliography," NASBM 38: 216-22 '65.

NITZE, William Albert, 1876-1957
1502. Woodbridge, B. M. "Analytical Bibliography of the Works of Professor William A. Nitze," Romance Philology 9:95-114 N '55.

NOE, Adolf Carl, 1873-1939
1503. Croneis, Carey "Memorial to Adolf Carl Noé," GSAP pp. 219-27 '39.

NOLAN, Paul T. , 1919-
1504. Finley, Katherine P. "Paul T. Nolan; an Example: The Teacher in Print: a Check List," Serif 3:9-16 Mr '66.

NOLL, Bink, 1927-
1505. Towers, Robert "A Checklist of the Writings of Bink Noll," PULC 25:114-15 Autumn '63.

NORRIS, Frank, 1870-1902
1506. French, Warren "Frank Norris (1870-1902)," ALR #1 pp. 84-89 Fall '67.
1507. White, William "Frank Norris: Bibliographical Addenda," BB 22:227-28 S-D '59.

NORTON, William Harmon, 1856-1944
1508. Fryxell, Fritiof M. "Memorial to William Harmon
124

NORTON, William Harmon (continued)
Norton," GSAP pp. 109-208 '46.

NORWOOD, Charles Joseph, 1853-1927
1509. Foerste, August F. "Memorial of Charles Joseph
Norwood," GSAB 39:40-47 '28.

NOTT, Josiah Clark, 1804-1873
1510. Carmichael, E. B. "Josiah Clark Nott," Bulletin of
the History of Medicine 22:255-62 My '48.

NOVY, Frederick George, 1864-1957
1511. Long, Esmond R. "Bibliography," NASBM 33:341-50
'59.

NOYES, Arthur Amos, 1866-1936
1512. Pauling, Linus "Bibliography," NASBM 31:331-46 '58.

NOYES, William Albert, 1857-1941
1513. Adams, Roger "Bibliography," NASBM 27:196-208 '52.

O

O'CONNOR, Flannery, 1925-1964
1514. Brittain, Joan T. "Flannery O'Connor; A Bibliography," BB 25:98-100 S-D '67; 25:123-24 Jan-Apr '68.
1515. Wedge, George F. "Two Bibliographies: Flannery
O'Connor and J. F. Powers," C 2:59-63 Fall '58.

OETTEKING, Bruno, 1871-1960
1516. Weiant, C. W. "Bruno Oetteking," AA62:675-80 Ag '60.

O'HARRA, Cleophas C., 1866-1935
1517. Connolly, Joseph P. "Memorial of Cleophas C. O'Harra," GSAP pp. 289-96 '35.

OLDSCHOOL, Oliver see DENNIE, Joseph.

OLIVER, James Edward, 1829-1895
1518. Hill, G. W. "List of the Published Scientific Papers
of James Edward Oliver," NASBM 4:74 '02.

OLMAN, Cecil Bernard, 1894-
1519. Sherrington, U. "List of C. B. Olman's Writings on
Music," Music Review 25:154-57 My '64.

O'NEAL, James, 1875-
1520. "Pamphlets by James O'Neal in the Tamiment Institute Library," Tamiment Institute Library. Bulletin 21:2-3 Mr '59.

O'NEALE, Lila Morris, 1886-1948
1521. Harrison, M. W. "Lila Morris O'Neale: 1886-1948," AA 50:664-65 O '48.

O'NEILL, Eugene, 1888-1953
1522. Bryer, Jackson R. "Forty Years of O'Neill Criticism: a Selected Bibliography," Modern Drama 4: 196-216 S '61.

O'REILLY, Miles see HALPINE, Charles Graham.

ORTON, Edward, 1829-1899
1523. Gilbert, G. K. "Memoir of Edward Orton," GSAB 11:542-50 1900.

OSBORN, Henry Fairfield, 1857-1935
1524. Gregory, William K. "Bibliography of Henry Fairfield Osborn," NASBM 19:89-119 '38.

OSBURNE, Thomas Burr, 1859-1929
1525. Vickery, Hubert Bradford "Bibliography," NASBM 14:285-304 '32.

O'SULLIVAN, Vincent, 1872-1940
1526. Sims, George "Some Uncollected Authors XV Vincent O'Sullivan," BC 6:395-402 Winter '57.

OSWALD, Brian see BYRNE, Donn.

OVERBECK, Robert Milton, 1887-1958
1527. Cloos, Ernst "Memorial to Robert Milton Overbeck," GSAP pp. 161-64 '58.

OVERHOLTS, Lee Oras, 1890-1946
1528. Kern, F. D. "Lee Oras Overholts," Mycologia 40: 3-5 Jan '48.

OWEN, Richard, d. 1890
1529. Stanley-Brown, Joseph "Geological Writings of Richard Owen," GSAB 5:571-72 1894.

PACKARD, Alpheus Spring, 1839-1905
1530. Cockerell, T. D. A. "Bibliography," NASBM 9:207-36 '19.

PADELFORD, Frederick Morgan, 1875-1942
1531. Griffith, D. D. and others "Frederick Morgan Padelford: February 27, 1875-December 3, 1942," Modern Language Quarterly 3:519-24 D '42.

PAGE, Stanton see FULLER, Henry Blake.

PAGE, Thomas Nelson, 1853-1922
1532. Gross, Theodore L. "Thomas Nelson Page (1853-1922)," ALR #1 pp. 90-92 Fall '67.

PALACHE, Charles, 1869-1954
1533. Daly, Reginald A. "Bibliography," NASBM 30:319-28 '57.
1534. Hurlbut, Cornelius S., Jr. "Memorial to Charles Palache," GSAP pp. 137-43 '57.

PARK, Willard Zerbe, 1906-1965
1535. Murdock, George Peter "Willard Z. Park," AA 68: 135-36 F '66.

PARKER, Arthur Caswell, 1881-1955
1536. Guthe, Alfred K. "Bibliography," AAY 21:294-95 Jan '56.
1537. Ritchie, W. A. "Arthur Caswell Parker - 1881-1955," AAY 21:294-5 Jan '56.

PARKER, George Howard, 1864-1955
1538. Romer, Alfred Sherwood "Bibliography," NASBM 39: 368-90 '67.

PARKINS, Almon Ernest, 1879-1940
1539. Whitaker, J. R. "Almon Ernest Parkins; with Bibliography of His Publications," Association of American Geographers. Annals 31:48-50 Mr '41.

PARKS, William Arthur, 1868-1936
1540. Moore, E. S. "Memorial to William Arthur Parks; with List of His Publications," GSAP pp. 231-36 '37.

PARMELEE, Cullen Warner, 1874-1947
1541. "Cullen Warner Parmelee; with List of His Publica-

PARMELEE, Cullen Warner (continued)
   tions," American Ceramic Society. Bulletin 21:119-
   21 Jl '42.

PARSONS, Arthur Leonard, 1873-1957
1542. Langford, G. B. "Memorial to Arthur Leonard Parsons," GSAP pp. 145-48 '57.

PATCH, Howard Rollin, 1889-1963
1543. Woodbridge, Benjamin M., Jr. "An Analytical Bibliography of the Writings of Howard Rollin Patch,"
   Romance Philology 19:143-54 N '65.

PATCHEN, Kenneth, 1911-
1544. See, Carolyn "Kenneth Patchen, 1934-1958; a Partial
   Bibliography," BB 23:81-84 Jan-Apr '61.

PATTERSON, John Thomas, 1878-1960
1545. Painter, Theophilus S. "Bibliography," NASBM 38:
   252-62 '65.

PATTON, Horace Bushnell, 1858-1929
1546. Butler, G. M. "Memorial of Horace Bushnell Patton,"
   GSAB 42:122-25 '32.

PATTON, Leroy Thompson, 1880-1957
1547. Trowbridge, A. C. "Memorial to Leroy Thompson,"
   GSAP pp. 149-51 '57.

PAULDING, James Kirke, 1778-1860
1548. Aderman, Ralph M. "James Kirke Paulding's Contributions to American Magazines," SB 17:141-51 '64.
1549. Aderman, Ralph M. "Publication Dates of Three
   Early Works of James Kirke Paulding," BSA 59:49-50
   '65.
1550. Robbins, J. Albert "Some Unrecorded Poems of
   James Kirke Paulding: an Annotated Checklist," SB
   3:229-40 '50-'51.
1551. Wegelin, Oscar "A Bibliography of the Separate Publications of James Kirke Paulding, Poet, Novelist,
   Humorist, Statesman, 1779-1860," BSA 12:34-40 '18.

PAVY, Paul David III, 1938-1968
1552. Edmonson, Munro S. "Bibliography of Paul David
   Pavy III," AA 72:820 Ag '70.

PAYNE, Enoch George, 1877-1953
1553. "Bibliography of E. G. Payne," Journal of Educational
128

PAYNE, Enoch George (continued)
Sociology 13:47-53 S '39.

PAYNE, John Howard, 1791-1852
1554. Heartman, Charles F. and Harry B. Weiss "John Howard Payne: a Bibliography," ABC 3:55-57, 181-84, 224-28, 305-07; 4:27-29, 79-82.

PEABODY, Frank Elmer, 1914-1958
1555. Camp, Charles L. "Memorial to Frank Elmer Peabody," GSAP pp. 165-67 '58.

PEACOCK, Martin Alfred, 1898-1950
1556. Palache, C. "Memorial to Martin Alfred Peacock," American Mineralogist 36:389-93 My '51.

PEARL, Raymond, 1879-1940
1557. Jennings, H. S. "Bibliography of Raymond Pearl," NASBM 22:311-47 '43.

PECK, Frederick Burritt, 1860-1926
1558. Shimer, Hervey W. "Memorial of Frederick Burritt Peck," GSAB 37:111-14 '26.

PEGRAM, George Braxton, 1876-1958
1559. Embrey, Lee Anna "Bibliography," NASBM 41:405-07 '70.

PEIRCE, Benjamin Osgood, 1854-1914
1560. Hall, Edwin H. "Bibliography of Benjamin Osgood Peirce," NASBM 8:464-66 '19.

PEIRCE, Charles Santiago Sanders, 1829-1914
1561. Potter, V. G. "Survey of Recent Peirce Literature," Philosophical Quarterly 8:593-618 D '68.

PENCK, Albrecht, 1858-1945
1562. von Engelin, O. D. "Memorial to Albrecht Penck," GSAP pp. 169-72 '58

PENFIELD, Samuel Lewis, 1856-1906
1563. Iddings, Joseph P. "Memoir of Samuel Lewis Penfield," GSAB 18:572-82 '07.
1564. Wells, Horace L. "The Works of Samuel Lewis Penfield," NASBM 6:141-46 '09.

PENHALLOW, David Pearce, 1854-1910
1565. Barlow, Alfred E. "Memoir of D. P. Penhallow,"

PENHALLOW, David Pearce (continued)
GSAB 22:15-19 '11.

PENROSE, Richard Alexander Fullerton, Jr., 1863-1931
1566. Stanley-Brown, Joseph "Memorial of Richard Alexander Fullerton Penrose," GSAB 43:68-108 '33.

PERCY, Florence see ALLEN, Elizabeth Ann Chase Taylor Akers.

PERKINS, Edward Henry, 1886-1936
1567. Mather, Kirtley F. "Memorial of Edward Henry Perkins," GSAP pp. 237-40 '36.

PERKINS, Eli see LANDON, Melville De Lancey.

PERKINS, George Henry, 1844-1933
1568. Fairchild, Herman L. "Memorial of George Henry Perkins," GSAP pp. 235-41 '33.

PERRY, Joseph Hartshorn, 1858-1934
1569. Alden, William C. "Memorial of Joseph Hartshorn Perry," GSAP pp. 297-300 '35.

PERRY, Thomas Sergeant, 1845-1928
1570. Monteiro, George "Addenda to Harlow: Two T. S. Perry Essays," BSA 62:612-13 '68.
1571. Monteiro, George "Thomas Sergeant Perry: Four Attributions," BSA 59:57 '65.

PETERS, John Punnett, 1887-1955
1572. Paul, John Rodman and Cyril Norman Hugh Long "Bibliography," NASBM 31:362-75 '58.

PETERS, William John, 1863-1942
1573. Haradon, H. D. "William John Peters, 1863-1942," Terrestrial Magnetism and Atmospheric Electricity 47: 191-93 S '42.

PETRY, Edward Jacob, 1880-1939
1574. "Edward Jacob Petry: with List of Publications," Phytopathology 30:990-91 D '40.

PETTEE, William Henry, 1836-1904
1575. Russell, Israel C. "Memoir of William Henry Pettee," GSAB 16:558-60 '05.

PFUND, August Herman, 1879-1949
1576. Worthing, A. G. "Doctor August Herman Pfund, Ives Medalist for 1939," Optical Society of America. Journal 30:181 Apr '40.

PHALEN, William Clifton, 1877-1949
1577. Burchard, Ernest F. "Memorial to William Clifton Phalen," GSAP pp. 213-16 '49.

PHILLIPS, Alexander Hamilton, 1866-1937
1578. Buddington, A. F. "Memorial of Alexander Hamilton Phillips," GSAP pp. 241-47 '36.

PHILLIPS, Charles John, 1908-
1579. "Publications," American Ceramic Society. Bulletin 20:421-22 N '41.

PHILLIPS, David Graham, 1867-1911
1580. Feldman, Abraham "David Graham Phillips - His Work and His Critics," BB 19:144-46 My-Ag '48; 19:177-79 S-D '48.
1581. Ravitz, Abe C. "David Graham Phillips (1867-1911)," ALR #3 pp. 24-29 Summer '68.
1583. Stallings, Frank L., Jr. "David Graham Phillips (1867-1911): a Critical Bibliography of Secondary Comment," ALR 3:1-35 Winter '70.

PHOENIX, John see DERBY, George Horatio.

PICKERING, Edward Charles, 1846-1919
1583. Bailey, Solon I. "Bibliography of Edward Charles Pickering," NASBM 15:179-89 '34.

PIERCE, George Washington, 1872-1956
1584. Saunders, Frederick A. and Frederick V. Hunt "Bibliography," NASBM 33:371-80 '59.

PIKE, James Albert, 1913-1969
1585. Crumb, Rev. Lawrence N. "James Albert Pike: an Author-Subject Bibliography," BB 27:1-6 Jan/Mr '70.

PILAT, Stanislaw, 1881-1942?
1586. "Professor Stanislaw Pilat," Institute of Petroleum Journal 28:176-77 Ag '42.

PILLSBURY, Walter Bowers, 1872-1960
1587. Miles, Walter R. "Bibliography," NASBM 37:286-91 '64.

PINTNER, Rudolf, 1884-1942
1588. Symonds, P. M. "Rudolf Pintner, 1884-1942,"
Teachers College Record 44:207-11 D '42.

PIROU, Gaëtan, 1886-1945
1589. "Memorial," American Economic Review 37:193 Mr
'47.

PIRSSON, Louis Valentine, 1860-1919
1590. Knopf, Adolph "Bibliography," NASBM 34:244-48 '60.

PLATT, Franklin, 1844-1900
1591. Frazer, Persifor "Memoir of Franklin Platt,"
GSAB 12:454-55 '01.

PLUMER, James Marshall, 1899-1960
1592. Usilton, B. M. "Bibliography of the Writings of
James Marshall Plumer," Ars Orientalis 5:331-36 '63.

PLUMMER, Frederick Byron, 1886-1947
1593. Moore, Raymond C. "Memorial to Frederick Byron
Plummer," GSAP pp. 155-65 '47.

POE, Edgar Allan, 1809-1849
1594. Benton, Richard P. "Current Bibliography on Edgar
Allan Poe," Emerson Society Quarterly 47:84-87.
1595. Benton, Richard P. "Edgar Allan Poe: Current Bibliography," Poe Newsletter 2:4-12.
1596. Campbell, Killis "Gleanings in the Bibliography of
Poe," Modern Language Notes 32:267-72 My '17.
1597. Dameron, J. Lasley "The State of the Complete Poe
Bibliography; 1827-1967," Poe Newsletter 2:3.
1598. Dedmond, Francis B. "A Check-list of Edgar Allan
Poe's Works in Book Form Published in the British
Isles," BB 21:16-20 My-Ag '53.
1599. Dedmond, Francis B. "Poe in Drama, Fiction, and
Poetry: a Bibliography," BB 21:107-14 S-D '54.
1600. Engel, Claire-Elaine "L'Etat des travaux sur Poe en
France," Modern Philology 29:482-88 '32.
1601. Englekirk, J. E. "Bibliography of Mexican Versions
and Criticisms of Poe," PMLA 52:524-26 Je '37.
1602. Gordan, John D. "Edgar Allan Poe: an Exhibition
on the Centenary of His Death October 7, 1849. A
Catalogue of the First Editions, Manuscripts, Auto-
graph Letters from the Berg Collection," NYPLB
53:471-91 O '49.
1603. Hyneman, Esther F. "The Contemporaneous Reputa-
tion of Edgar Allan Poe with Annotated Bibliography of
132

POE, Edgar Allan (continued)
Poe Criticism: 1827-1967," Dissertation, Columbia
University, 1969.
1604. Marrs, Robert L. "Fugitive Poe References: a Bibliography," Poe Newsletter 2:12-18.
1605. Randall, David "Edgar Allan Poe," Publishers' Weekly 125:1540-43 '34.
1606. Randall, David A. "The J. K. Lilly Collection of
Edgar Allan Poe," Indiana University Bookman #4 pp.
46-58 Mr '60.
1607. "Recent Books About Poe," Studies in Philology 24:
474-79 '27.
1608. Rede, Kenneth and Charles F. Heartman "A Census
of First Editions and Source Materials by or Relating
of Edgar Allan Poe in American Public and Private
Collections," ABC 2:28-36, 141-53, 232-34, 338-42 '32.
1609. Staats, Armin "Edgar Allan Poes Symbolistische
Erzählkunst," Jahrbuch für Amerikastudien 20:171-80
Winter '67.
1610. Tanselle, G. Thomas "The State of Poe Bibliography," Poe Newsletter 2:1-3.
1611. Tanselle, G. Thomas "Two More Appearances of 'The
Raven,'" BSA 57:229-30 '63.
1612. Tanselle, G. Thomas "Unrecorded Early Reprintings
of Two Poe Tales," BSA 56:252 '62.
1613. Woodbridge, Hensley C. "Poe in Spanish America:
a Bibliographical Supplement," Poe Newsletter 2:18-19.

PORTER, Katherine Anne, 1890-
1614. Schwartz, Edward "Katherine Anne Porter: a Critical Bibliography: with an Introduction by Robert Penn
Warren," NYPLB 57:211-47 My '53.
1615. Sylvester, William A. "Selected and Critical Bibliography of the Uncollected Works of Katherine Anne
Porter," BB 19:36 Jan-Apr '47.

PORTER, William Sidney, 1862-1910
1616. Long, E. Hudson "O. Henry (William Sidney Porter)
(1862-1910)," ALR #1 pp. 93-99 Fall '67.

POSTAN, Michael Moissey, 1898-
1617. "Bibliography of the Writings of Professor M. M.
Postan," Economic History Review 18 3 pp. at front.

POUND, Ezra, 1885-
1618. Agresti, Olivia Rosetti "Bibliography," Pound Newsletter #5 pp. 30-35; #6 pp. 24-30; #7 pp. 6-10; #8
pp. 33-35.

POUND, Ezra (continued)
1619. "A Checklist of Explications: II The Cantos," Pound Newsletter #6 pp. 16-19.
1620. "A Checklist of Explications: I The pre-Canto Poetry," Pound Newsletter #5 pp. 20-21.

POURTALES, Louis Francois de, 1824-1880
1621. Agassiz, Alexander "Bibliography," NASBM 5:87-89 '05.

POWERS, J. F., 1917-
1622. Wedge, George F. "Two Bibliographies: Flannery O'Connor and J. F. Powers," C 2:63-70 Fall '58.

POWERS, Sidney, 1890-1932
1623. De Golyer, E. "Memorial of Sidney Powers," GSAP pp. 243-57 '33.

PRATT, Joseph Hyde, 1870-1942
1624. Stuckey, Jasper L. "Memorial to Joseph Hyde Pratt," GSAP pp. 201-15 '42.

PRESCOTT, William Hickling, 1796-1859
1625. Patterson, Jerry E. "A Checklist of Prescott Manuscripts," Hispanic American Historical Review 39:116-28.
1626. Woodbridge, Hensley C. "William Hickling Prescott: a Bibliography," Revista Interamericana de Bibliografía 9:48-77.

PRICE, Miles Oscar, 1890-1968
1627. Ruffier, A. J. "Miles Oscar Price: a Bibliographical Sketch," Law Library Journal 62:2-4 F '69.

PRINDLE, Louis Marcus, 1865-1956
1628. Mertie, John B., Jr. "Memorial to Louis Marcus Prindle," GSAP pp. 139-41 '60.

PROSSER, Charles Smith, 1860-1916
1629. Cumings, E. R. "Memorial of Charles Smith Prosser," GSAB 28:70-80 '17.

PROUTY, William Frederick, 1879-1949
1630. Berkey, Charles P. "Memorial to William Frederick Prouty," GSAP pp. 115-17 '50.

PROVINSE, John H., 1897-1965
1631. Spicer, Edward H. "John H. Provinse," AA 68:990-

PROVINSE, John H. (continued)
94 Ag '66.

PRUDDEN, Theophil Mitchell, 1849-1924
1632. Hektoen, Ludvig "Bibliography of Theophil Mitchell Prudden," NASBM 12:94-98 '29.

PUMPELLY, Raphael, 1837-1923
1633. Willis, Bailey "Bibliography," NASBM 16:61-62 '36.
1634. Willis, Bailey "M emorial of Raphael Pumpelly," GSAB 36:45-84 '25.

PUPIN, Michael Idvorsky, 1858-1935
1635. Davis, Bergen "Bibliography," NASBM 19:318-23 '38.

PURDUE, Albert Homer, 1861-1917
1636. Ashley, George H. "Memorial of Albert Homer Purdue," GSAB 29:55-64 '18.

PUTNAM, Frederic Ward, 1839-1915
1637. Tozzer, Alfred M. "Bibliography of Frederic Ward Putnam," NASBM 16:139-53 '36.

PUTNAM, Samuel, 1892-1950
1638. "List of Publications of Samuel Putnam," Books Abroad 24:252-53 Summer '50.

Q

QUIRKE, Terence Thomas, 1886-1947
1639. Chapman, Carleton A. "Memorial to Terence Thomas Quirke," GSAP pp. 167-72 '47.

R

RANDLE, Martha Champion, 1910-1965
1640. Slobodken, Richard "Martha Champion Randle," AA 68:995-96 Ag '66.

RANSOM, John Crowe, 1888-
1641. Stallman, Robert W. "John Crowe Ransom: a Checklist," Sewanee Review 56:442-76 '48.

RANSOME, Frederick Leslie, 1868-1935
1642. Bastin, Edson S. "Bibliography of Frederick Leslie Ransome," NASBM 22:164-70 '43.

RANSOME, Frederick Leslie (continued)
1643. Lindgren, Waldemar "Memorial of Frederick Leslie Ransome," GSAP pp. 249-57 '36.

RANSON, Stephen Walter, 1880-1942
1644. Sabin, Florence R. "Bibliography," NASBM 23:383-97 '45.

RAVENAL, Mazyck Porcher
1645. "Bibliography of Mazyck P. Ravenal, M. D. from 1891 to Date," American Journal of Public Health 31:7-9 Jan '41.

RAYMOND, Percy Edward, 1879-1952
1646. Stetson, Henry C. "Memorial to Percy Edward Raymond," GSAP pp. 121-25 '52.

READ, Opie Percival, 1852-1939
1647. Martin, T. L. "Requiem for Giants: Opie Read and the Frontier Humorists," Southern Observer 4:184-85 Jl '56.

REDFIELD, Robert, 1897-1958
1648. Cole, Fay-Cooper and Fred Eggan "Robert Redfield," AA 61:652-62 Ag '59.

REED, Ralph Daniel, 1889-1940
1649. Woodford, A. O. "Memorial to Ralph Daniel Reed," GSAP pp. 233-42 '40.

REED, William Wharton, 1877-1942
1650. "Papers by W. W. Reed," American Meteorological Society. Bulletin 23:303 S '42.

REESE, Charles Lee, 1862-1940
1651. "Published Technical Papers of Charles L. Reese," American Chemical Society. Journal 62:1890-91 Ag '40.

REESIDE, John Bernard, Jr., 1889-1958
1652. Dane, Carle H. "Bibliography," NASBM 35:285-91 '61.
1653. Imlay, Ralph W. "Memorial to John Bernard Reeside, Jr.," GSAP pp. 173-78 '58.

REGER, David Bright, 1882-1958
1654. Singewald, Joseph T., Jr. "Memorial to David Bright Reger," GSAP pp. 179-82 '58.

REICHARD, Gladys Armanda, 1893-1955
1655. Smith, Martin W. "Gladys Armanda Reichard," AA
58:913-16 O '56.

REID, Harry Fielding, 1859-1944
1656. Alvey, Mary F. "Bibliography of Harry Fielding
Reid," NASBM 26:5-12 '51.
1657. Berry, Edward W. "Memorial to Harry Fielding
Reid," GSAP pp. 293-98 '44.

REITER, Paul David, 1909-1953
1658. Stubbs, Stanley "Bibliography," AAY 19:68 Jl '53.

REMSEN, Ira, 1846-1927
1659. Noyes, William Albert and James Flack Norris "Investigations carried Out by Ira Remsen or Under His
Direction Chronologicall Arranged," NASBM 14:230-
40 '32.

RESSER, Charles Elmer, 1889-1943
1660. Howell, B. F. "Memorial to Charles Elmer Resser,"
GSAP pp. 217-23 '43.

RHEAD, Frederick Hurten, 1880-1942
1661. "Frederick Hurten Rhead," American Ceramic Society.
Bulletin 21:306-07 D '42.

RICE, Elmer, 1892-1967
1662. Hogan, Robert "Elmer Rice: a Bibliography,"
Modern Drama 8:44-73 F '66.

RICE, John L., 1884-1956
1663. Bucher, Walter H. "Memorial to John L. Rich,"
GSAP pp. 183-90 '58.

RICE, William North, 1845-1928
1664. Westgate, Lewis D. "Memorial of William North
Rice," GSAB 40:50-57 '30.

RICHARDS, Laura, 1850-1943
1665. Calhoun, Philo and Howell J. Heaney "A Checklist
of the Separately Published Works of Laura E. Richards," CLQ 5:337-43 D '61.
1666. Cary, Richard "Some Richards Manuscripts and Correspondence," CLQ 5:344-56 D '61.

RICHARDSON, Charles Henry, 1862-1935
1667. Ruedemann, Rudolf "Memorial of Charles Henry
137

RICHARDSON, Charles Henry (continued)
Richardson," GSAP pp. 301-04 '35.

RICHARDSON, George Burr, 1892-1949
1668. Richards, Ralph W. "Memorial to George Burr Richardson," GSAP pp. 135-39 '51.

RICHARDSON, Roland George Dwight, 1878-1949
1669. Archibald, R. C. "R. G. D. Richardson 1878-1949," American Mathematical Society. Bulletin 56:264-65 My '50.

RICHARZ, Stephen, 1874-1934
1670. Ritzek, Henry "Memorial of the Rev. Stephen Richarz, S. V. D. ," GSAP pp. 253-57 '34.

RICHTMYER, Floyd Karker, 1881-1939
1671. Ives, Herbert E. "Bibliography of Floyd K. Richtmyer," NASBM 22:77-81 '43.

RICKETSON, Oliver Garrison, Jr. , 1894-1952
1672. Lothrop, S. K. "Bibliography," AAY 19:71-72 Jl '53.

RIDGWAY, Robert, 1850-1929
1673. Wetmore, Alexander "Bibliography," NASBM 15:69-101 '34.

RIES, Heinrich, 1871-1951
1674. Anderson, A. L. "Memorial to Heinrich Ries," American Mineralogist 37:269-75 Mr '52.
1675. Moore, E. S. "Memorial to Heinrich Ries," GSAP pp. 141-44 '51.

RITT, Joseph Fels, 1893-1951
1676. Lorch, E. R. "Joseph Fels Ritt," American Mathematical Society. Bulletin 57:315-18 Jl '51.
1677. Smith, Paul A. "Bibliography," NASBM 29:259-64 '56.

RIVERS, Thomas Milton, 1888-1962
1678. Horsfall, Frank L. , Jr. "Bibliography," NASBM 38: 280-94 '65.

ROARK, Louis, 1890-1950
1679. Miser, Hugh D. "Memorial to Louis Roark," GSAP pp. 145-48 '51.

ROBERTS, Elizabeth Madox, 1886-1941
1680. Tate, Allen "The Elizabeth Madox Roberts Papers,"
LCQJ 1:29-31 '44.

ROBERTS, Frank Harold Hanna, Jr., 1897-1966
1681. Judd, Neil M. "Frank H. H. Roberts, Jr.," AA 68:
1226-32 O '66.
1682. Stephenson, Robert L. "Frank H. H. Roberts, Jr.,
1897-1966," AAY 32:84-94 Jan '67.

ROBERTS, Kenneth, 1885-1957
1683. Albert, George "Bibliography of Kenneth Lewis
Roberts," BB 17:191-92 S-D '42; 17:218-19 Jan-Apr '43.
1684. Ellis, Marjorie Mosser "Supplementary Bibliography
of Kenneth Roberts," CLQ 6:99-105 S '62.
1685. Stemple, Ruth "Kenneth Roberts: A Supplementary
Checklist," BB 22:228-30 S-D '59.
1686. Stone, F. "American First Editions: Kenneth (Lewis)
Roberts," Publishers' Weekly 132:1595-96 '37.

ROBERTS, Lydia Jane, 1879-1965
1687. Martin, E. A. "Life Works of Lydia Jane Roberts,"
American Dietetic Association. Journal 49:299-302 O
'66.

ROBERTSON, William Spence, 1872-1955
1688. Humphreys, R. A. "William Spence Robertson, 1872-
1955," Hispanic American Historical Review 36:264-
67 My '56.

ROBINSON, Benjamin Lincoln, 1864-1935
1689. Fernald, M. L. "Bibliography," NASBM 17:314-30
'37.

ROBINSON, Edwin Arlington, 1869-1935
1690. Adams, Léonie "The Ledoux Collection of Edwin Arlington Robinson," LCQJ 7:9-13.
1691. Cary, Richard "Robinson, Books and Periodicals: I,"
CLQ 8:266-77 Mr '69; 8:334-43 Je '69; 8:399-413 S '69.
1692. Cary, Richard "Robinson Manuscripts and Letters,"
CLQ 8:479-87 D '69.
1693. Hogan, Charles Beecher "Edwin Arlington Robinson:
New Bibliographical Notes," BSA 35:115-44 '41.
1694. Isaacs, Edith J. R. "Edwin Arlington Robinson: a
Descriptive List of the Lewis M. Isaac Collection of
Robinsoniana," NYPLB 52:211-33 My '48.
1695. White, William "A Bibliography of Edwin Arlington
Robinson, 1941-1963," CLQ 7:1-26 Mr '65.

ROBINSON, Edwin Arlington (continued)
1696. White, William "A Bibliography of Edwin Arlington Robinson, 1694-1969," CLQ 8:448-62 D '69.

ROBINSON, Henry Hollister, d. 1928
1697. Bowman, Isaiah "Memorial of Henry Hollister Robinson," GSAB 41:25-27 '31.

ROBINSON, Rowland E. , 1833-1900
1698. Baker, Ronald L. "Rowland E. Robinson, (1833-1900)," ALR 2:156-59 Summer '69.

RODDY, Harry Justin, 1856-1943
1699. Miller, Benjamin L. "Memorial to Harry Justin Roddy," GSAP pp. 225-28 '43.

RODEBUSH, Worth Huff, 1887-1959
1700. Marvel, Carl S. and Frederick T. Wall "Bibliography," NASBM 36:281-88 '62.

ROETHKE, Theodore, 1908-1963
1701. Hollenberg, Susan Weidman "Theodore Roethke: Bibliography," TCL 12:216-21 Jan '67.

ROGERS, Austin Flint, 1877-1957
1702. Donnay, J. D. H. "Memorial to Austin Flint Rogers," GSAP pp. 191-95 '58.

ROGERS, Bruce, 1870-1957
1703. Haas, I. "Bruce Rogers Bibliography," Packet 3:19-20 S '38.

ROGERS, Fairman, 1833-1900
1704. Smith, Edgar F. "Bibliography of Fairman Rogers," NASBM 6:107 '09.

ROGERS, Gaillard Sherburne, 1889-1919
1705. Kemp, James F. "Memorial of Gaillard Sherburne Rogers," GSAB 31:96-100 '20.

ROGERS, Malcolm Jennings, 1890-1960
1706. Ezell, Paul H. "Bibliography," AAY 26:534 Apr '61.

ROGERS, Robert Empie, 1813-1884
1707. Smith, Edgar Fahs "Bibliography of R. E. Rogers," NASBM 5:309 '05.

ROGERS, William A. , 1832-1898
1708. Morley, Edward W. "Bibliography of William A. Rogers," NASBM 6:113-17 '09.

ROOD, Ogden Nicholas, 1831-1902
1709. Nichols, Edward L. "Bibliography," NASBM 6:469-72 '09.

ROOSEVELT, Theodore, 1858-1919
1710. "Catalog of the Theodore Roosevelt Centennial Exhibit," LCQJ 15:106-64 My '58.

ROOT, William Campbell, 1904-1969
1711. Johnson, Frederick "Bibliography," AAY 35:364 Jl '70.

ROSA, Edward Bennett, 1861-1921
1712. Coblentz, W. W. "Bibliography of Papers Published by Edward B. Rosa," NASBM 16:364-68 '36.

ROSS, Clarence Samuel, 1880-1953?
1713. Hooker, M. "Bibliography of Clarence Samuel Ross," American Mineralogist 38:1272-75 N '53.

ROSS, Frank Elmore, 1874-1960
1714. Morgan, W. W. "Bibliography," NASBM 39:396-402 '67.

ROSSBY, Carl-Gustaf Arvid, 1898-1957
1715. Byers, Horace R. "Bibliography," NASBM 34:264-70 '60.

ROTH, Walter E. , 1861-1933
1716. Herskovits, Melville J. "Bibliography," AA 36:269-70 '34.

ROUNDY, Paul Vere, 1884-1937
1717. "Bibliography of Paul Vere Roundy," American Association of Petroleum Geologists. Bulletin 21:1369-70 O '37.

ROWAN, William, 1891-1957
1718. Salt, W. R. "In Memoriam: William Rowan," Auk 75:389-90 O '58.

ROWLAND, Henry Augustus, 1848-1901
1719. Mendenhall, Thomas C. "Bibliography," NASBM 5:135-40 '05.

ROYCE, Josiah, 1855-1916
1720. Woodworth, Robert S. "Selected Bibliography,"
NASBM 33:392-96 '59.

RUEDEMANN, Rudolf, 1864-1956
1721. Goldring, Winifred "Memorial to Rudolf Ruedemann,"
GSAP pp. 153-61 '57.

RUMSEY, James, 1743-1792
1722. "List of Works in the New York Public Library Relating to Henry Hudson, the Hudson River, Robert Fulton, Early Steam Navigation, etc.," NYPLB 13:585-
613 '09.

RUPPERT, Karl, 1895-1960
1723. Lambert, Marjorie F. "Bibliography," AAY 27:102-
03 Jl '61.

RUSSELL, Henry Norris, 1877-1957
1724. Shapley, Harlow "Bibliography," NASBM 32:363-78
'58.

RUSSELL, Israel C., d. 1906
1725. Willis, Bailey "Memoir of Israel C. Russell," GSAB
18:582-92 '07.

RUSSELL, William Fletcher, 1890-1956
1726. Cremin, L. A. and C. E. Derring "Writings of William F. Russell," Teachers College Record 59:174-78
D '57.

RUTHERFORD, Ralph Leslie, 1894-1952
1727. Allan, John A. "Memorial to Ralph Leslie Rutherford," GSAP pp. 127-30 '52.

RUTLEDGE, John Joseph, 1870-1952
1728. Singewald, Joseph T., Jr. "Memorial to John Joseph
Rutledge," GSAP pp. 131-35 '52.

RYAN, Harris Joseph, 1866-1934
1729. Durant, W. F. "Bibliography," NASBM 19:302-06 '38.

S

SABIN, Florence Rena, 1871-1953
1730. McMaster, Philip D. and Michael Heidelberger "Bibliography," NASBM 34:309-19 '60.

SABINE, Wallace Clement Ware, 1868-1919
1731. Hall, Edwin H. "Bibliography," NASBM 11:19 '23.

SAFFORD, James Merrill, 1822-1907
1732. Stevenson, J. J. "Memoir of James Merrill Safford,"
GSAB 19:522-27 '08.

ST. JOHN, Charles Edward, 1857-1935
1733. Adams, Walter S. "Bibliography 1887-1933," NASBM
18:298-304 '38.

SAINT JOHN, Orestes Hawley, 1841-1920
1734. Keyes, Charles R. "Memorial of Orestes Hawley
Saint John," GSAB 33:31-44 '22.

SALINGER, J. D., 1919-
1735. Beebe, Maurice, and Jennifer Sperry "Criticism of
J. D. Salinger: a Selected Checklist," MFS 12:377-91
Autumn '66.
1736. Davis, Tom "J. D. Salinger: A Checklist," BSA 53:
69-71 '59.
1737. Fiene, Donald M. "J. D. Salinger: a Bibliography,"
Wisconsin Studies in Contemporary Literature 4:109-49.

SALISBURY, Rollin D., 1858-1930
1738. Chamberlin, Rollin T. "Memorial of Rollin D. Salisbury," GSAB 42:216-38 '32.

SANBORN, Franklin Benjamin, 1831-1917
1739. Clarkson, John W. "A Bibliography of Franklin Benjamin Sanborn," BSA 60:73-85 '66.

SANDBURG, Carl, 1878-1967
1740. "Books by Carl Sandburg," Southern Packet 4:8 Ag '48.
1741. Newman, Ralph G. "A Selective Checklist of Sandburg's Writings," Illinois State Historical Society.
Journal 65:402-06 '52.
1742. Schenk, William P. "Carl Sandburg - a Bibliography," BB 16:4-7 S-D '36.

SANTAYANA, George, 1863-1952
1743. Cory, Daniel "The George Santayana Collection,"
Columbia Library Chronicle 5:23-25 F '56.

SAPIR, Edward, 1884-1939
1744. Benedict, Ruth "Edward Sapir," AA 41:469-77 Jl '39.
1745. Swadesh, M. "Bibliografías de antropólogos: Edward
Sapir," Boletín Bibliográfico de Antropología Americana
143

SAPIR, Edward (continued)
3:80-86 Jan '39.

SARDESON, Frederick William, 1866-1959
1746. Howell, B. F. "Memorial to Frederick William Sardeson," GSAP pp. 143-45 '59.

SARGENT, Charles Sprague, 1841-1927
1747. Rehder, Alfred "Bibliography of the Published Writings of Charles Sprague Sargent," NASBM 12:259-70 '29.

SARGENT, Daniel, 1890-1952
1748. Ketrick, P. J. "Contemporary Catholic Authors: Daniel Sargent, Metaphysical Poet and Biographer of a New World; with List of his Publications," Catholic Library World 12:176 Mr '41.

SAUNDERS, Frederick Albert, 1875-1963
1749. Olson, Harry F. "Bibliography," NASBM 39:414-16 '67.

SAUNTER, Samuel see DENNIE, Joseph.

SAUVEUR, Albert, 1863-1939
1750. Daly, Reginald A. "Bibliography," NASBM 22:126-33 '43.

SAVAGE, Thomas Edmund, 1866-1947
1751. Sulton, A. H. "Memorial to Thomas Edmund Savage," GSAP pp. 173-76 '47.

SAYLES, Robert Wilcox, 1878-1942
1752. Larsen, Esper S., Jr. "Memorial to Robert Wilcox Sayles," GSAP pp. 229-33 '43.

SCHAFER, Joseph, 1867-1941
1753. Powers, A. "Debt of the Pacific Northwest to Dr. Joseph Schafer; with Bibliography of His Writings," Oregon Historical Quarterly 42:95-97 Mr '41.

SCHAIRER, John Frank, 1904-
1754. "J. F. Schairer; with List of His Publications," American Ceramic Society. Bulletin 21:68-69 My '42.

SCHALLER, Waldemar Theodore, 1882-1967
1755. Hooker, M. "Bibliography of Waldemar Theodore Schaller 1954-1963," American Mineralogist 48:1412

SCHALLER, Waldemar Theodore (continued)
N '63.

SCHENCK, William Egbert, 1884-1956
1756. Gifford, E. W. "William Egbert Schenck," AA 59:
326-27 Apr '57.

SCHEVILL, Rudolph, 1874-1946
1757. Schevill, K. E. "Bibliography of the Publications of
Rudolph Schevill," Hispanic Review 14:259-63 Jl '46.

SCHLESINGER, Frank, 1871-1943
1758. Brouwer, Dirk "Bibliography of Frank Schlesinger,"
NASBM 24:127-44 '47.

SCHMITT, Karl, 1915-1952
1759. Bell, Robert E. "Bibliography," AAY 18:260 Jan '53.
1760. Eggan, Fred "Karl Schmitt, 1915-1952," AA 55:237-
39 '53.

SCHNEIDER, Hyrum, 1882-1955
1761. Eardley, A. J. "Memorial to Hyrum Schneider,"
GSAP pp. 201-02 '58.

SCHOTT, Charles Anthony, 1826-1901
1762. Abbe, Cleveland "A Catalogue of the Works (abridged
titles) of Charles Anthony Schott," NASBM 8:116-33 '19.

SCHRADER, Frank Charles, 1860-1944
1763. Mendenhall, W. C. "Memorial to Frank Charles
Schrader," GSAP pp. 259-70 '45.

SCHRAMM, Edward, 1886-
1764. "Publications," American Ceramic Society. Bulletin
19:480 D '40.

SCHUCHERT, Charles, 1858-1942
1765. Dunbar, Carl Owen "Bibliography of Charles Schuchert," NASBM 27:377-89 '52.
1766. Dunbar, Carl O. "Memorial to Charles Schuchert,"
GSAP pp. 217-40 '42.

SCHULTZ, Alfred Reginald, 1876-1943
1767. Ball, Max W. "Memorial to Alfred Reginald Schultz,"
GSAP pp. 299-304 '44.

SCHUMPETER, Joseph Alois, 1883-1950
1768. "Bibliography," Quarterly Journal of Economics 64:

SCHUMPETER, Joseph Alois (continued)
373-84 Ag '50.
1769. "J. A. Schumpeter, 1883-1950," American Economic
Review 40:646-48 S '50.

SCOTT, Gayle, 1894-1948
1770. Winton, W. M. "Memorial to Gayle Scott," GSAP pp.
207-10 '48.

SCOTT, Irving Day, 1877-1955
1771. Hussey, Russell C. "Memorial to Irving Day Scott,"
GSAP pp. 163-64 '57.

SCOTT, William Berryman, 1858-1947
1772. Jepsen G. L. and Genevieve Cobb "Bibliography,"
NASBM 25:192-203 '49.
1773. Jepsen, Glenn L. "Memorial to William Berryman
Scott," GSAP pp. 211-27 '48.

SCRIBER, Peter see DAVIS, Charles Augustus.

SCUDDER, Samuel Hubbard, 1837-1911
1774. Mayor, Alfred Goldsborough "Bibliography," NASBM
10:87-104 '19.

SEAGER, Allen, 1906-1968
1775. Hanna, Allan "An Allen Seager Bibliography," C 5:
75-90 Winter '62-'65.

SEALSFIELD, Charles, 1793-1864
1776. Heller, O. and T. H. Leon "Charles Sealsfield: Bibliography of His Writings Together with a Classified
and Annotated Catalogue of Literature Relating to His
Works and His Life," Washington University. Studies
in Language and Literature n. s. 8:1-88 '39.

SEARES, Frederick Hanley, 1873-1964
1777. Joy, Alfred "Bibliography," NASBM 39:432-44 '67.

SEASHORE, Carl Emil, 1866-1949
1778. Miles, Walter R. "Bibliography," NASBM 29:304-16
'56.

SEELY, Henry Martyn, 1828-1917
1779. Perkins, George H. "Memorial to Henry Martyn
Seely," GSAB 29:65-69 '18.

SELIGMAN, Charles G., 1873-1940
1780. Fortes, M. "Charles G. Seligman, 1873-1940; with List of His Publications," Man (London) 41:6 Jan '41.
1781. Herskovits, Melville J. "Charles Gabriel Seligman; with List of Works Published since 1934," AA 43:438-39 Jl '41.

SELLARDS, Elias Howard, 1875-1961
1782. Krieger, Alex D. "Bibliography," AAY 27:227-28 O '61.

SELLARS, Roy Wood, 1880-
1783. Myers, G. E. "Bibliography of the Writings of Roy Wood Sellars," Philosophy and Phenomenological Research 15:98-103 S '54.

SETCHELL, William Albert, 1864-1943
1784. Goodspeed, T. H. and Lee Bonar "Bibliography of William Albert Setchell," NASBM 23:137-47 '45.

SHAFFER, Philip Anderson, 1881-1960
1785. Doisy, Edward A. "Bibliography," NASBM 40:330-36 '69.

SHALLER, Millard King, 1880-1942
1786. Ball, Sydney H. "Memorial to Millard King Shaler," GSAP pp. 305-08 '44.

SHALER, Nathaniel Southgate, 1841-1906
1787. Wolff, John E. "Memoir of Nathaniel Southgate Shaler," GSAB 18:592-609 '07.

SHARP, Donald Ellsworth, 1896-
1788. "D. E. Sharp, Glass Division Trustee," American Ceramic Society. Bulletin 17:183-84 Apr '38.

SHATTUCK, George Burbank, 1869-1934
1789. Mathews, Edward B. "Memorial of George Burbank Shattuck," GSAP pp. 271-76 '34.

SHAW, Eugene Wesley, 1881-1935
1790. Westgate, Lewis G. "Memorial of Eugene Wesley Shaw," GSAP pp. 311-18 '35.

SHEAR, Cornelius Lott, 1865-1956
1791. Stevenson, J. A. "Cornelius Lott Shear," Mycologia 49:291-97 Mr '57.

SHEDD, Solon, 1860-1941
1792. Jenkins, Olaf P. "Memorial to Solon Shedd," GSAP
pp. 187-91 '41.

SHEEN, Fulton, 1895-
1793. Heffron, E. J. "Contemporary Catholic Authors:
Monsignor Fulton J. Sheen, Theologian, Philosopher,
Orator; with List of His Publications," Catholic Library
World 12:207 Apr '41.

SHEPARD, Edward Martin, 1854-1934
1794. Buehler, H. A. "Memorial of Edward Martin Shepard," GSAP pp. 277-80 '34.

SHERRILL, Richard E., 1899-1952
1795. Dickey, Parke A. "Memorial to Richard E. Sherrill,"
GSAP pp. 149-51 '53.

SHETRONE, Henry Clyde, 1876-1954
1796. Baby, Raymond S. "Bibliography," AAY 21:298-99
Jan '56.
1797. Setzler, F. M. "Henry Clyde Shetrone - 1876-1954,"
AAY 21:298-99 Jan '56.

SHIDELER, William H., 1886-1958
1798. Dunn, Paul H. "Memorial to William H. Shideler,"
GSAP pp. 147-50 '59.

SHIMEK, Bohumil, 1861-1938
1799. Kay, George F. "Memorial to Bohumil Shimek,"
GSAP pp. 169-73 '38.

SHORT, Maxwell Naylor, 1889-1952
1800. McKee, Edwin D. "Memorial to Maxwell Naylor
Short," GSAP pp. 137-38 '52.

SHORTFIELD, Luke see JONES, John Beauchamp.

SHULER, Ellis William, 1881-1954
1801. Foscue, Edwin J. "Memorial to Ellis William Shuler,"
GSAP pp. 133-36 '54.
1802. Geiser, S. W. "Ellis William Shuler," Field and
Laboratory 21:9-10 Jan '53.

SIEBENTHAL, Claude Ellsworth, 1869-1930
1803. Lindgren, Waldemar "Memorial of Claude Ellsworth
Siebenthal," GSAB 42:138-47 '32.

SIEGEL, Morris, 1906-1961
1804. Joffe, Natalie F. "Morris Siegel," AA 66:395-96
Apr '64.

SILLIMAN, Benjamin, 1816-1885
1805. Wright, Arthur W. "Bibliography," NASBM 7:133-41
'13.

SILVERMAN, Alexander, 1881-1962
1806. "Alexander Silverman; with List of His Publications,"
American Ceramic Society. Bulletin 20:455-56 D '41.

SIMCOE, George, 1878-1941
1807. "George Simcoe; with List of His Publications and
Patents," American Ceramic Society. Bulletin 20:418
N '41.

SIMMS, Charles Carroll
1808. Welsh, John R. "The Charles Carroll Simms Collection," South Atlantic Bulletin XXI: iv, 1-3.

SIMMS, William Gilmore, 1806-1870
1809. Wegelin, Oscar "Simms' First Publication," New
York Historical Society Quarterly Review 25:26-27 '41.
1810. Wegelin, Oscar "William Gilmore Simms; A Short
Sketch, with a Bibliography of His Separate Writings,"
ABC 3:113-16, 149-51, 216-18, 284-86.

SIMONDS, Frederic William, 1853-1941
1811. Deussen, Alexander "Memorial to Frederic William
Simonds," GSAP pp. 193-200 '41.

SIMPSON, Howard Edwin, 1875-1938
1812. Norton, W. H. "Memorial to Howard Edwin Simpson,"
GSAP pp. 175-83 '38.

SINCLAIR, Upton, 1878-1968
1813. Bantz, Elizabeth "Upton Sinclair: Book Reviews and
Criticisms Published in German and French Periodicals
and Newspapers," BB 18:204-06 Jan-Apr '46.
1814. Evans, I. O. "List of Books, Pamphlets, Leaflets by
Upton Sinclair," Tamiment Institute Library. Bulletin
17:2-7 S '58.

SINCLAIR, William John, 1877-1938
1815. Scott, W. B. "Memorial to William John Sinclair,"
GSAP pp. 185-89 '38.

SISK, John P.
1816. Seelhammer, Ruth "John P. Sisk; a Selected Checklist," BB 23:179 My-Ag '62.

SISLER, James Donaldson, 1896-1935
1817. Ashley, George H. "Memorial of James Donaldson
Sisler," GSAP pp. 319-22 '35.

SKARLAND, Ivar, 1899-1965
1818. West, Frederick Hadleigh "Ivar Skarland," AA 68:
132-33 F '66.

SKINNER, Alanson Buck, 1885-1925
1819. Harrington, M. R. "Bibliography of Alanson Skinner,"
AA 28:277-80 '26.

SLOAN, Earle, 1858-1926
1820. Vaughan, Thomas Wayland "Memorial of Earle
Sloan," GSAB 40:57-61 '30.

SLOSSON, Edwin Emery, 1854-1929
1821. Barton, D. "Edwin Emery Slosson: a Chemist of the
West; with List of His Publications," Journal of Chemical Education 19:19 Jan '42.

SLOTKIN, James Sydney, 1913-1958
1822. Tax, Sol "James Sydney Slotkin," AA 61:844-47 O
'59.

SMALL, Lyndon Frederick, 1897-1959
1823. Mosettig, Erich "Bibliography," NASBM 33:408-13 '59.

SMITH, Alexander, 1865-1922
1824. Noyes, William A. "Bibliography of Scientific Papers,"
NASBM 11:5-7 '23.

SMITH, Burnett, 1877-1958
1825. Palmer, Katherine Van Winkle "Memorial to Burnett
Smith," GSAP pp. 151-55 '59.

SMITH, Edgar Fahs, 1854-1928
1826. Meeker, George H. "Scientific Papers of Edgar Fahs
Smith," NASBM 17:140-49 '37.

SMITH, Elmer R., 1909-1960
1827. Dibble, Charles "Elmer R. Smith," AA 62:1047-49
D '60.

150

SMITH, Ernest Rice, 1891-1952
1828. Maxwell, John C. "Memorial to Ernest Rice Smith,"
GSAP pp. 139-41 '52.

SMITH, Erwin Frink, 1854-1927
1829. Rand, Frederick V. "The Published Writings of Erwin Frink Smith," NASBM 21:47-71 '41.

SMITH, Eugene Allen, 1841-1927
1830. Butts, Charles "Memorial of Eugene Allen Smith,"
GSAB 39:51-65 '28.

SMITH, George Otis, 1871-1944
1830a. Smith, Philip S. "Memorial to George Otis Smith,"
GSAP pp. 309-39 '44.

SMITH, Gilbert Morgan, 1885-1959
1831. Wiggins, Ira L. "Bibliography," NASBM 36:308-13
'62.

SMITH, Homer William, 1895-1962
1832. Pitts, Robert F. "Bibliography," NASBM 39:458-70
'67.

SMITH, James Perrin, 1864-1931
1833. Blackwelder, Eliot "Bibliography," NASBM 38:304-
08 '65.

SMITH, John Lawrence, 1818-1883
1834. Silliman, Benjamin "Bibliography," NASBM 2:239-48
1886.

SMITH, Logan Pearsall, 1865-1946
1835. "The Logan Pearsall Smith Papers; Catalogue," Serif
II iv, 28-30.
1836. "Writings in Prose and Verse," London Mercury 3:
436 F '21.

SMITH, Marian Wesley, 1907-1961
1837. de Laguna, Frederica "Selected Publications in
American Archaeology and Ethnology," AAY 27:570
Apr '62.

SMITH, Philip Sydney, 1877-1949
1838. Moffit, F. H., J. C. Reid, and A. L. Washburn
"Memorial to Philip Sydney Smith," GSAP pp. 217-25
'49.

SMITH, Sidney Irving, 1843-1926
1839. Coe, Wesley R. "Bibliography," NASBM 14:11-16 '32.

SMITH, Theobald, 1859-1934
1840. Zinsser, Hans "Bibliography of Theobald Smith,"
NASBM 17:288-303 '37.

SMITH, Warren Dupré, 1880-1950
1841. Staples, Lloyd W. "Memorial to Warren Dupré
Smith," GSAP pp. 119-24 '50.

SMOCK, John Conover, 1842-1926
1842. Kummel, Henry B. "Memorial of John Conover
Smock," GSAB 38:93-100 '27.

SMYTH, Charles Henry, 1866-1937
1843. Buddington, A. F. "Memorial to Charles Henry
Smyth, Jr.," GSAP pp. 195-202 '37.

SMYTH, Henry Lloyd, 1862-1944
1844. Graton, L. C. "Memorial to Henry Lloyd Smyth,"
GSAP pp. 177-90 '47.

SMYTH, Herbert Weir, 1857-1937
1844a. Jackson, C. N. "Herbert Weir Smyth," Harvard
Studies in Classical Philology 49:17-28 '38.

SMYTHE, Samuel see DAWES, Rufus.

SNIDER, Luther Crocker, 1882-1947
1845. Gould, Charles N. "Memorial to Luther Crocker
Snider," GSAP pp. 191-93 '47.

SNODGRASS, W. D., 1926-
1846. White, William "Snodgrass Peoples His Universe II,"
BSA 57:94 '63.

SOLLAS, William Johnson, 1849-1936
1847. Guppy, E. M. "Memorial to William Johnson Sollas:
with List of His Publications," GSAP pp. 207-19 '38.

SPECK, Frank Gouldsmith, 1881-1950
1848. Witthoft, John "Anthropological Bibliography 1903-
1950," AA 53:75-87 '51.

SPENCER, Joseph William Winthrop, 1851-1924
1849. Shaw, Eugene Wesley "Memorial of Joseph William
Winthrop Spencer," GSAB 35:25-37 '24.

SPERRY, Elmer Ambrose, 1860-1930
1850. Hunsaker, J. C. "List of the More Important Scientific Papers of Elmer Ambrose Sperry," NASBM 28: 248-60 '54.

SPIER, Leslie, 1893-1961
1851. Basehart, Harry W., and W. W. Hill "Leslie Spier," AA 67:1271-77 O '65.
1852. Taylor, Walter W. "Archaeological Bibliography of Leslie Spier," AAY 28:380-81 Jan '63.

SPRINGER, Frank, 1848-1927
1853. Schuchert, Charles "Memorial of Frank Springer," GSAB 39:65-80 '28.

SQUIER, Ephraim George, 1821-1888
1854. Patterson, Jerry E. and William R. Stanton "The Ephraim George Squier Manuscripts in the Library of Congress: a Checklist," BSA 53:309-26 '59.

SQUIER, George Owen, 1865-1934
1855. Kennelly, Arthur E. "Bibliography of George Owen Squier," NASBM 20:157-59 '39.

STADLER, Lewis John, 1896-1954
1856. Rhoades, M. M. "Bibliography," NASBM 30:342-47 '57.

STAINBROOK, Merrill Addison, 1897-1956
1857. Trowbridge, A. C. "Memorial to Merrill Addison Stainbrook," GSAP pp. 167-70 '56.

STANTON, Timothy William, 1860-1953
1858. Reeside, John B., Jr. "Memorial to Timothy William Stanton," GSAP pp. 137-41 '54.

STARR, Betty Warren, 1906-1964
1859. Casagrande, Joseph B. "Betty Warren Starr," AA 68:128-31 F '66.

STEBINGER, Eugene, 1883-1951
1860. Bauer, C. Max "Memorial to Eugene Stebinger," GSAP pp. 153-54 '53.

STEIDTMANN, Edward, 1881-1948
1861. Bevan, Arthur "Memorial to Edward Steidtmann," GSAP pp. 229-31 '48.

STEIN, Gertrude, 1874-1946
1862. Sawyer, Julian "Gertrude Stein: a Bibliography 1941-1948," BB 19:152-56 My-Ag '48; 19:183-87 S-D '48.
1863. Sawyer, Julian "Gertrude Stein (1874-   ) a Checklist Comprising Critical and Miscellaneous Writings About her Work, Life and Personality from 1913-1942," BB 17:211-12 Jan-Apr '43.
1864. Sawyer, Julian "Gertrude Stein (1874-1946): a Checklist Comprising Critical and Miscellaneous Writings About Her Work, Life, and Personality from 1913-1948," BB 19:128-31 Jan-Apr '48; 19:187 S-D '48.

STEINBECK, John, 1902-1968
1865. Beebe, Maurice and Jackson R. Bryer "Criticism of John Steinbeck: a Selected Checklist," MFS 11:90-103 Spring '65.
1866. Hayashi, Tetsumaro "A Brief Survey of John Steinbeck Bibliographies," Kyushu American Literature 9: 54-61 Jl '66.
1867. Hayashi, Tetsumaro "A Checklist of Steinbeck Criticism after 1965," Steinbeck Newsletter v. 1 #3 S '68.
1868. Hayashi, Tetsumaro "John Steinbeck: a Checklist of Unpublished Ph.D. Dissertations (1946-1967)," Serif 5:30-31 D '68.
1869. Powell, Lawrence C. "Toward a Bibliography of John Steinbeck," Colophon n.s. 3:558-68 '38.
1870. Remordas, Georges "John Steinbeck - Note Bibliographique," Bulletin de La Faculté des Lettres de Strasbourg 28:301-95 Apr '50.
1871. Steele, Joan "John Steinbeck: a Checklist of Biographical, Critical, and Bibliographical Material," BB 24:149-52 My-Ag '65.

STEINITZ, Kate, 1889-
1872. Edelstein, J. M. "Kate's Writings: a Selected Bibliography," Wilson Library Bulletin 44:529-34 Jan '70.

STEINMETZ, Charles Proteus, 1865-1923
1873. Lazarus, L. "List of References on Steinmetz in the Socialist Literature," Tamiment Institute Library. Bulletin #44 pp. 4-7 Apr '64.

STEJNEGER, Leonhard Hess, 1851-1943
1874. Wetmore, Alexander "Bibliography," NASBM 24:171-95 '47.

STETSON, Henry Crosby, 1900-1955
1875. "Henry Crosby Stetson," Deep Sea Research 3:292-
154

STETSON, Henry Crosby (continued)
   93 S '56.
1875a. Frask, Parker D. "Memorial to Henry Crosby
   Stetson," GSAP pp. 171-74 '56.

STETSON, Raymond Herbert, 1872-1950
1876. Reid, C. "Bibliography of R. H. Stetson," Journal
   of Speech and Hearing Disorders 23:268-69 Ag '58.

STEVENS, Wallace, 1879-1955
1877. Bryer, Jackson R. and Joseph N. Riddel "A Checklist of Stevens Criticism," TCL 8:124-42 O '62.
1878. Ford, W. T. "Some Notes on Stevens' Foreign Bibliography," Wallace Stevens Newsletter 1:1-3.
1879. Mitchell, Roger S. "Wallace Stevens: a Checklist
   of Criticism," BB 23:208-11 S-D '62; 23:232-33 Jan-
   Apr '63.

STEVENSON, John James, 1841-1924
1880. White, I. C. "Memorial of John James Stevenson,"
   GSAB 36:100-15 '25.

STEVENSON, Matilda Coxe, d. 1915
1881. Holmes, W. H. "List of Mrs. Stevenson's Scientific
   Publications," AA 18:558-59 '16.

STEVENSON, Philip
1882. Brüning, Eberhard "Bibliographie der bisher erschien-
   enen Werke von Philip Stevenson (Lars Laurence),"
   Zeitschrift für Anglistik und Amerikanistik (East Ber-
   lin) 14:381-85.

STEWART, George W., 1876-1956
1883. Fletcher, Harvey "Bibliography," NASBM 32:392-98
   '58.

STICKNEY, Joseph Trumbull, 1870-1904
1884. Lopez, Manuel D. "Joseph Trumbull Stickney (1870-
   1904)," BB 26:83-85 Jl/S '69.
1885. Myers, J. William "A Complete Stickney Bibliography," TCL 9:209-12 Jan '64.

STIEGLITZ, Julius, 1867-1937
1886. Noyes, William Albert "Bibliography of Julius Stieglitz," NASBM 21:299-314 '41.

STILLWELL, Lewis Buckley, 1863-1941
1887. Condit, Kenneth H. "A Partial Bibliography," NASBM

STILLWELL, Lewis Buckley (continued)
34:326-28 '60.

STIMPSON, William, 1832-1872
1888. Mayer, Alfred Goldsborough "Bibliography of Scientific Papers by William Stimpson," NASBM 8:429-33 '19.

STOCK, Chester, 1892-1950
1889. Simpson, George Gaylord "Bibliography," NASBM 27: 353-62 '52.
1890. Woodring, W. P. "Memorial to Chester Stock," GSAP pp. 149-55 '51.

STONE, Roland Elisha, 1881-1939
1891. Howitt, J. E. "Roland Elisha Stone; With List of His Publications," Phytopathology 30:880 N '40.

STOSE, George Willis, 1869-1960
1892. Miser, Hugh D. "Memorial to George Willis Stose," GSAP pp. 143-49 '60.

STOVALL, John Willis, 1891-1953
1893. Branson, Carl C. "Memorial to John Willis Stovall," GSAP pp. 155-57 '53.

STOW, Marcellus Henry, 1902-1957
1894. Thom, W. Taylor, Jr. "Memorial to Marcellus Henry Stow," GSAP pp. 165-66 '57.

STOWE, Harriet Beecher, 1811-1896
1895. Adams, John R. "Harriet Beecher Stowe (1811-1896)," ALR 2:160-64 Summer '69
1896. Johnson, Merle "American First Editions: Harriet (Elizabeth) Beecher Stowe," Publishers' Weekly 121: 1738-40 '32.

STRATTON, George Malcolm 1865-1957
1897. Tolman, Edward C. "Bibliography," NASBM 35:297-306 '61.

STRATTON, Samuel Wesley, 1861-1931
1898. Kennelly, A. E. "Published Papers of Samuel Wesley Stratton," NASBM 17:259-60 '37.

STREETER, Georg Linius, 1873-1948
1899. Corner, George W. "Bibliography," NASBM 28:279-87 '54.

STRONG, William Duncan, 1899-1962
1900. Solecki, Ralph and Charles Wagley "William Duncan Strong," AA 65:1102-11 O '63.

STUART, Jesse, 1907-
1901. Woodbridge, Hensley C. "Articles by Jesse Stuart: a Bibliography," Kentucky Library Association. Bulletin #23 pp. 89-91 '59.
1902. Woodbridge, Hensely C. "First Supplement to Jesse and Jane Stuart: a Bibliography," Jack London Newsletter 2:118-20.
1903. Woodbridge, Hensley C. "Jesse Stuart: a Bibliographical Note," ABC 9:8-22 S '58.
1904. Woodbridge, Hensley C. "Jesse Stuart: a Critical Bibliography," ABC 16:11-13 F '66.
1905. Woodbridge, Hensley C. "Jesse Stuart's Contributions to Newspapers," Kentucky Library Association. Bulletin #23 pp. 45-47 '59.

STUBBS, Stanley A., 1906-1959
1906. Ellis, Bruce T. "Bibliography," AAY 25:588 Apr '60.

STYRON, William, 1925-
1907. Schneider, Harold W. "Two Bibliographies: Saul Bellow and William Styron," C 3:86-91 Summer '60.

SULLIVAN, John D., 1900-
1908. "J. D. Sullivan; Refractories Division Trustee," American Ceramic Society. Bulletin 19:234-35 Je '40.

SUMNER, Francis Bertody, 1874-1945
1909. Child, Charles Manning "Bibliography," NASBM 25:164-73 '49.

SUMNER, James Batcheller, 1887-1955
1910. Maynard, Leonard A. "Bibliography," NASBM 31:387-96 '58.

SWAIN, George Fillmore, 1857-1931
1911. Hovgaard, William "Bibliography," NASBM 17:348-

SWAIN, George Fillmore (continued)
    50 '37.

SWANTON, John Reed, 1873-1958
1912. Fenton, William N. "John Reed Swanton," AA 61:663-
    68 Ag '59.
1913. Steward, Julian H. "Bibliography," NASBM 34:339-
    49 '60.

SWARTZ, Charles Kephart, 1861-1949
1914. Singewald, Joseph T., Jr. "Memorial to Charles
    Kephart Swartz," GSAP pp. 131-34 '50.

SWINNERTON, Allyn Coats, 1897-1952
1915. Garrels, Robert M. "Memorial to Allyn Coats Swin-
    nerton," GSAP pp. 143-45 '52.

SZILARD, Leo, 1898-1964
1916. Wigner, Eugene P. "Bibliography," NASBM 40:342-
    47 '69.

T
—

TABB, John Banister, 1845-1909
1917. Starke, Aubrey "Father John B. Tabb: a Checklist,"
    ABC 6:101-04 '35.

TAFF, Joseph Alexander, 1862-1944
1918. Miser, Hugh D. "Memorial to Joseph Alexander
    Taff," GSAP pp. 227-35 '49.

TALBOT, Mignon, 1869-1950
1919. Hoff, John C. "Memorial to Mignon Talbot," GSAP
    pp. 157-58 '51.

TALMAGE, James Edward, 1862-1933
1920. Miller, Benjamin L. "Memorial of James Edward
    Talmage," GSAP pp. 259-71 '33.

TANNENBAUM, Jane Belo, 1904-1968
1921. Metraux, Rhoda "Jane Belo Tannenbaum," AA 70:
    1168-69 D '68.

TARR, Ralph Stockman, 1864-1912
1922. Woodworth, J. B. "Memoir of Ralph Stockman Tarr,"
    GSAB 24:29-43 '13.

TARR, William Arthur, 1881-1939
1923. Branson, E. B. "Memorial to William Arthur Tarr,"
GSAP pp. 241-47 '39.

TATE, Allen, 1899-
1924. Korges, James "Allen Tate: a Checklist Continued,"
C 10:35-52 '68.
1925. Thorp, Willard "Allen Tate: a Checklist," PULC
3:85-98 Apr '42.
1926. Thorp, Willard "Allen Tate: A Checklist," C 10
#2:17-34 '68.

TAYLOR, Charles Vincent, 1885-1946
1927. Danforth, C. H. "Bibliography of Charles Vincent
Taylor," NASBM 25:222-25 '49.

TAYLOR, David Watson, 1864-1940
1928. Hovgaard, William "Bibliography," NASBM 22:151-
53 '43.

TAYLOR, Edward, 1642-1729
1929. Elkins, Mary Jane "Edward Taylor: a Checklist,"
Early American Literature 4:56-63.
1930. Hoffmann, Carol Ann "Edward Taylor: A Selected
Bibliography," BB 23:85-87 Jan-Apr '61.

TAYLOR, Frank Bursley, 1860-1938
1931. Leverett, Frank "Memorial to Frank Bursely Taylor,"
GSAP pp. 191-99 '38.

TAYLOR, Griffith, 1880-1963
1932. "Griffith Taylor: Principal Publications," Australian
Geographical Studies 2:3-9 Apr '64.

TAYLOR, Henry Charles, 1873-
1933. Taylor, A. D. "Bibliographic Guide to the Writings
of Henry C. Taylor, Agricultural Economist, Covering
the Years 1893-1957," Agricultural History 32 Supplement 1-28 Jl '58.

TAYLOR, Peter, 1917-
1934. Smith, James Penny "A Peter Taylor Checklist,"
C 9:31-36 '67.

TEASDALE, Sara, 1884-1933
1935. Buchan, Vivian "Sara Teasdale (1884-1933)," BB 25:
94-97 S-D '67; 25:120-23 Jan-Apr '68.

TENNENT, David Hilt, 1873-1941
1936. Gardiner, Mary S. "Bibliography," NASBM 26:116-19 '51.

TERMAN, Lewis Madison, 1877-1956
1937. Oden, Melita H. "Bibliography," NASBM 33:442-61 '59.

THAXTER, Roland, 1858-1932
1938. Clinton, G. P. "Bibliography of Roland Thaxter," NASBM 17:64-68 '37.

THIELEN, Benedict
1939. Carlson, Eric W. "Benedict Thielen: an Introduction and a Checklist," PULC 13:143-55 Spring '52.

THOM, Charles, 1872-1956
1940. Raper, Kenneth B. "Bibliography," NASBM 38:335-44 '65.

THOMAS, Abram Owen, 1876-1931
1941. Lees, James H. "Memorial of Abram Owen Thomas," GSAB 43:108-14 '33.

THOMPSON, Daniel Pierce, 1795-1868
1942. Johnson, Merle "American First Editions: Daniel Pierce Thompson (1795-1869)," Publishers' Weekly 121:2218 '32.

THOMPSON, David Grosh, 1888-1943
1943. Meinzer, Oscar E. "Memorial to David Grosh Thompson," GSAP pp. 235-41 '43.

THOMPSON, Elihu, 1853-1937
1944. Compton, Karl T. "Selected List of the Publications of Elihu Thompson," NASBM 21:163-79 '41.

THOMPSON, John Eric, 1898-
1945. "Bibliografías de Antropólogos: J. Eric Thompson," Boletín Bibliográfica de Antropólogia Americana 4:161-63 My '40.

THOREAU, Henry D., 1817-1862
1946. Burnham, Philip E. and Carvel Collins "Contribution to a Bibliography of Thoreau, 1938-1945," BB 19:16-18 S-D '46; 19:37-39 Jan-Apr '47.
1947. Dedmond, F. B. "A Checklist of Manuscripts Relating to Thoreau in the Huntington Library, the Houghton
160

THOREAU, Henry D. (continued)
Library of Harvard University and the Berg Collection
of New York Public Library," Thoreau Society Bulletin #43 pp. 3-4.
1948. Harding, Walter "Additions to the Thoreau Bibliography," Thoreau Society Bulletin #18 pp. 3-4; #19 pp.
3-4; #20 p. 4; #21 p. 4; #23 p. 4; #24 p. 4; #25 p.
4; #26 p. 4; #27 p. 4; #28 p. 4; #29 p. 4; #30 p. 4;
#31 p. 4; #32 p. 4; #34 p. 4; #38 pp. 39-44; #43 p.
1; #54 p. 4; #55 pp. 3-4; #56 p. 4; #57 p. 4; #58 pp.
3-4; #59 p. 4; #60 p. 4; #61 pp. 3-4; #62 pp. 3-4;
#63 pp. 2-4; #64 p. 4; #65 pp. 5-6; #66 pp. 3-4;
#67 p. 4; #68 p. 4; #69 pp. 3-4; #70 pp. 3-4; #71
pp. 3-4; #72 p. 4; #73 pp. 7-8; #74 pp 6-7; #75 pp.
3-4; #76 pp. 2-3; #77 pp. 2-3; #78 pp. 2-4; # 79 pp.
3-4; #81 pp. 2-4; #82 pp. 3-4; #83 pp. 3-4; #84 pp.
3-4; #85 p. 3; #86 pp. 2-3; #87 pp. 1-3; #89 pp. 2-
4; #90 pp. 2-4; #91 pp. 2-3; #93 pp. 3-4; #101 pp.
3-5; #102 pp. 7-8; #103 pp. 4-6; #104 pp. 3-5.
1949. Harding, Walter "A Centennial Checklist of the Editions of Henry David Thoreau's Walden," Secretary's
News Sheet Bibliographical Society of the University of
Virginia #28:1-32.
1950. Harding, Walter "A Preliminary Checklist of the Editions of Walden," Thoreau Society Bulletin #39 pp. 2-3.
1951. Harding, Walter "Some Forgotten Reviews of Walden,"
Thoreau Society Bulletin #46.
1952. Harding, Walter and Carl Bode "Henry David Thoreau: a Check List of His Correspondence," NYPLB
59:227-52 My '55.
1953. "Henry David Thoreau, 1817-1862: Books, Manuscripts, and Association Items in Detroit and Ann
Arbor," Thoreau Society Booklet #18 pp. 1-13.
1954. Kent, H. W. "A Catalog of the Thoreau Collection
in the Concord Antiquarian Society," Thoreau Society
Bulletin #47.
1955. Kern, Alexander "Thoreau Manuscripts at Harvard,"
Thoreau Society Bulletin #53 pp. 1-2.
1956. Morrisson, Helen B. "Thoreau and the New York
Tribune: a Checklist," Thoreau Society Bulletin #77
pp. 1-2.
1957. Wade, Joseph S. "A Contribution to a Bibliography
from 1909 to 1936 of Henry David Thoreau," New York
Entomological Society. Journal 47:163-203 '39.
1958. White, William "A Henry David Thoreau Bibliography, 1908-1937," BB 16:90 Jan-Apr '38; 16:111-13 My-
Ag '38; 16:131-32 S-D '38; 16:163 Jan-Apr '39; 16:181-
82 My-Ag '39; 16:199-202 S-D '39.

THORNDIKE, Edward Lee, 1874-1949
1959. "Annotated Chronological Bibliography of Publications,"
Teachers' College Record 27:466-515 F '26.
1960. Lorge, I. "Edward Thorndike's Publications for 1940
to 1949," Teachers' College Record 51:42-50 '49.
1961. "Publications from 1898 to 1940 by E. L. Thorndike,"
Teachers' College Record 41:699-725 My '40.
1962. Woodworth, Robert S. "Bibliography," NASBM 27:222-
37 '52.

THORPE, Thomas Bangs, 1815-1878
1963. Richels, Milton "A Bibliography of the Writings of
Thomas Bangs Thorpe," AL 29:171-79 Mr '57.

THURBER, James, 1894-1961
1964. Bowden, Edwin T. "The Thurber Carnival: Bibliography and Printing History," TSLL 9:555-66 Winter
'68.

THURNWALD, Richard, 1869-1954
1965. Baldus, H. "Richard Thurnwald, 1869-1954," Revista
de Antropologia 2:49-52 Je '54.
1966. Lowie, R. H. "Richard Thurnwald, 1869-1954," AA
56:867 O '54.

THURSTONE, Louis Leon, 1887-1955
1967. Guilford, J. P. "Bibliography," NASBM 30:360-82 '57.

TIGHT, William George, 1865-1910
1968. Bownocker, J. A. "Memorial of William George
Tight," GSAB 22:19-22 '11.

TILTON, John Littlefield, 1863-1930
1969. Reger, David B. "Memorial of John Littlefield Tilton," GSAB 42:147-59 '32.

TODD, James Edward, 1846-1922
1970. Leverett, Frank "Memorial of James E. Todd,"
GSAB 34:44-51 '23.

TODD, Thomas Wingate, 1885-1938
1971. Shapiro, H. L. "Bibliography," AA 41:461-64 '39.

TOEPELMAN, Walter Carl, 1894-1958
1972. Worcester, P. G. "Memorial of Walter Carl Toepelman," GSAP pp. 159-60 '59.

TOLMACHOFF, Innokenty Pavlovich, 1872-1950
1973. Johnson, Helgi "Memorial to Innokenty Pavlovich Tolmachoff," GSAP pp. 147-54 '52.

TOLMAN, Edward Chace, 1886-1959
1974. Ritchie, Benbow F. "Bibliography," NASBM 37:318-24 '64.

TOLMAN, Richard Chace, 1881-1948
1975. Kirkwood, John G., Oliver R. Wulf, and P. S. Epstein "Bibliography," NASBM 27:145-53 '52.

TONE, Frank Jerome, 1868-1944
1976. "Bibliography of Articles Written by F. J. Tone," American Ceramic Society. Bulletin 17:334 Ag '38.

TORRENCE, Ridgely, 1874-1950
1977. Thorp, Willard "The Achievement of Ridgely Torrence with a List of His Works," PULC 12:103-17 Spring '51.

TOURGÉE, Albion W., 1838-1905
1978. Keller, Dean H. "A Checklist of the Writings of Albion W. Tourgée (1838-1905)," SB 18:269-79 '65.

TOZZER, Alfred Marston, 1876-1954
1979. Lothrop, S. K. "Alfred Marston Tozzer 1876-1954," AA 57:614-18 '55.
1980. Peabody Museum. Harvard University "Bibliography," AAY 21:76-80 Jl '55.
1981. Spinden, Herbert Joseph "Bibliography," NASBM 30: 389-97 '57.

TREGANZA, Adán Eduardo, 1916-1968
1982. Hohenthal, W. D. "Adán Eduardo Treganza, 1916-1968," AAY 34:462-66 O '69.

TRELEASE, William, 1857-1945
1983. Yuncker, Truman George "Bibliography," NASBM 35:317-32 '61.

TRENT, Josia C., 1914-1948
1984. Ditrick, H. "Bibliography of Dr. Josiah C. Trent," Bulletin of the History of Medicine 23:97-100 Jan '49.

TROSTEL, Louis Jacob, 1893-
1985. "Louis Jacob Trostel, President of the American Ceramic Society, 1942-1943; with List of Publications on Ceramics," American Ceramic Society. Bulletin

TROSTEL, Louis Jacob (continued)
21:64-65 My '42.

TROWBRIDGE, Augustus, 1870-1934
1986. Compton, Karl T. "Bibliography of Scientific Papers by Augustus Trowbridge," NASBM 18:242-44 '38.

TROWBRIDGE, John, 1843-1923
1987. Hall, Edwin H. "Papers," NASBM 14:201-04 '32.

TRUMBULL, James Hammond, 1821-1897
1988. Wright, Arthur W. "Bibliography," NASBM 7:161-69 '13.

TSCHOPIK, Harry, Jr., 1915-1956
1989. Rowe, John Howland "Harry Tschopik, Jr.," AA 60: 132-40 F '58.

TUCKERMAN, Louis Bryant, 1879-1962
1990. "Biographical Sketch; with List of His Publications," American Ceramic Society. Bulletin 25:38-39 Mr '42.

TURNER, Charles Henry, 1867-1923
1991. Ferguson, E. "Revised List of Papers Published by Charles Henry Turner," Journal of Negro Education 9:658-60 O '40.

TURNER, Henry Ward, 1857-1937
1992. Lawson, Andrew C. "Memorial to Henry Ward Turner," GSAP pp. 201-07 '38.

TURNER, William Ernest Stanley, 1881-
1993. "List of Original Investigations Published by W. E. S. Turner," American Ceramic Society. Bulletin 17:307-14 Jl '38.

TWAIN, Mark see CLEMENS, Samuel Langhorne.

TWENHOFEL, William Henry, 1875-1957
1994. Dunbar, Carl O. "Memorial to William Henry Twenhofel," GSAP pp. 151-56 '60.

TWITCHELL, Mayville W., 1868-1927
1995. Kümmel, Henry B. "Memorial of Mayville W. Twitchell," GSAB 39:47-51 '28.

TYLER, Harry Walter, 1863-1938
1996. Bigelow, R. P. "Harry Walter Tyler: with Bibliog-

TYLER, Harry Walter (continued)
raphy of His Publications," Isis 31:60-64 N '39.

TYRRELL, Joseph Burr, 1858-1957
1997. Moore, E. S. "Memorial to Joseph Burr Tyrrell,"
GSAP pp. 167-70 '57.

U

ULRICH, Edward Oscar, 1857-1944
1998. Bassler, Ray S. "Memorial to Edward Oscar Ulrich,"
GSAP pp. 331-51 '44.
1999. Ruedemann, Rudolf "Bibliography of More Important
Works of Edward Oscar Ulrich," NASBM 24:276-80 '47.

UNTERMEYER, Louis, 1885-
2000. "Louis Untermeyer; a Bibliography," Demcourier 10
#2:5-10 '40.

UPHAM, Warren, 1850-1934
2001. Emmons, W. H. "Memorial of Warren Upham," GSAP
pp. 281-94 '34.

V

VAIL, Curtis Churchill Doughty, 1903-1957
2002. Reed, C. E. "Curtis C. D. Vail," Modern Language
Quarterly 18:178-82 S '57.

VAILLANT, George Clapp, 1901-1945
2003. "Bibliografías de Antropólogos: George Clapp Vaillant,"
Boletín Bibliográfica de Antropologia Americana 2:156-
58 O '39.
2004. Kidder, A. V. "Bibliography," AA 47:598-602 '45.

VALENTINER, Wilhelm Reinhold, 1880-1958
2005. Insley, M. "Bibliography of the Writings of Wilhelm
R. Valentiner from 1903 to 1940," Detroit Institute of
Arts. Bulletin 19:91-111 My '40.

VAN AMRINGE, Erwin Verne, 1899-1956
2006. Hill, H. Stanton "Memorial to Erwin Verne Van Amringe," GSAP pp. 203-05 '58.

VAN CLEAVE, Harley Jones, 1886-1953
2007. Mizelle, J. D. "Memorial to Harley Jones Van

VAN CLEAVE, Harley Jones (continued)
Cleave," American Midland Naturalist 49:687-95 My
'53.

VAN DEVENTER, William Carlstead, 1908-
2008. Pruitt, C. M. "William Carlstead Van Deventer,"
Science Education 52:212-13 Apr '68.

VAN DINE, S. S. see WRIGHT, Willard Huntington.

VAN HISE, Charles Richard, 1857-1918
2009. Chamberlin, Thomas C. "Bibliography," NASBM 10:
150-51 '19.
2010. Leith, C. K. "Memorial of Charles Richar Van
Hise," GSAB 31:100-10 '20.

VAN HORN, Frank Robertson, 1872-1933
2011. Hyde, Jesse E. "Memorial of Frank Robertson Van
Horn," GSAP pp. 273-87 '33.

VAN INGEN, Gilbert, 1869-1925
2012. Howell, B. F. "Memorial of Gilbert Van Ingen,"
GSAB 42:159-63 '32.

VAN VECHTEN, Carl, 1880-1964
2013. Jonas, Klaus W. "Additions to the Bibliography of
Carl Van Vechten," BSA 55:42-45 '61.

VAN VLECK, Edward Burr, 1863-1943
2014. Langer, Rudolph E. and Mark H. Ingraham "Bibliography," NASBM 30:407-09 '57.

VAUGHAN, Thomas Wayland, 1870-1952
2015. Thompson, Thomas G. "Bibliography," NASBM 32:
410-37 '58.

VEATCH, Arthur Clifford, 1878-1941
2016. Heroy, William B. "Memorial to Arthur Clifford
Veatch," GSAP pp. 201-09 '41.

VEBLEN, Oswald, 1880-1960
2017. MacLane, Saunders "Bibliography," NASBM 37:336-
41 '64.

VENABLE, Francis Preston, 1856-1934
2018. Cameron, F. K. "Publications of Francis Preston
Venable," American Chemical Society. Journal 59:
supplement 30-32 Ag '37.

VERPLANCK, Gulian Crommelian, 1786-1870
2019. Harvey, Sara K. "A Bibliography of the Miscellaneous Prose of Gulian Crommelian Verplanck," AL 8: 199-203 '36-'37.

VERRILL, Addison Emery, 1839-1926
2020. Coe, Wesley R. "Bibliography," NASBM 14:40-66 '32.

VER STEEG, Karl, 1891-1952
2021. Strahler, Arthur N. "Memorial to Karl Ver Steeg," GSAP pp. 155-58 '52.

VIDAL, Gore, 1925-
2022. Nichols, L. "Bibliography," New York Times Book Review p. 8 F 21 '65.

VIVIAN, Richard Gordon, 1908-1966
2023. Richert, Roland "Richard Gordon Vivian, 1908-1966," AAY 32:100-03 Jan '67.

VOGDES, Anthony Wayne, 1843-1923
2024. Dumble, E. T. "Memorial of Anthony Wayne Vogdes," GSAB 35:37-42 '24.

VON KÁRMÁN, Theodore, 1881-1963
2025. Dryden, Hugh L. NASBM 38:369-84 '65.

von NEUMANN, John, 1903-1957
2026. Bochner, S. "Bibliography," NASBM 32:448-57 '58.
2027. Ulam, S. "John von Neumann, 1903-1957," American Mathematical Society. Bulletin 64:42-49 My '58.

W

WACHSMUTH, Charles, 1829-1895
2028. Calvin, Samuel "Memoir of Charles Wachsmuth," GSAB 8:374-76 1897.

WADSWORTH, Marshman E., 1847-1923
2029. Lane, Alfred C. "Memorial of Marshman E. Wadsworth," GSAB 35:15-25 '24.

WAGNER, Henry Raup, 1862-1957
2030. Axe, R. F. "More Published Writings of Henry R. Wagner, Including Tributes and Bibliographies," California Historical Society Quarterly 47:273-84 S '68.

WAGNER, Henry Raup (continued)
2031. Hammond, G. P. and J. E. Patterson "Henry Raup
Wagner, 1862-1957," Hispanic American Historical Review 37:489-94 N '57.

WALCOTT, Charles Doolittle, 1850-1927
2032. Darton, Nelson H. "Memorial of Charles Doolittle
Walcott," GSAB 39:80-116 '28.
2033. Yochelson, Ellis L. "Bibliography," NASBM 39:516-
40 '67.

WALKER, Francis Amasa, 1840-1897
2034. Billings, John S. "Bibliography of Francis A.
Walker's Work," NASBM 5:214-18 '05.

WALLACE, Robert Charles, 1881-1955
2035. Hawley, J. E. "Memorial to Robert Charles Wallace,"
GSAP pp. 177-82 '55.

WALTHER, Johannes, 1860-1937
2036. Twenhofel, W. H. "Memorial to Johannes Walther:
with Selected List of His Publications," GSAP pp. 227-
29 '38.

WANDKE, Alfred, 1887-1941
2037. Graton, L. C. "Memorial of Alfred Wandke: with
List of His Publications," American Mineralogist 27:
206 Mr '42.
2038. Short, M. N. "Memorial to Alfred Wandke," GSAP
pp. 211-14 '41.

WARD, Artemus see BROWNE, Charles Farrar.

WARD, Freeman, 1879-1943
2039. Miller, Benjamin L. "Memorial to Freeman Ward,"
GSAP pp. 243-48 '43.

WARD, James, 1843-1925
2040. "List of Writings of James Ward," Monist 36:170-76
Jan '26.

WARDLE, Harriet Newell, 1875-1964
2041. Mason, J. Alden "H. Newell Wardle," AA 67:1512-
15 D '65.

WARING, Antonio J., Jr., 1915-1964
2042. Williams, Stephen "Antonio J. Waring, Jr., 1915-
1964," AAY 31:552-54 Apr '66.

WARNER, Langdon, 1881-1955
2043. Plumer, J. M. "Langdon Warner, 1881-1955," Ars Orientalia 2:635-36 '57.

WARREN, Charles Hyde, 1876-1950
2044. Knopf, Adolph "Memorial to Charles Hyde Warren," GSAP pp. 159-64 '51.

WARREN, Robert Penn, 1905-
2045. Beebe, Maurice and Erin Marcus "Criticism of Robert Penn Warren: a Selected Checklist," MFS 6:83-88 Spring '60.
2046. McDowell, Frederick P. "Robert Penn Warren's Criticism," Accent 15:173-96.
2047. Stallman, Robert W. "Robert Penn Warren: a Checklist of His Critical Writings," University of Kansas City Review 14:78-83 '47.
2048. Stallman, Robert Wooster "Robert Penn Warren: a Checklist of his Critical Writings," Western Review 14:78-83.

WASHBURN, Edward Wight, 1881-1934
2049. Noyes, William Albert "Bibliography of Edward Wight Washburn," NASBM 17:77-81 '37.

WASHBURN, Margaret Floy, 1871-1939
2050. Kambouropoulou, P. "Bibliography of the Writings of Margaret Floy Washburn: 1928-1939," American Journal of Psychology 53:19-20 Jan '40.
2051. Woodworth, Robert S. "Bibliography," NASBM 25:287-95 '49.

WASHINGTON, George, 1732-1799
2052. "Bibliography on George Washington and 150 Years," Story Behind the Headline Bulletin 2:22-23 Mr 7 '39.
2053. Stillwell, Margaret B. "Checklist of Eulogies and Funeral Orations on the Death of George Washington December, 1799-February, 1800," NYPLB 20:403-50 '16.
2054. Williams, M. "Washington Bookshelf," Our World Weekly 2:48 F 16 '25.

WASHINGTON, Henry Stephens, 1867-1934
2055. Merwin, Herbert E. "Memorial to Henry Stephens Washington," GSAP pp. 165-73 '51.

WATERMAN, Thomas Talbot, 1885-1936
2056. Kroeber, A. L. "Anthropological Bibliography," AA

WATERMAN, Thomas Talbot (continued)
39:528-29 '37.

WATSON, James Craig, 1838-1880
2057. Comstock, George C. "A List of the More Important
Published Writings of James C. Watson," NASBM 3:
56 1895.

WATSON, Sereno, 1820-1892
2058. Brewer, William H. "Bibliography," NASBM 5:285-
90 '05.

WATSON, Thomas Leonard, 1871-1924
2059. Ries, H. "Memorial of Thomas L. Watson," GSAB
36:116-28 '25.

WEAVER, Charles Edwin, 1880-1958
2060. Goodspeed, G. E. "Memorial to Charles Edwin
Weaver," GSAP pp. 207-09 '58.

WEBB, William Synder, 1882-1964
2061. Haag, William G. "William Synder Webb, 1882-1964,"
AAY 30:470-73 Apr '65.

WEBER, Carl J., 1894-1966
2062. "A Bibliography of the Publications of Carl J. Weber,"
CLQ 5:25-33 Je '59.

WEBSTER, Arthur Gordon, 1863-1923
2063. Baker, Edith M. "Bibliography," NASBM 18:342-47
'38.

WECKLER, Joseph Edwin, Jr., 1906-1963
2064. Hoijer, Harry "Joseph Edwin Weckler, Jr.," AA 66:
1348-50 D '64.

WEGELIN, Oscar, 1876-
2065. Stoddard, Roger E. "Oscar Wegelin, Pioneer Bibliographer of American Literature," BSA 56:237-47 '62.

WEGEMANN, Carroll Harvey, 1879-1952
2066. Dobbin, Carroll E. "Memorial to Carroll Harvey
Wegemann," GSAP pp. 159-62 '52.

WEIDMAN, Samuel, 1870-1945
2067. Decker, Charles E. "Memorial to Samuel Weidman,"
GSAP pp. 275-77 '45.

WEITLANER, Robert J., 1883-1968
2068. Foster, George M. "Bibliography of Robert J. Weitlaner," AA 73:345-48 Apr '70.

WELCH, William Henry, 1850-1934
2069. Flexner, Simon "Bibliography of William Henry Welch,"
NASBM 22:224-31 '43.

WELLER, Stuart, 1870-1927
2070. Chamberlin, Thomas C. and Raymond C. Moore
"Memorial of Stuart Weller," GSAB 39:116-26 '28.

WELLS, Harry Gideon, 1875-1943
2071. Long, Esmond R. "Bibliography of H. Gideon Wells,"
NASBM 26:233-63 '51.

WELLS, Horace Lemuel, 1855-1924
2072. Foote, H. W. "Bibliography," NASBM 12:283-85 '29.

WELLS, Roger Clark, 1877-1944
2073. Schaller, Waldemar T. "Memorial to Roger Clark
Wells," GSAP pp. 279-84 '45.

WELTY, Eudora, 1909-
2074. Cole, McKelva "Book Reviews by Eudora Welty: a
Check-list," BB 23:240 Jan-Apr '63.
2075. Gross, Seymour L. "Eudora Welty: a Bibliography
of Criticism and Comment," Secretary's News Sheet.
Bibliographical Society of the University of Virginia #45
pp. 1-32.
2076. Jordan, Leona "Eudora Welty: Selected Criticism,"
BB 23:14-15 Jan-Apr '60.
2077. Keller, Dean H. "A Footnote to Eudora Welty: a
Checklist," BB 24:138 Jan-Apr '65.
2078. McDonald, W. U., Jr. "Eudora Welty Manuscripts;
An Annotated Finding List," BB 24:44-46 S-D '63.
2079. Smythe, Katherine Hinds "Eudora Welty: a Checklist," BB 21:207-08 Jan-Apr '56.

WESSEL, Bessie Bloom, 1888-1969
2080. Simmons, Leo W. "Bibliography of Bessie Bloom
Wessel," AA 72:557 Je '70.

WEST, Nathanael, 1904-1940
2081. Kraus, W. Keith "Nathanael West: a Further Bibliographical Note," Serif 4:i:32.
2082. White, William "Nathanael West: a Bibliography,"
Serif 2:5-18 Mr '65; 2:28-31 S '65.

WEST, Nathanael (continued)
2083. White, William "Nathanael West: a Bibliography,"
SB 11:207-24 '58.
2084. White, William "Nathanael West's 'Balso Snell' in
Cloth," BSA 60:474-76 '66.
2085. White, William "Some Uncollected Authors XXXII Nathanael West, 1903?-1940," BC 11:206-10 Summer '62.

WESTCOTT, Glenway, 1901-
2086. Kahn, Sy M. "Glenway Westcott; A Bibliography,"
BB 22:156-60 S-D '58.

WESTGATE, Lewis Gardner, 1868-1948
2087. Bevan, Arthur "Memorial to Lewis Gardner Westgate," GSAP pp. 243-48 '48.

WHARTON, Edith, 1862-1937
2088. Nevius, Blake " 'Pussie' Jones's verses: a Bibliographical Note of Edith Wharton," AL 23:494-97 '51-
'52.

WHEELER, Joseph L., 1884-
2089. Bell, Marion V. "Joseph L. Wheeler; A Bibliography," BB 23:127-32 S-D '61.

WHEELER, William Morton, 1865-1937
2090. Parker, George Howard "Bibliography of William
Norton Wheeler," NASBM 19:222-41 '38.

WHITE, Charles Abiathar, 1826-1910
2091. Dall, William H. "Bibliography," NASBM 7:230-43
'13.

WHITE, David, 1862-1935
2092. Mendenhall, W. C. "Memorial of David White,"
GSAP pp. 271-91 '36.
2093. Postley, Olive C. "Bibliography of David White,
1862-1935," NASBM 17:210-21 '37.

WHITE, Helen Constance, 1896-1967
2094. App, A. J. "Contemporary Catholic Authors: Helen
C. White, Scholar and Historical Novelist," Catholic
Library World 11:202 Apr '40.

WHITE, Henry Seely, 1861-1943
2095. Coble, Arthur B. "Bibliography of Henry Seely White,"
NASBM 25:31-33 '49.

WHITE, Israel C., 1848-1927
2096. Fairchild, Herman L. "Memorial of Israel C. White,"
GSAB 39:126-45 '28.

WHITE, Newman Ivey, 1892-1948
2097. "Newman Ivey White," South Atlantic Bulletin 14:3 Jan
'49.

WHITE, Theodore Greely, 1872-1901
2098. Kemp, J. F. "Memoir of Theodore Greely White,"
GSAB 13:516-17 '02.

WHITE, William Allen, 1868-1944
2099. Johnson, W. and P. Pantle "Bibliography of the Published Works of William Allen White," Kansas Historical Quarterly 15:22-41 F '47.
2100. Pady, Donald S. "A Bibliography of the Poems of
William Allen White," BB 25:446-47 Jan-Apr '67.

WHITE, William Lawrence, 1908-1952
2101. Siu, R. G. H. and E. T. Reese "William Lawrence
White," Mycologia 45:611-12 Jl '53.

WHITEHEAD, John Boswell, 1872-1954
2102. Kouvenhoven, William Bennett "Bibliography,"
NASBM 37:354-60 '64.

WHITFIELD, Robert Parr, 1828-1910
2103. Clarke, John M. "Memoir of Robert Parr Whitfield,"
GSAB 22:22-32 '11.

WHITLOCK, Brand, 1869-1934
2104. Thorburn, Neil "Brand Whitlock (1869-1934)," ALR
#3 pp. 30-35 Summer '68.

WHITLOCK, Herbert Percy, 1868-1948
2105. Pough, Frederick H. "Memorial to Herbert Percy
Whitlock," GSAP pp. 249-51 '48.
2106. Pough, F. H. "Memorial to Herbert Percy Whitlock," American Mineralogist 34:265-66 Mr '49.

WHITMAN, Alfred Russell, 1882-1940
2107. Grant, U. S. "Memorial to Alfred Russell Whitman,"
GSAP pp. 243-45 '40.

WHITMAN, Charles Otis, 1842-1910
2108. Morse, Edward S. "Bibliography," NASBM 7:268-66
'13.

WHITMAN, Walt, 1819-1892

2109. Allen, Evie A. and Gay W. Allen "Walt Whitman Bibliography 1944-1954," Walt Whitman Foundation Bulletin Apr '55.
2110. Allen, Gay Wilson "Walt Whitman Bibliography, 1918-1934," BB 15:84-88 S-D '34; 15:106-09 Jan-Apr '35.
2111. Allen Gay Wilson "Walt Whitman Bibliography, 1935-1942," BB 17:209-10 Jan-Apr '43.
2112. Amy, Ernest Francis "An Evaluation of Ohio Wesleyan University's Recently Acquired Walt Whitman Collection," Ohio Wesleyan Magazine Je '55.
2113. Bowen, Dorothy and Philip Durham "Walt Whitman Materials in the Huntington Library," HLQ 19:81-96 N '55.
2114. McCain, Rea "Walt Whitman in Italy," BB 17:66-67 Jan-Apr '41; 17:92-93 My-Ag '41.
2115. Miller, F. DeWolfe "Whitman Bibliography in Russia," Walt Whitman Review xi, pp. 77-79.
2116. Tanner, James T. F. "Walt Whitman Bibliographies: a Chronological Listing, 1902-1964," BB 25:131-32 Jan-Apr '68.
2117. Tanselle, G. Thomas "Whitman's Short Stories: Another Reprint," BSA 56:115 '62.
2118. "Walt Whitman: the Man and the Poet: Catalog of the Sesquicentennial Exhibit Held in the Library of Congress from May, 1969 to January, 1970," LCQJ 27: 171-76 Apr '70.
2119. White, William "Addenda to Whitman's Short Stories," BSA 57:221-22 '63.
2120. White, William "Bibliography," Walt Whitman Newsletter 2:14, 29, 54.
2121. White, William "Walt Whitman's Journalism: a Bibliography," Walt Whitman Review S '68. Reprinted Detroit, Wayne State University Press, 1968.
2122. White, William "Walt Whitman's Short Stories: Some Comments and a Bibliography," BSA 52:300-06 '58.
2123. White, William "Whitman: Current Bibliography," Walt Whitman Newsletter 3:13-14, 33; 4:81-82, 97-99 113-14; 5:18, 37-38, 57-58, 77-78; 7:16-18, 38, 57-59, 78-79; 8:21-23, 46-47, 71; 8:94-95; 9:21-22, 45-46, 70-71, 93-94; 10:46-47, 77-78, 102-03; 11:21-23, 56-57, 80-81, 104-05; 12:22-23, 45-46, 72-73, 102-03; 13:33-34, 68-69, 102-03, 128-29.
2124. "The Whitman Collection: Some New Manuscripts," PULC 14:29-31 Apr '57.
2125. Woodbridge, Hensley C. "Walt Whitman: Additional Bibliography in Spanish," Walt Whitman Review 12:

WHITMAN, Walt (continued)
70-71.

WHITMORE, Frank Clifford, 1887-1947
2126. Marvel, C. S. "Bibliography," NASBM 28:296-311 '54.

WHITNEY, Willis Rodney, 1868-1958
2127. Suits, Guy "Bibliography," NASBM 34:361-67 '60.

WHITTIER, John Greenleaf, 1807-1892
2128. Taylor, C. Marshall "Some Whittier First Editions
Published in the British Isles," Journal of the Friends'
Historical Society 42:41-45 '50.
2129. "Whittier Bibliography for 1967, etc.," Whittier Newsletter 4:1-2; 6:1-3.

WHORF, Benjamin Lee, 1897-1941
2130. Hackett, Herbert "Bibliography of the Writings of
Benjamin Lee Whorf," Etc.: a Review of General Semantics 9:189-91 Spring '52. Reprinted AA 55:153-55
'53.

WIENER, Norbert, 1894-1964
2131. "Bibliography of Norbert Wiener," American Mathematical Society. Bulletin v. 72 pt. 2 pp. 135-45 Jan
'66.

WIGGLESWORTH, Michael, 1631-1705
2132. Jones, Matt B. "Notes for a Bibliography of Michael
Wigglesworth's Day of Doom and Meat Out of the
Eater," American Antiquarian Society. Proceedings
n. s. 39:77-84 '30.

WILCZYNSKI, Ernest Julius, 1876-1932
2133. Lane, Ernest P. "Bibliography," NASBM 16:319-27
'36.

WILDE, Richard Henry, 1789-1847
2134. Starke, Aubrey H. "Richard Henry Wilde; Some
Notes and a Check-list," ABC 4:226-32, 285-95.

WILDER, Frank Alonzo, 1870-
2135. Bain, H. Foster "Memorial of Frank Alonzo Wilder,"
GSAB 42:163-65 '32.

WILDER, Thornton, 1897-
2136. Bryer, Jackson R. "Thornton Wilder and the Reviewers," BSA 58:35-49 '64.

WILDER, Thornton (continued)
2137. Kosok, Heinz "Thornton Wilder: a Bibliography of Criticism," TCL 9:93-100 Jl '63.
2138. Kosok, H. Thornton Wilder: ein Literaturbericht," Jahrbuch für Amerikastudien 9:196-227 '64.

WILE, Henry, 1857-1887
2139. Gilman, R. L. "Henry Wile: Pioneer in Dermatological Research," Annals of Medical History s3: 4:17 Jan '42.

WILKINS, Ernest Hatch, 1880-1966
2140. Cecchetti, G. and others "Analytical Bibliography of the Writings of Dr. Ernest Hatch Wilkins," Romance Philology 13:193-217 F '60.

WILKINS, Lawrence Augustus, 1878-1945
2141. Alpern, H. "Written Legacy of Lawrence A. Wilkins," Hispania 29:178-80 My '46.

WILL, George Francis, 1884-1955
2142. Woolworth, Alan R. and Waldo R. Wedel "Bibliography," AAY 22:75-76 Jl '56.

WILLIAMS, Ben Ames, 1889-1953
2143. Cary, Richard "Ben Ames Williams in Books," CLQ 6:293-302 S '63.

WILLIAMS, Edward Higginson, Jr., 1849-1933
2144. Miller, Benjamin L. "Memorial of Edward Higginson Williams, Jr.," GSAP pp. 289-97 '33.

WILLIAMS, Espy, 1852-1908
2145. Nolan, P. T. "Espy Williams: New Orleans Playwright," Louisiana Library Association. Bulletin 21: 138-39 Winter '58.

WILLIAMS, George Huntington, 1856-1895
2146. Clark, William B. "Memorial to George Huntington Williams," GSAB 6:432-40 1895.

WILLIAMS, Henry Shaler, 1847-1918
2147. Cleland, Herdman F. "Memorial of Henry Shaler Williams," GSAB 30:47-65 '19.

WILLIAMS, Ira Abraham, 1876-1934
2148. Williams, J. W. "Memorial of Ira A. Williams," GSAP pp. 295-306 '34.

WILLIAMS, James Steele, 1896-1957
2149. Woodring, W. P. "Memorial to James Steele Williams," GSAP pp. 171-74 '57.

WILLIAMS, Joshua, 1813-1881
2150. Moys, E. M. "Mr. Joshua Williams, Q. C.: His Life and Writings," Law Library Journal 51:122-24 My '58.

WILLIAMS, Tennessee, 1914-
2151. Brown, Andreas "Tennessee Williams by Another Name," BSA 57:377-78 '63.
2152. Carpenter, Charles A., Jr. and Elizabeth Cook "Addenda to Tennessee Williams: a Selected Bibliography," Modern Drama 1:181-91; 2:22-23.

WILLIAMS, William Carlos, 1883-1963
2153. Wagner, Linda Welshimer "A Decade of Discovery, 1953-1963: Checklist of Criticism of William Carlos Williams' Poetry," TCL 10:166-69 Jan '65.
2154. Wallace, Emily Mitchell "William Carlos Williams Bibliography," Literary Review (Fairleigh Dickinson University) 9:501-12.
2155. White, William "William Carlos Williams: Bibliography Review with Addenda," ABC 19:9-12 Mr '69.

WILLIAMSON, George, 1895-
2156. Kolb, G. J. "List of George Williamson's Book and Articles," Modern Philology 61:238-39 F '64.

WILLIS, Bailey, 1857-1949
2157. Blackwelder, Eliot "Bibliography," NASBM 35:343-50 '61.

WILLISTON, Samuel Wendell, 1852-1918
2158. Hathaway, J. T. and Clara M. Le Vene "Bibliography," NASBM 10:136-41 '19.

WILLOUGHBY, Charles Clark, 1857-1943
2159. Hooton, Ernest A. "Bibliography," AAY 9:237-39 O '43.

WILSON, Alfred W. G., 1873-1954
2160. Wilson, Alice E. "Memorial to Alfred W. G. Wilson," GSAP pp. 143-45 '54.

WILSON, Arthur Herman, 1905-
2161. Wilson, A. H. "Bibliography of the Published Writings

WILSON, Arthur Herman (continued)
(1927-1955)," Susquehanna University Studies 5:174-78
My '55.

WILSON, Edmund, 1895-
2162. Lewis, William J. "Edmund Wilson: a Bibliography,"
BB 25:145-49 My-Ag '68.
2163. Mizener, Arthur "Edmund Wilson; A Checklist,"
PULC 5:62-78 N '43.

WILSON, Edmund Beecher, 1856-1939
2164. Morgan, T. H. "Publications of Edmund Beecher
Wilson," NASBM 21:336-42 '41.

WILSON, Edward Arthur, 1886-
2165. Bolton, T. "Book Illustrations of Edward A. Wilson
(1886-   )," American Artist 22:9 F '58; 22:9 Mr '58.

WILSON, Henry Van Peters, 1863-1939
2166. Costello, Donald Paul "Bibliography," NASBM 35:
375-83 '61.

WILSON, Hewitt, 1891-
2167. "Publications by Hewitt Wilson," American Ceramic
Society. Bulletin 16:263-64 Je '37.

WILSON, Louis Round, 1876-
2168. Thornton, M. L. "Bibliography of Louis Round Wilson," Library Quarterly 12:339-52 Jl '42.

WILSON, Ralph Elmer, 1886-1960
2169. Joy, Alfred H. "Bibliography," NASBM 36:324-29 '62.

WILSON, Samuel McKay, 1871-1946
2170. Clift, G. G. "Samuel McKay Wilson, 1871-1946; an
Appreciation," Kentucky State Historical Society Regis-
ter 45:34-38 Jan '47.

WILSON, Walter Byron, 1885-1951
2171. Howell, J. V. "Memorial to Walter Byron Wilson,"
GSAP pp. 175-76 '51.

WILSON, Woodrow, 1856-1924
2172. "Catalogue of an Exhibition in the Princeton University
Library February 18 through April 15, 1956 Commem-
orating the Centennial of His Birth," PULC 17:113-62
Spring '56.
2173. "Catalog of the Woodrow Wilson Centennial Exhibit,"

WILSON, Woodrow (continued)
    LCQJ 13:73-105 F '56.
2174. Kusielewicz, E. "Wilson and Poland," Polish Review
    1:119-21 Autumn '56.

WINCHELL, Alexander, 1824-1891
2175. "Geological Writings of Alexander Winchell," GSAB
    5:557-64 1893.

WINCHELL, Alexander Newton, 1874-1958
2176. Corbett, Clifton S. "Memorial to Alexander Newton
    Winchell," GSAP pp. 211-18 '58.

WINCHELL, Horace Vaughn, 1865-1923
2177. Kemp, James F. "Memorial of Horace Vaughn Win-
    chell," GSAB 35:46-56 '24.

WINCHELL, Newton Horace, 1839-1914
2178. Upham, Warren "Memoir of Newton Horace Winchell,"
    GSAB 26:27-46 '15.

WINCHESTER, Dean Eddy, 1883-1936
2179. Emery, W. B. "Dean Eddy Winchester (1883-1936),"
    American Association of Petroleum Geologists. Bulle-
    tin 21:137 Jan '37.

WINSLOW, Arthur, 1860-1938
2180. Lane, Alfred C. "Memorial to Arthur Winslow,"
    GSAP pp. 209-17 '38.

WINTERS, Yvor, 1900-
2181. Lohf, Kenneth A. and Eugene P. Sheehy "Yvor
    Winters: a Bibliography," TCL 5:27-51 Apr '59.

WINTHROP, Theodore, 1828-1861
2182. Colby, Elbridge "Bibliographical Notes on Theodore
    Winthrop," NYPLB 21:3-13 Jan '17.

WIRT, William
2183. Wellford, B. Randolph "Check-list of Editions of
    William Wirt's The Letters of the British Spy,"
    Secretary's News Sheet. Bibliographical Society of
    the University of Virginia #31 pp. 10-16 '54.

WISE, John Sergeant, 1846-1913
2184. Davis, Curtis Carroll "Wise Words from Virginia:
    the Published Writings of John S. Wise, of the Eastern
    Shore and New York City," BSA 54:273-85 '60.

WOLFE, Thomas, 1900-1938
2185. Beebe, Maurice and Leslie A. Field "Criticism of Thomas Wolfe; a Selected Checklist," MFS 11:315-28 Autumn '65.
2186. Holman, C. Hugh "Thomas Wolfe; a Bibliographical Study," TSLL 1:427-45 Autumn '59.
2187. Hutsell, J. K. "Thomas Wolfe and Altamount," Southern Packet 4:1-10 Apr '48.
2188. Kauffman, Bernice "Bibliography of Periodical Articles on Thomas Wolfe," BB 17:162-65 My-Ag '42.

WOLFF, John Eliot, 1857-1940
2189. Palache, Charles "Memorial to John Eliot Wolff," GSAP pp. 247-53 '40.

WOLFF, Mary Evaline see MADELVA, Sister Mary.

WOOD, Harry Oscar, 1879-1958
2190. Richter, Charles F. "Memorial to Harry Oscar Wood," GSAP pp. 219-24 '58.

WOOD, Horatio C., Jr., 1841-1920
2191. Roth, George B. "Bibliography," NASBM 33:475-84 '59.

WOODBERRY, George Edward, 1855-1930
2192. Doyle, Joseph "George Edward Woodberry: a Bibliography," BB 21:136-40 Jan-Apr '55; 21:163-68 My-Ag '55; 21:176-81 S-D '55; 21:209-14 Jan-Apr '56.
2193. Hawkins, R. R. "A List of Writings by and About George Edward Woodberry," NYPLB 34:279-96 My '30.

WOODMAN, Joseph Edmund, 1873-1939
2194. Lilley, Ernest R. "Memorial to Joseph Edmund Woodman," GSAP pp. 249-53 '39.

WOODWARD, Joseph Janvier, 1833-1884
2195. Billings, J. S. "List of the Publications of Dr. J. J. Woodward, U.S. Army," NASBM 2:300-07 1886.

WOODWARD, Robert Simpson, 1849-1924
2196. Wright, F. E. "Bibliography," NASBM 19:16-24 '38.
2197. Wright, Fred E. "Memorial of Robert Simpson Woodward," GSAB 37:115-34 '26.

WOODWORTH, Jay Backus, 1865-1925
2198. Keith, Arthur "Memorial of Jay Backus Woodworth," GSAB 37:134-41 '26.

WOODWORTH, Robert Sessions, 1869-1962
2199. Graham, Clarence H. "Bibliography," NASBM 39:
560-72 '67.

WOOLSON, Constance Fenimore, 1840-1894
2200. Moore, Rayburn S. "Constance Fenimore Woolson
(1840-1894)," ALR #3 pp. 36-38 Summer '68.

WORTHEN, Amos Henry, 1813-1888
2201. White, Charles A. "Bibliography," NASBM 3:348-62
1895.

WRIGHT, Albert Allen, 1846-1905
2202. Wilder, Frank A. "Memoir of Albert Allen Wright,"
GSAB 17:687-90 '06.

WRIGHT, Arthur Williams, 1836-1915
2203. Dana, Edward S. "Bibliography," NASBM 15:254-57
'34.

WRIGHT, Frank James, 1888-1954
2204. Sharp, Henry S. "Memorial to Frank James Wright,"
GSAP pp. 183-85 '55.

WRIGHT, Frederick Eugene, 1877-1953
2205. Fleming, John A. and Charles S. Piggot "Bibliography," NASBM 29:345-59 '56.
2206. Piggot, Charles S. "Memorial to Frederick Eugene
Wright," GSAP pp. 159-69 '53.
2207. Schairer, J. F. "Memorial to Frederick Eugene
Wright," American Mineralogist 39:286-92 Mr '54.

WRIGHT, George Frederick, 1835-1921
2208. Upham, Warren "Memorial of George Frederick
Wright," GSAB 33:15-30 '22.

WRIGHT, Orville, 1871-1948
2209. Durand, William F. "List of Principal Contributions
to Science by Orville Wright," NASBM 25:274 '49.

WRIGHT, Richard, 1908-1960
2210. Bryer, Jackson R. "Richard Wright: a Selected
Checklist of Criticism," Wisconsin Studies in Contemporary Literature 1:22-23.
2211. Fabre, Michel and Edward Margolies "Richard Wright
(1908-1960): a Bibliography," BB 24:313-33 Jan-Apr '65.
2212. Gibson, Donald B. "Richard Wright: a Bibliographical Essay," CLA 12:360-65 Je '69.

WRIGHT, Richard (continued)
2213. Kinnamon, Keneth "Richard Wright Items in the Fales Collection," Bulletin of the Society for the Libraries of New York University #66 p. 4.
2214. Sprague, M. D. "Richard Wright: a Bibliography," BB 21:39 S-D '53.
2215. Webb, Constance "Richard Wright; a Bibliography," Negro Digest 18:86-92.

WRIGHT, Willard Huntington, 1887-1939
2216. Crawford, Walter B. "Willard Huntington Wright: a Bibliography," BB 24:11-16 My-Ag '63.

WYMAN, Jeffries, 1814-1874
2217. Packard, A. S. "List of Scientific Papers and Works," NASBM 2:118-26 1886.

Y

YARMOLINSKY, Avraham, 1890-
2218. Lydenberg, Harry Miller "Avraham Yarmolinsky," NYPLB 59:110-32 Mr '55.
2219. Yachnin, Rissa "Avraham Yarmolinsky: a List of His Published Writings 1955-1967 with Addenda of Earlier Materials," NYPLB 72:414-19.

YERKES, Robert Mearnes, 1876-1956
2220. Hilgard, Ernest R. "Bibliography," NASBM 38:412-25 '65.

YOUNG, Charles Augustus, 1834-1908
2221. Frost, Edwin B. "Bibliography," NASBM 7:108-14 '13.

YOUNG, Edward
2222. Templeman, William D. "Additions to the Checklist of Young's 'Night-Thoughts' in America," BSA 43:348-49 '49.

Z

ZABRISKIE, George Albert, 1868-1954
2223. Baker, C. E. "Writings of George A. Zabriskie," New York Historical Society Quarterly 38:172-84 Apr '54.

ZINSSER, Hans, 1878-1940
2224. Walbach, Simeon Burt "Bibliography of Hans Zinsser," NASBM 24:348-60 '47.

ZUBIN, Joseph, 1900-
2225. "Writings," Psychiatry 4:663 N '41

AUTHOR INDEX

Numerals refer to entry numbers.

185

187

Couch, J. N. , 382
Cox, Doak C. , 355
Crawford, H. , 236
Crawford, Walter B. , 2216
Craycraft, Carl L. , 291
Cremin, L. A. , 1726
Cressey, G. B. , 68
Cressman, P. , 521
Crew, Henry, 41, 1393
Cronies, Carey, 1503
Crosby, W. O. , 1045
Cross, Charles R. , 421
Cross, Whitman, 591, 1005
Crowley, J. Donald, 888
Crumb, Rev. Laurence N. ,
1585
Culver, Harold E. , 450, 852
Cumberland, C. C. , 821
Cumings, E. R. , 1265, 1629
Currier, L. S. , 214
Cushing, Harvey, 416

Dake, C. L. , 417
Dall, William Healy, 135,
740, 770, 2091
Daly, Reginald A. , 489,
1533, 1750
Dameron, J. Lasley, 1597
Dana, Edward S. , 247, 2203
Dana, James D. , 820
Dane, Carle H. , 1652
Danforth, C. H. , 1927
Daniel, Robert, 635
Daniels, Farrington, 13
Dapples, E. C. , 93
Darrow, Karl K. , 1057
Darton, Nelson H. , 494,
1346, 2032
Davenport, Charles B. , 107,
481, 1372
Davis, Bergen, 1635
Davis, Curtis Carroll, 2184
Davis, Hallowell, 622
Davis, Tom, 1736
Davis, W. M. , 328
Day, Arthur L. , 133
Dean, Bashford, 581

Decker, Charles E. , 2067
Dedmond, Francis B. , 1598,
1599, 1947
De Golyer, Everett, 1623
De Gruson, Gene, 871, 1429
Deiss, Charles, 346
de Laguna, Frederica, 1837
Dell'Isola, Frank, 1406
Denison, A. Rodger, 505
Derrenbacher, Merle, 221
Derring, C. E. , 1726
Deussen, Alexander, 1811
DeWinter, U. J. , 805
De Wolf, Frank W. , 86
Dibble, Charles, 1827
Dickey, Parke A. , 1795
Dickson, L. E. , 1450
Diechmann, Elisabeth, 1064
Diller, J. S. , 574
Dinwiddie, Shirley W. , 24
Ditrick, H. , 1984
Dobbin, Carroll E. , 910, 2066
Dochez, A. R. , 76, 754
Doisy, Edward A. , 1785
Dole, M. , 1109
Dolton, R. K. , 1067
Donnay, J. D. H. , 1702
Dott, Robert H. , 120
Douglas, George Vibert, 558
Douglas, Jesse, 1122
Dow, S. , 1171
Downey, Jean, 403
Doyle, Joseph, 2192
Doyle, Paul A. , 1132, 1210
Dragstedt, Lester R. , 293
Dryden, Hugh L. , 2025
Du Bois, Eugene F. , 144, 1303
Du Bose, La Rocque, 310
DuBridge, Lee A. , 1433
Dumble, E. T. , 2024
Dunbar, Carl Owen, 1167,
1765, 1766, 1994
Dunbar, Viola R. , 1074
Dunn, L. C. , 307
Dunn, Oliver C. , 1458
Dunn, Paul H. , 1798
Durand, William F. , 1235,
1442, 2209

189

Durant, W. F. , 1729
Durham, Philip, 280, 2113

Eagan, J. M. , 902
Eardley, A. J. , 1761
Easby, Dudley T. Jr. , 1284
Eckert, Robert P. Jr. , 841
Edelstein, J. M. , 1872
Edmonson, Munro S. , 1552
Eggan, Fred, 383, 1648, 1760
Egly, William H. , 778
Eichelberger, Clayton L. , 1004, 1100, 1161, 1308
Eissenstat, Martha Turnquist, 1420
Elderfield, Robert C. , 79
Elias, Robert H. , 556
Elkins, Mary Jane, 1929
Ellis, Bruce T. , 1906
Ellis, Marjorie Mosser, 1684
Elvehjem, Conrad A. , 869
Embrey, Lee Anna, 1559
Emerson, Sterling Howard, 614
Emery, W. B. , 2179
Emmons, Samuel Franklin, 1153
Emmons, Winfred S. , Jr. , 1289, 2001
Engel, Claire-Elaine, 1600
Englekirk, J. E. , 1601
Epstein, Paul S. , 1433, 1975
Erdelyi, Gabor, 973
Erlanger, Joseph, 1009
Esdall, John T. , 381
Etulain, Richard W. , 411, 818
Eubank, E. , 1329
Evans, I. O. , 1814
Evans, Isabel P. , 134
Ezell, Paul H. , 1706

Fabre, Genevieve, 18
Fabre, Michael, 2211
Fairchild, Herman L. , 1217, 1568, 2096

Fairchild, Salome Cutler, 605
Farrington, Oliver C. , 446
Fatout, Paul, 163
Feaster, John, 364, 916
Feldman, Abraham, 1580
Fenn, Wallace O. , 693
Fenneman, Nevin M. , 511
Fenton, William N. , 1912
Ferguson, Alfred R. , 1075
Ferguson, E. , 1991
Fernald, M. L. , 1689
Field, Leslie, 2185
Fiene, Donald M. , 1737
Finley, Katherine P. , 1504
Finn, Fenton H. , 654
Fischer, Russell G. , 88
Fitzpatrick, Harry M. , 67
Flaxman, N. , 1087
Fleischer, Michael, 33
Fleming, John A. , 192, 589, 2205
Fletcher, Frank, 245
Fletcher, Harvey, 1425, 1883
Flexner, Simon, 2069
Foerste, August F. , 1509
Foote, H. W. , 2072
Foote, Paul D. , 1379
Forbes, George Shannon, 1059
Ford, W. T. , 1878
Fortes, M. , 1780
Foscue, Edwin J. , 1801
Foshag, William F. , 1344
Foster, George M. , 2068
Foster, W. R. , 1313
Fraser, Robert S. , 433
Frask, Parker D. , 1875a
Frazer, Persifor, 1591
Frederic, G. , 1331
French, Warren, 1506
Fried, Lewis, 278
Frodin, R. , 1043
Frost, Edwin B. , 2221
Frost, John E. , 1101
Fry, Varian, 592
Fryxell, Fritiof, 1365, 1435, 1508
Furcon, A. S. , 1371

Gardiner, H. C., 1314
Gardiner, Mary S., 1936
Garner, Stanton, 719
Garrels, Robert M., 1915
Garrison, Joseph M. Jr.,
264
Gasteyer, Charles E., 1469
Geiser, S. W., 1802
Genthe, Charles V., 936
Getty, R. E., 1321
Gibbs, J. Willard, 1494
Gibbs, William Francis,
1000
Gibson, Anna J., 1177
Gibson, Donald B., 2212
Gibson, Judith Ann, 1176
Gibson, William M., 1014
Gifford, E. W., 1756
Gilbert, G. K., 397, 1523
Gilbert, Vedder M., 50
Gilbertson, Albert N., 320
Gill, Theodore, 967
Gilliland, Edwin R., 1473
Gillin, John, 1253
Gillson, J. L., 45
Gilman, R. L., 2139
Glancy, Eileen K., 526
Glavin, Mary A., 973
Glemser, Karlena, 861
Glenn, L. C., 1851
Gohdes, Clarence, 1279
Goldenweiser, E. A., 958
Goldring, Winifred, 319,
1491, 1721
Goldschmidt, Richard B.,
1172
Goldsmith, Robert H., 1201
Goodale, George Lincoln, 17
Goodpasture, Ernest W.,
1264
Goodspeed, G. E., 1187,
2060
Goodspeed, T. H., 1784
Gordon, John D., 606, 1602
Gould, Charles N., 1157,
1845
Gould, Laurence M., 965

Gozzi, Raymond D., 55
Graf, Dorothy W., 1002
Graf, John E., 1002
Graham, Clarence H., 1039,
2199
Graham, Philip, 1015
Granger, Walter, 1282
Granick, S., 1411
Grant, I. F., 687
Grant, U. S., 949, 2107
Graton, L. C., 394, 1844,
2037
Green, David B., 232, 1102
Green, Morton, 255
Gregore, William King, 329
Gregory, Herbert E., 111,
913
Gregory, William K., 495,
1524
Griffen, James B., 1457
Griffith, A. H., 1241
Griffith, D. D., 1531
Grinnell, Hilda W., 1397
Griscom, John, 792
Gropp, Arthur E., 1136
Gross, Seymour L., 2075
Gross, Theodore L., 1532
Grout, F. F., 802
Guilford, J. P., 1967
Gullason, Thomas A., 430
Gunderson, R. G., 1242
Gunter, Herman, 281, 289
Gunther, Erna, 480
Guppy, E. M., 1847
Guthe, Alfred K., 1536
Guzman, Jessie Parkhurst,
301

Haag, William G., 2061
Haas, G. C. O., 1058
Haas, I., 1703
Hackett, Herbert, 2130
Hagemann, E. R., 280, 501,
502, 503, 1076
Hague, Arnold, 616, 617
Halberstadt, Baird, 955
Hall, Edwin H., 1560, 1731,
1987

Hall, George Martin, 793
Hallowell, A. Irving, 480
Hamilton, Eunice C., 1077
Hammond, G. P., 2031
Hamson, C. J., 819
Handen, Ralph D., 129, 132
Hanna, Allen, 1775
Harding, Eugene, 749
Harding, Walter, 1948, 1949,
1950, 1951, 1952
Haring, Douglas G., 140
Harradon, H. D., 192, 1573
Harrington, M. R., 1819
Harrison, Margaret W., 1461,
1521
Harrison, Thomas S., 662
Hart, James D., 473
Hart, William L., 1060,
1061
Harvey, E. Newton, 393
Harvey, Sara K., 2019
Haskell, John D., Jr., 992
Hassid, W. Z., 94, 664
Hastings, Charles S., 761,
1125
Hastings, Robert, 895
Hathaway, J. T., 2158
Haughton, Sidney H., 830
Hawkins, R. R., 2193
Hawkins, Sherman, 1156
Hawley, J. E., 246, 2035
Hayashi, Tetsumaro, 1421,
1866, 1867, 1868
Haydock, James, 1268
Haynes, Barrie, 1441
Hazen, E. L., 150
Heald, K. C., 350
Heaney, Howell J., 1665
Heartman, Charles F., 1554,
1608
Heck, Nicholas H., 193
Heffron, E. J., 1793
Heidelberger, Michael, 1189,
1730
Heizer, Robert F., 766
Hektoen, Ludvig, 1632
Heller, O., 1776

Hellman, Florence S., 137
Henbest, Lloyd G., 457
Henry, Joseph, 78
Henson, Clyde E., 1162
Heroy, William B., 2016
Herrick, C. Judson, 379, 935
Herrnstadt, Richard L., 24
Herskovits, Melville J.,
1165, 1716, 1781
Hesler, L. R., 1095
Hewett, D. F., 741, 1224
Hewitt, A. B., 813
Hildebrand, Joel Henry, 211,
1207, 1236
Hilgard, Ernest R., 2220
Hilgard, Eugene W., 1218
Hilgard, J. E., 27
Hill, Frank A., 64
Hill, G. W., 1518
Hill, H. Stanton, 2006
Hill, Robert T., 900
Hill, W. W., 1851
Hillier, R. L., 371
Hinz, John P., 311
Hipkiss, Robert A., 109
Hobbs, William H., 1230,
1231
Hobbs, William K., 396
Hoff, John C., 1919
Hoffmann, Carol Ann, 1930
Hofman, H. O., 298
Hogan, Charles Beecher, 1693
Hogan, Robert, 1662
Hohenthal, W. D., 1982
Hoijer, Harry, 103, 205, 2064
Holden, Edward S., 116
Hollenberg, Susan Weidman,
1701
Hollingworth, H. L., 972
Hollister, J. C., 912
Holloway, Jean, 827
Holman, C. Hugh, 2186
Holmes, Chauncey D., 1024
Holmes, Thomas J., 1362
Holmes, W. H., 1456, 1881
Hooker, M., 1713, 1755
Hooton, Ernest A., 2159

192

Hoots, Harold W. , 745
Horigan, William D. , 831
Horsfall, Frank L. , Jr. ,
1678
Hotchkiss, William Otis, 39
Hough, Walter, 655, 656,
686, 984, 1359
Houston, W. V. , 184
Hovey, Edmund Otis, 736
Hovgaard, William, 1911,
1928
Howard, L. O. , 1464
Howell, B. F. , 1660, 1746,
2012
Howell, J. V. , 2171
Howell, William H. , 1382
Howitt, J. E. , 1891
Howland, A. L. , 93
Hrdlička, Aleš, 1040
Hudspeth, Robert N. , 434,
435
Humphrey, James III, 508
Humphreys, R. A. , 1688
Humphreys, W. J. , 1
Hunsaker, J. C. , 559, 1850
Hunt, D. E. , 424
Hunt, Frederick V. , 1584
Hunter, W. S. , 60
Hurlbut, Cornelius S. , Jr. ,
1534
Hussey, Russell C. , 1771
Hutchinson, Phyllis Martin,
312
Hutsell, J. K. , 2187
Hyde, Jesse E. , 2011
Hyman, Libbie H. , 338
Hyneman, Esther F. , 1603

Iddings, Joseph P. , 823, 824,
1563
Imlay, Ralph W. , 1653
Ingerson, Earl, 1345
Ingraham, Mark H. , 2014
Insley, M. , 2005
Ireland, Alexander, 607
Isaacs, Edith J. R. , 1694
Ives, Herbert E. , 1671

Ives, Sidney, 1386

Jackson, C. N. , 1844a
Jackson, Charles Loring, 401,
957
Jackson, Robert Tracy, 790
Jacobs, Walter A. , 1229
James, John E. , 1417
Jeffries, Zy, 990, 1145, 1396
Jenkins, James A. , 361
Jenkins, Olaf P. , 1792
Jennings, J. S. , 1557
Jennings, L. B. , 306
Jepsen, Glenn L. , 1772, 1773
Jessup, Mary E. , 56, 313
Jewell, W. B. , 780, 781
Jewett, Frank B. , 300
Joffe, Natalie F. , 1804
Johnson, E. D. H. , 418
Johnson, F. R. , 422
Johnson, Frank H. , 874
Johnson, Frederick, 1711
Johnson, H. , 470
Johnson, Helgi, 1973
Johnson, Meredith E. , 1180
Johnson, Merle, 147, 234,
474, 551, 726, 844, 917,
1140, 1896, 1942
Johnson, W. , 2099
Johnston, L. C. , 1297
Jonas, Klaus W. , 2013
Jones, Buford, 890
Jones, Claude E. , 436
Jones, Dan Burne, 1143
Jones, Donald F. , 579
Jones, Gardner Maynard, 608,
891, 892
Jones, Matt B. , 2132
Jordan, George F. , 1475
Jordan, Leona, 2076
Joy, Alfred H. , 12, 1277,
2169
Joyce, H. E. , 1294
Judd, Neil M. , 1681
Jugaku, Bunsho, 609
Just, Evan, 1482

Moore, Raymond C., 1593, 2070
Morgan, T. H., 215, 2164
Morgan, W. W., 1714
Morley, Edward W., 1708
Morner, M., 63
Morris, Elizabeth Ann, 1462
Morris, Frederick K., 1046
Morrisson, Helen B., 1956
Morrow, Patrick, 872
Morse, Edward S., 1436, 2108
Mosettig, Erich, 1823
Moys, E. M., 2150
Mumm, B., 774
Murdock, George Peter, 1336, 1535
Murnaghan, F. D., 124
Murphy, James B., 624
Murray, Donald, 919
Myers, G. E., 1783
Myers, J. William, 1885

Napier, James J., 932
Neal, D. C., 1415
Nevius, Blake, 2088
Newcomb, Simon, 930
Newland, D. H., 1480
Newman, Ralph G., 1741
Newton, H. A., 1281
Nichol, John W., 1271
Nicholas, J. S., 517
Nichols, Edward L., 1497, 1709
Nichols, L., 2022
Nichols, Robert L., 1191
Nolan, P. T., 2145
Norris, James Flack, 1659
Norton, W. H., 1812
Notestein, F. W., 1285
Noyes, William Albert, 1659, 1824, 1886, 2049

O'Connor, Roger B., 723
O'Daniel, Therman B., 1028, 1029
Oden, Melita H., 1937

O'Donnell, Thomas F., 714
Odum, H. W., 812
Oesterling, H. C., 694
Oftedal, Ivar, 786
Oko, D. K., 561
Olson, Harry F., 1749
Olsson, Axel A., 863
Oppenheimer, Jane M., 1495
Oreans, G. Harrison, 1184
Oros, Margaret O., 1163
Orton, Vrest, 920
Osborn, Henry Fairfield, 409, 1222, 1366
Osborne, Harold S., 139
Osborne, Lilly de Johgh, 261
Osborne, Thomas B., 1106
Ottley, A. R., 774

Packard, A. S., Jr., 349, 2217
Pady, Donald S., 2100
Page, Leigh, 256
Pagenstecher, Ann, 1155
Painter, Theophilis S., 1545
Palache, Charles, 577, 1556, 2189
Palmer, Katherine Van Winkle, 1825
Paltsits, Victor Hugo, 893
Pantle, P., 2099
Parameswaran, Uma, 733
Parker, Franklin, 849
Parker, George Howard, 2090
Parker, Joyce, 849
Parrish, W., 795
Patrick, J. Max, 170
Patterson, J. E., 167, 1625, 1854, 2031
Patton, John B., 507
Patton, John J., 1419
Paul, John Rodman, 173, 1572
Pauling, Linus, 1512
Peabody Museum. Harvard University, 1980
Peirce, B. Osgood, 1291
Pelletier, R. A., 96
Penchef, E., 304
Pendergast, Daniel M., 43

Penrose, R. A. F., Jr., 208, 209, 230, 710
Perez, C. B., 241
Perez Gallego, Candido, 921
Perkins, Edward H., 703
Perkins, George H., 1779
Perry, Bradley T., 637, 638
Perry, Ralph Barton, 1086
Perry, Vincent D., 1151
Peters, Sir Rudolph A., 1410
Pettengill, G. E., 709
Pettijohn, F. J., 322
Phillips, Maurice E., 284, 700
Phillips, Robert S., 894, 895, 1065, 1066, 1317
Phillips, Venia T., 700
Pietrangeli, A., 1118, 1119
Piggot, Charles S., 2205, 2206
Pikelis, Anna, 597
Pillsbury, W. B., 317, 523
Piper, Henry Dan, 680, 684
Piquet, A. P. D., 629
Pirsson, Louis V., 469
Pitts, Robert F., 1832
Pizer, Donald, 750, 751
Ploger, Louis W., 991
Plumer, J. M., 2043
Polsgrove, Carol, 596
Porter, Bernard H., 681, 1390
Postley, Olive C., 2093
Potter, V. G., 1561
Pough, Frederick H., 2105
Poulton, Helen J., 496
Powell, Lawrence Clark, 75, 1869
Powers, A., 1753
Pratt, H. E., 1246
Pratt, Joseph Hyde, 975
Pratt, Wallace E., 117, 506
Price, M. T., 1333
Price, R., 316
Proskouriakoff, Tatiana, 1416
Protor, V., 391

Prouty, William F., 372
Pruitt, C. M., 48, 452, 2008
Pumpelly, Ralph, 1037

Quenenbery, W. D., Jr., 779

Rabinowitch, Eugene, 613
Radhuber, Stanley G., 426
Rainey, Froelich, 764
Rand, Frederick V., 1829
Randall, David, 1605, 1606
Randel, William, 588
Raper, Kenneth B., 1940
Ravitz, Abe C., 1581
Raymond, Percy E., 125, 363
Raymond, Rossiter W., 175
Rede, Kenneth, 1608
Reed, C. E., 2002
Reed, John C., 647
Reeds, Chester A., 1368
Rees, Robert A., 601
Reese, E. T., 2101
Reeside, John B., Jr., 1343, 1858
Reeves, John K., 1018
Reger, David B., 928, 929, 1969
Rehder, Alfred, 1747
Reichart, Walter A., 1055
Reid, C., 1876
Reid, J. C., 1838
Reinhardt, J. M., 772
Reinhart, Virginia S., 547
Remordas, Georges, 1870
Remsen, Ira, 1465
Renken, Maxime, 1428
Rhoades, M. M., 1856
Rice, Howard C., Jr., 71, 340
Rich, A. L., 1357
Richards, A. N., 1334
Richards, Irving T., 1481
Richards, Ralph W., 1668
Richardson, G. B., 385
Richardson, Madge D., 1298
Richels, Milton, 1963
Richert, Roland, 2023

Treis, Susan, 529
Trimble, Harry C. , 690
Trowbridge, A. C. , 1124,
 1547, 1857
True, Michael D. , 187, 189
Tunnell, George, 797
Turner, Arlin, 866
Turner, F. E. , 942
Tuve, Merle A. , 685
Twenhofel, W. H. , 2036
Tyrell, James B. , 1431

Uhler, Horace S. , 876
Ulam, S. , 2027
Ungar, Harriet, 1422
Upham, Warren, 963, 2178,
 2208
Usilton, B. M. , 1592

Vallette, Jacques, 682
Van den Bos, Willem H. , 20
Vandersee, Charles, 9
Vann, J. Don, 1388
Van Name, Ralph G. , 789
Van Royen W. , 149
Van Slyke, Donald D. , 1229
Van Tuyl, F. M. , 912
Van Valkenberg S. , 224
Van Vleck, J. H. , 1392
Vaughan, Bess, 1154
Vaughan, Thomas Wayland,
 959, 1820
Vickery, Hubert Bradford,
 54, 341, 1107, 1525
Visher, Stephen S. , 541,
 1092, 1093
Visscher, Maurice B. , 1340
Von Engelin, O. D. , 1562
Voss, E. G. , 115
Voss, H. E. , 1301

Wade, Joseph S. , 1957
Wagley, Charles, 1437, 1900
Wagner, Linda Welshimer,
 2153
Wainwright, Alexander D. ,
 266, 744

Walbach, Simeon Burt, 2224
Walcott, Charles D. , 1193
Wales, Lucy, 1166
Walker, Dale L. , 1273
Walker, J. C. , 565, 1111
Walkom, A. B. , 58
Wall, Frederick, T. , 1700
Wall, Richard J. , 291
Wallace, Edith M. , 1458
Wallace, Emily Mitchell, 2154
Wallis, Wilson D. , 784
Walsh, James E. , 1280
Walter, Paul A. F. , 943
Walts, Robert W. , 1020
Warren, Charles H. , 1005
Warren, P. S. , 28
Washburn, A. E. , 1838
Washburne, Chester W. , 347
Watson, Thomas L. , 691
Wauchope, Robert, 1149
Weaver, Charles E. , 44
Weaver, Warren, 1358
Webb, Constance, 2215
Webb, Harold W. , 482
Weber, Richard B. , 620
Wedel, Waldo R. , 954, 2142
Wedge, George F. , 1515,
 1622
Weeks, Elizabeth Harriet,
 1449
Weeks, Lewis G. , 392, 1023
Wegelin, Oscar, 400, 1551,
 1809, 1810
Weiant, C. W. , 1516
Weidman, Samuel, 46
Weiss, Harry B. , 1554
Wellford, B. Randolph, 2183
Wells, Horace L. , 1564
Welsh, John R. , 1808
Wendorf, Fred, 497
West, Frederick Hadleigh,
 1818
Westbrook, Perry D. , 724
Westgate, Lewis D. , 1664,
 1790
Westheimer, Frank H. , 1148
Wetherbee, Winthrop, Jr. ,
 275

Wetmore, Alexander, 1673, 1874
Wheeler, B. E. , 1248
Wheeler, Martha Thorne, 1295
Whitaker, J. R. , 1539
White, C. , 1249
White, Charles A. , 901, 1378, 1487, 2201
White, David, 1170, 1182
White, G. F. , 113
White, George W. , 787
White, Helen, 632
White, I. C. , 1880
White, William, 429, 530, 531, 548, 549, 683, 924, 925, 1091, 1347, 1348, 1349, 1507, 1695, 1696, 1846, 1958, 2082, 2083, 2084, 2085, 2119, 2120, 2121, 2122, 2123, 2155,
Whitney, Willis R. , 615
Wiggins, Ira L. , 1831
Wigner, Eugene P. , 1916
Wilder, Frank A. , 2202
Wilens, Sally, 868
Willard, Bradford, 308, 666, 911
Willey, Gordon R. , 695, 1150
Williams, Edwin E. , 1409
Williams, F. E. , 1354
Williams, J. W. , 2148
Williams, James S. , 777
Williams, Kenny Jackson, 735
Williams, Lucia K. , 357
Williams, M. , 2054
Williams, M. Y. , 220
Williams, Stephen, 2042
Williamson, G. M. , 896
Willier, B. H. , 1239
Willis, Bailey, 324, 1633, 1634, 1725
Wilson, A. H. , 2161
Wilson, Alice E. , 2160
Wilson, C. W. Jr. , 780, 781

Wilson, John A. , 212
Wilson, Louis N. , 838
Wilson, Olin C. , 1404
Wilson, W. B. , 1316
Winchell, Newton H. , 833
Winser, B. , 470
Winship, George Parker, 1257
Winton, W. M. , 1770
Witthoft, John, 625, 1848
Wold, H. , 52
Wolff, John E. , 1787
Wolfrom, Melville L. , 946, 1026, 1483
Wood, B. D. , 767
Woodbridge, Benjamin M. , 1232, 1493, 1502, 1543
Woodbridge, Hensley C. , 1274, 1613, 1626, 1901, 1902, 1903, 1904, 1905, 2125
Woodford, A. O. , 207, 1649
Woodress, James, 1021
Woodring, W. P. , 462, 1890, 2149
Woodward, Robert H. , 715, 716, 717, 718, 719, 1275
Woodworth, J. B. , 1922
Woodworth, Robert S. , 1369, 1720, 1962, 2051
Woodworth, S. D. , 643
Woolworth, Alan R. , 2142
Worcester, P. G. , 444, 1972
Worthing, A. G. , 1576
Wrather, W. E. , 1141, 1320
Wright, Anna Z. , 1104
Wright, Arthur W. , 1805, 1988
Wright, Frank J. , 1104
Wright, Fred E. , 649, 2196, 2197
Wright, L. , 239
Wright, William H. , 290, 1451
Wulf, Oliver R. , 1975
Wyman, Jeffries, 798

Yachnin, Rissa, 2219
Yochelson, Ellis L. , 2033